Making the Most of Field Placement

Helen Cleak & Jill Wilson

THOMSON
TM

Australia · New Zealand · Canada · Mexico · Singapore · Spain · United Kingdom · United States

Level 7, 80 Dorcas Street
South Melbourne, Victoria
Australia 3205

Email: highereducation@thomsonlearning.com.au
Website: www.thomsonlearning.com.au

First published in 2004, this second edition published in 2007
10 9 8 7 6 5 4 3 2 1
10 09 08 07

Copyright © 2007 Nelson Australia Pty Limited.

National Library of Australia
Cataloguing-in-Publication data

Cleak, Helen Mary.
Making the most of field placement.

    2nd ed.
    Bibliography.
    Includes index.
    ISBN 978 0 17 013198 8 (pbk.).

    1. Social service – Field work – Handbooks, manuals, etc.
    I. Wilson, Jill, 1946– . II. Title.

361.32

Publishing manager: Michael Tully
Project editor: Ronald Chung
Publishing editor: Liz Male
Cover designer: Olga Lavecchia
Editor: Robyn Flemming
Indexer: Julie King
Typeset in Minion 11.5 pt and Avenir 10.5 pt by Chris Ryan
Production controller: Zoe Whatmore
Printed in Australia by Ligare Book Printing

This title is published under the imprint of Thomson.
Nelson Australia Pty Limited ACN 058 280 149 (incorporated in Victoria)
trading as Thomson Learning Australia.

The URLs contained in this publication were checked for currency during the production process.
Note, however, that the publisher cannot vouch for the ongoing currency of URLs.

CONTENTS

Preface   viii
Introduction   x
Acknowledgements   xi

PART ONE   PRE-PLACEMENT PLANNING   1
Chapter 1 – Preparing for placement – student   2
    Introduction   2
    What is field placement?   2
    Goals of a placement   3
    How to choose a placement   4
    Planning for placement   4
    Summary   11

Chapter 2 – Preparing for placement – supervisor   12
    Introduction   12
    Preparing for placement   13
    Meeting the student   22
    Summary   24

PART TWO   BEGINNING PLACEMENT   25
Chapter 3 – Getting started – student   26
    Introduction   26
    The first weeks   26
    Surviving in a human service agency   27
    Summary   30

Chapter 4 – Getting started – supervisor   31
    Introduction   31
    The first weeks   31
    Starting work   32
    Summary   38

Chapter 5 – Charting the course for placement – contracts and agreements   39
    Introduction   39
    The learning agreement   39
    Other types of agreements   45
    Summary   47

PART THREE   TEACHING AND LEARNING ON PLACEMENT   49
Chapter 6 – Critical reflection for teaching and learning   50
    Introduction   50
    Educational approaches   50
    Summary   54

Chapter 7 – Developing good supervisory practices   55
    Introduction   55
    The functions of supervision   55
    Expectations of supervision   56
    Developing the supervisory relationship   59

Supervision sessions 64
Other types of supervision 68
Summary 72

Chapter 8 – Teaching and learning tools 73
Introduction 73
The teaching and learning approach 74
Discussion tools 75
Observation tools 83
Teaching and learning activities 86
Summary 89

Chapter 9 – Linking learning and practice in placement 90
Introduction 90
What are theories? 91
Integrating theory and practice 93
Summary 97

PART FOUR   METHODS AND CONTEXTS OF PRACTICE 99
Chapter 10 – Community work 100
Introduction 100
How does change occur? 100
The political realities 102
Knowledge and practice skills 103
Documentation 106
Finishing placement 108
Summary 108

Chapter 11 – Research and policy 109
Introduction 109
Research practice 110
Policy practice 111
Summary 117

Chapter 12 – Working with teams and groups 118
Introduction 118
What are teams and groups? 118
Teamwork 119
Groupwork 122
Methods of practice 123
Summary 127

Chapter 13 – Rural and overseas placements 128
Introduction 128
Rural practice 128
Starting out 129
The issues for placement 130
Overseas placements 136
Summary 137

PART FIVE   KEEPING ON COURSE 139
Chapter 14 – Challenging issues in supervision 140
Introduction 140

General issues 140
Specific issues 145
Summary 149

Chapter 15 – Working with difference 150
Introduction 150
Understanding ourselves 150
Understanding difference 151
Difference – teaching and learning methods 155
Summary 157

Chapter 16 – Ethical and legal issues 158
Introduction 158
Legal responsibilities 158
Ethical practice 163
Summary 166

Chapter 17 – Roles and responsibilities of the training institution 167
Introduction 167
The teaching and learning framework 167
Resources 168
Liaison 168
Summary 172

PART SIX   EVALUATING, ASSESSING AND FINISHING PLACEMENT 173
Chapter 18 – Assessment and evaluation – students and supervisors 174
Introduction 174
Evaluating students' practice 174
Evaluating supervisors' practice 178
Assessment events 182
Summary 184

Chapter 19 – Finishing well 185
Introduction 185
How to begin the ending! 185
Planning for the future 187

References 190
Index 194

PREFACE

This workbook is written from our combined experiences of over 50 years of involvement in field education from a range of perspectives: as students, supervisors, liaison staff, practice teachers and lecturers. The impetus for writing the book came from the lack of a local textbook that offered a 'how to' for students and supervisors preparing for a field placement. Many practitioners also requested a more practical and applied learning text that reflected contemporary field education practice within the constraints of working in the human services in the 21st century.

This second edition of the book builds on the success of the first edition and incorporates feedback and ideas from the range of readers who used the text. We have made a number of changes throughout the text in response to this information. This edition also contains a new chapter on critical reflection for teaching and learning, and a section on overseas placements. The book's exercises and ideas come from a variety of sources: our own experiences and ideas; exercises in an array of field education manuals; tools used by our colleagues; and some well-used tools whose origins are long since lost.

Purpose

A placement offers students the opportunity to apply their classroom learning to real-life situations and to learn how to cope with the complex and contested nature of helping. It offers supervisors the opportunity to reflect on their own practice and to learn effective ways of helping others to become proficient practitioners. The purpose of this book is to provide a practical and user-friendly teaching and learning resource to assist human service field educators and students progress through the various stages of a field placement.

The text provides the bridge between classroom and placement and concentrates on describing exercises and tools that can be used by both supervisors and students to maximise their teaching and learning opportunities throughout the placement experience.

The text assumes an understanding of social work and human services theories and frameworks underpinning professional practice. A number of theoretical perspectives are implicit in the examples and exercises. Its purpose is to illustrate or promote the mastery of a particular learning experience in learning to be a human services practitioner.

Audience

We decided to write a book that addressed the two central players in the placement experience – students and supervisors – since the ideas and concepts should be familiar and useful to both. Students need to understand the issues and concerns inherent in their supervision, and supervisors can benefit from insight into the concerns and learning needs of the student.

The text is appropriate for students and supervisors working in direct services, community work, policy and project placements.

The text also provides a useful teaching resource for those involved in the education and preparation of students, field teachers and other academic staff in various human service courses. These would include social work, welfare studies, case management, community development, disability studies, family studies, psychology and nursing.

Ideological approach

The book follows an adult-learning model which advocates that not all the expertise and knowledge lies with the supervisor; responsibility is placed on the student to contribute to the learning process.

The new edition contains a new chapter on critical reflection and how to use a reflective approach in supervision, which is consistent with anti-oppressive practice and a values-based approach that includes tolerance of difference, creative practice and professional integrity.

Format

The structure of the book follows the various stages of the placement from both the student's and field educator's perspective. It addresses the range of critical learning issues that may emerge at each stage and suggests various educational strategies to deal with these. These sequences can be followed according to the particular fieldwork program in which the student is enrolled. That is, the student can be undertaking a part-time or full-time placement, or it could be a block or concurrent placement.

A major feature of this book is its practice orientation. Each chapter begins by introducing the main topic and important features of the relevant stage of the placement. A brief chapter outline and discussion of the relevant sub-topics follows. The sub-topics include a range of exercises, examples, checklists, ideas and other helpful material, which offer the student and supervisor ways to positively engage with each stage of the placement.

How to use this book

The book follows the stages of a placement and these parallel the stages that human service workers follow when working with a client, family, group or community: preparing, beginning, exploring, assessing, evaluating and terminating.

Throughout the book, responsibility is placed on the student to be a curious and responsible learner and to be proactive in planning and managing his or her placement. Likewise, supervisors are encouraged to explore and demonstrate the values and qualities consistent with the helping profession, such as empathy, respect and professional integrity, as they assist students to practise and learn on placement.

Each human service course differs in how it administers its field education programs. This book is designed to accommodate these differences. It presents the core practice issues and ideas that can be adapted to individual course requirements.

Students and supervisors can use this workbook as a guide as the placement progresses, or the exercises may be selected to enhance specific stages of the placement.

INTRODUCTION

It is a common observation that human service practitioners work with the most vulnerable people in our society, dealing with the complex and intractable problems that confront them. Education to prepare professional helpers requires students to be skilled and knowledgeable in a broad range of practice areas, to be able to work with people who are living difficult lives, and hence to be challenged on a daily basis. Many students in human services courses have a range of diverse range of life situations to face in maintaining body and soul while studying, and in coping with the demands of the course, particularly during placement.

This book has been written to acknowledge and respond to the changing context of practice that supervisors and students must work within. The context of human service delivery in contemporary society has changed over time and will continue to respond to periodic shifts in ideologies, structures and processes of service delivery. These changes include funding cuts, downsizing, amalgamations and increased privatisation, which have resulted in an increasingly bureaucratic and accountable work environment.

Supervisors are essential to the success of a field placement; yet they are working within this difficult and complex context and are expected to provide a series of learning experiences on placement and to serve as mentors and role models. This book affirms their contribution to the process of teaching students and offers a variety of ideas and techniques to help them with their endeavours.

Educational theories have also developed over time, and some of them challenge the traditional beliefs about how people learn. Preferred learning styles and reflective practice are two models that need to be incorporated into teaching and learning in a placement. The first suggests that individuals may have one learning style that predominates over others. Critical reflection is a personal process that 'fosters an integration of self, theory and practice in a way that sharpens our view and understanding of factors that influence the way we think and behave towards others' (Maidment & Egan 2004, p. 14). Awareness of these models encourages students to identify the skills and knowledge they already have and how they contribute to their approach to learning on placement. They also engage the student in the process of self-reflection, increased self-knowledge and developing their capacity for critical thinking and how to communicate and understand people in the context of their environment.

Finally, this book offers students, supervisors and training courses ways to structure a learning environment and specific criteria for designing and specifying what is to be learned on placement.

ACKNOWLEDGEMENTS

I am grateful to the La Trobe School of Social Work and Social Policy for giving me precious time off from teaching to write the book, and to school colleagues who covered my workload in my absence. Thanks to the School of Social Work and Applied Human Sciences, University of Queensland, who accommodated me for six months while we wrote the book.

Helen Cleak

I sincerely thank all the students and field educators who taught me what I know about field education, and the staff in the Field Education Unit at the University of Queensland who gave me very valuable feedback on drafts – thanks, Diana and Mary.

Jill Wilson

We also wish to thank the talented team at Thomson Learning who nurtured the book from manuscript to finished product, especially Rebekah Jardine-Williams, who believed in the concept of this book from the start and was the linchpin of the whole project.

We are indebted to all the students, field educators and social work colleagues who have shared their fieldwork stories and experiences over the decades. Special thanks to colleagues from the Victorian Combined Schools of Social Work who supported the initial concept for this book and to colleagues in the field education unit at the School of Social Work and Applied Human Sciences, whose contributions over many years are reflected in the book. All continue to develop ideas around best practice in fieldwork education.

The outline and/or sample chapters were reviewed with care and insight. Our thanks go to the following reviewers, who provided incisive and helpful feedback:

University

- Janet Bradshaw (University of Ballarat)
- Dr Susan Gair (James Cook University)
- Rosalie Hearne (La Trobe University)
- Karen Heycox (University of New South Wales)
- Judy Kulisa (Edith Cowan University)
- Kym MacFarlane (Griffith University)
- Rob Nabben (RMIT)
- Delia O'Donohue (Monash University)
- Claire Perry (University of Otago)
- Heather Stewart (Australian Catholic University)

TAFE

- Catherine Cusack (Hunter Institute of TAFE)
- Jeanie Feros (Bremer Institute of TAFE)
- Susan Monti (Northern Sydney Institute of TAFE)
- Gill Rimmer (Wide Bay Institute of TAFE)
- Cheryl Payne (Box Hill Institute of TAFE)

Finally, thanks to family and friends who contributed ideas and who understood that we were not available for other activities during the last hectic months. Your support is invaluable.

Helen Cleak
Jill Wilson

The authors and publisher would like to gratefully credit or acknowledge permission to reproduce extracts from the following sources:

Australian Social Work for figure 'A model of professional knowledge for social work practice' by J. Drury in *Australian Social Work Journal*, vol. 50 no. 3, 1997; La Trobe University for adapted extract from *The Information and Evaluation Handbook*, School of Social Work and Social Policy, La Trobe University, 2003; Pearson Education Australia for extract reproduced from *Social Work and Welfare Practice* by O'Connor, Wilson and Setterland © Pearson Education Australia, 2003.

Every attempt has been made to trace and acknowledge copyright holders. Where the attempt has been unsuccessful, the publisher welcomes information that would redress the situation.

PRE-PLACEMENT PLANNING

Planning for field placement is an important activity for the student and supervisor, as well as the agency and the training institution. For the student, placements mark particular stages of their studies – points they have reached by successfully completing a range of courses or subjects. Pre-placement planning helps students to decide which placements may be suitable for them, what opportunities and constraints may affect the successful completion of a placement and, perhaps, whether this is the right time to undertake a placement.

The current economic and managerial environment means that the agencies that offer field placements are under increasing pressure from funding bodies to improve their efficiency and productivity. Agencies may need to be assured by supervisors that offering a placement won't compromise their resources. Students might feel that they are embarking on a period of unpaid labour, often at considerable financial cost to themselves, and that they are doing the agency a favour. These realities have to be negotiated by all concerned. Taking the time to prepare for field placement will increase the likelihood of its being successful. The processes outlined in the following two chapters help in this planning process.

1

1

PREPARING FOR PLACEMENT – STUDENT

Introduction

The period of learning during which a student is located in a human service agency is called a placement. It may also be called a field placement or, in North America, a practicuum. A placement is usually valued by students and remembered long after many other aspects of academic courses are forgotten (Shardlow & Doel 1996, p. 4). Real-life experiences can be very influential in shaping hopes and fears for subsequent placements (O'Connor, Wilson & Setterlund 2003), as well as offering significant models of practice for the future.

Preparing for placement could be the most important activity you do at this time. The success of a placement will be enhanced by spending some time thinking through a number of important steps before the placement begins. This chapter will help you to lay the foundations for a successful placement by clarifying your preliminary expectations and learning needs and offering some strategies to negotiate a successful placement.

If this is your first placement, you are likely to want to test out whether a career in human services is for you. Perhaps you want to know if you can do it without too much personal pain. Does your developing identity as a human service worker 'fit' with who you are? Are you ready for placement?

If this is your second or subsequent placement, you will have a good idea of the issues involved in selecting and making the most of a placement. If your previous placement was a great experience, you will be keen to repeat it. If it was less than satisfactory, or if it is a repeat placement, you will have specific agendas about what you want and need to achieve. However good, or less than good, the first placement was, you need, as much as possible, to try not to let unfinished business from your first placement affect your new one. The person in the agency who is primarily responsible for the student's learning tasks and who undertakes the final evaluation of the student may be called field educator, field instructor, practice teacher, clinical teacher, teacher or supervisor; we will refer to 'supervisors' in this manual. Talking with your new supervisor about your gains and losses in previous experiences is one way of helping to keep the two placements separate.

What is field placement?

Field placement offers you the opportunity to learn about yourself and how you generate and use information as a human service practitioner. It also gives you an opportunity to understand the nature of your future professional role. A good placement engages you in a range of tasks that extend your professional skills and knowledge, and tests out your real interest in and suitability for this career.

There are tasks associated with planning the beginning, middle and end of placement. At each stage there is the opportunity to capitalise on the opportunities offered and learn from mistakes. These stages are characterised in the following diagram.

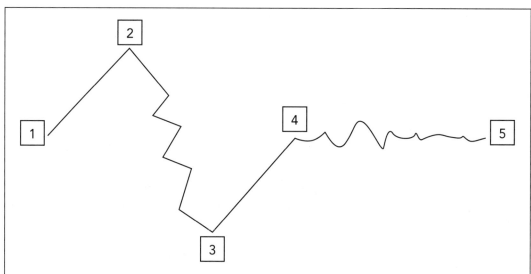

STAGES

1 Exiting from your training institution and anticipating placement:
  a 'This placement will be great.'
  b 'This placement meets many of my needs, but there are still some niggles.'
  c 'This placement is not great, really, but is the best I could get at the time.'

2 Getting started:
  a Does your supervisor meet your expectations?
  b Can you engage with the tasks outlined in the learning agreement?
  c How have you been received by other staff and clients?

3 During placement:
  You feel disappointed because your placement doesn't meet all your expectations.
  a Can you learn to successfully manage frustration and feelings of aloneness?
  b Can you learn from situations that don't go well?

4 Later in the placement:
  You develop a more realistic perspective about:
  a the quality of your relationship with your supervisor
  b balancing the 'wins' and 'losses'
  c placing yourself in the broader context that impacts on your work with clients.

5 Finishing up:
  a you reflect on what has been achieved
  b you learn from missed opportunities
  c you develop self-awareness and maturity as a human service practitioner.

Stages of placement

Goals of a placement

Each training institution has its own requirements and goals; however, some general fieldwork goals, as suggested by Corey and Corey (1998), include:

- to provide students with knowledge and skills in the various approaches and methods used in human service programs
- to help students extend self-awareness and achieve a sense of professional identity
- to broaden students' sociocultural understanding of the individual, the family and relevant social systems
- to help students recognise and respect diversity and to apply this understanding in practice
- to help students expand their awareness of the range of professional roles and relationships in the organisation, and the context of practice in the wider community.

A goal that could be added to this list is to help students develop skills as reflective practitioners. These skills are needed so that students can increase their insight and self-knowledge, and can evaluate the effectiveness of their practice against stated objectives.

How to choose a placement

Matching a placement to your personal and professional goals is not easy. What may be challenging to one student might be overwhelming to another and boring to someone else (Collins, Thomlison & Grinnell 1992, p. 3).

Collins, Thomlison and Grinnell (1992) compare the process of choosing a placement to that of children going to a lolly shop with their parents. The children are able to choose one item and are given some time to ponder their decision, but once it is made, it is final and the item is paid for. Never mind that the child did not know that their lolly had peanuts! The choice of placements can be tempting, but the selection process is limited and knowing about the peanuts is your responsibility and must be lived with unless the circumstances are extreme (p. 37). Your choice can be guided by the following three questions: What is in it? Will I like it? Can I have it?

Training institutions have different ways of organising placements for students in their human service programs. In some, placements are organised with very little input from students; in others, students are expected to negotiate their own placement, or they have some choice. It is more likely that there is a scarcity of available placements, and this may result in fierce competition between students and between programs to secure placements. Some agencies, by the nature of their service, have very clear requirements that may stop you from doing placement there: for example, a male student would not usually be placed in a domestic violence refuge, a family therapy service may not want to take an inexperienced student, and a multicultural agency may require a student to speak a particular language.

If your program offers some choice, you need to prepare for the process of selecting a placement well before you begin the stage of final negotiation.

Where you do your placement will often be a compromise between important considerations, such as:

- the availability of placements
- the factors that best help you to learn
- your expectations for the placement and your ambitions for practice when you graduate
- the practical considerations in balancing placement with the rest of your life.

A successful placement will have the necessary ingredients to make it workable and meet your personal and educational needs.

Of course, the course coordinator is responsible for helping you with your academic preparation for placement, as well as providing information about the variety of available placements. They will probably give you specific guidelines and expectations for placement, so read this chapter in conjunction with these. If your program allows you some choice, it is helpful to work through a self-assessment process to ensure that you can make an informed choice.

Planning for placement

Students often worry that their lack of practical experience will disadvantage them, and they forget that they usually have had some experiences that will help them with the demands of placement (Royse, Dhooper & Rompf 1993, p. 28).

The following steps provide you with the basic information you need to consider in planning for your placement. If you have already done a placement, then include that experience in your review.

Step 1: Self-assessment

The first step is to conduct an audit of the things that you bring to the placement. It comprises the skills, knowledge and experience that you have gained throughout your life and includes the following:

1 Education history, including specialisations such as politics, women's studies, criminology, and mental health. Education provides useful background knowledge in most placements. The learning achievements of a previous placement would also be relevant.
2 Work history, including paid and voluntary work in welfare-oriented or other fields. Previous work experience gives you important knowledge and skills.
3 Personal history, including any significant life events, such as being a parent, suffering the death of a significant person, having a disability, migrating from another country, travelling, or other experiences that have shaped your thinking and maturity.

All these experiences help in the next stage of identifying your practice framework.

In Chapter 2, there is an inventory for assessing your learning style (pp. 19–21). It may be helpful to do this as part of the planning process to include in your skills and knowledge audit. Learning styles are not fixed and it is important to consider ways in which you can expand your learning approaches on placement to improve your capacity to maximise your learning experience. Your assessment could enable you to identify, at the beginning of placement, what will help you learn during the placement.

Identifying your framework

The combination of knowledge, skills and values forms a framework for understanding the world of practice, and how you use this framework in part depends on how you like to think things through. In explaining your framework, maybe you move from big ideas to particular incidents. For instance, say you believe that the particular issues people face are a result of broader inequalities in society; this overarching idea will affect your understanding of situations (your knowledge), and hence what approach you will adopt (your skills). This knowledge and these skills are supported by a set of values – for example, you believe in empowerment or self-determination. You might like to test out your broad ideas by thinking about particular situations. Consider the following example.

> You are discussing with your siblings who should pay for repairs to a house that was bequeathed to your widowed mother. Your mother has an adequate but not extensive income. The will states that if your mother dies, the house will become the property, in equal shares, of the surviving siblings. You feel that you should not be hoping to maximise any potential gain for yourself in this situation, as, unlike your siblings, you don't have any dependants. The discussion covers issues about whether your mother should contribute to the cost of repairs, whether all the siblings should contribute, and to whom the house really belongs.
>
> Your responses indicate something about what you believe and know in this situation. You think that as it is your mother's house you should support her to stay there as long as she likes. As she looks after the house, you feel that she should not have to make a further contribution now. Would you feel differently if you had a family of your own for whom you had to provide? Would you think equal shares were fair when the other siblings have spouses who work? The different situations of each of your siblings might highlight different value positions.

Workers often experience a gap between what they say in principle and what they ought to do in practice. Exploring this gap helps them to identify their ideal in relation to what is real in a given situation. Thinking about these gaps may give you ideas about areas of knowledge, skills and values you might like to work on in placement.

Your self-assessment will help you to explain to your potential supervisor what matters to you about human services, what you know about and what you know how to do.

EXERCISE 1

Fill out this table to identify your knowledge, skills and values in the three key areas of education, work and personal history.

	What do you know?	What skills do you have?	What are the main values that you hold?
From your studies			
From your work experience			
From your life in general			
From this review you will be able to identify:			

- what is of core interest to you at this time
- what framework of skills, knowledge and values currently underpins your hopes for achievement in your chosen profession
- where your framework needs to be developed further.

Step 2: The placement setting

Once you have identified what interests you in relation to your current abilities, the next stage is to make the link between these interests and the type of agency that you consider would help you to capitalise on your assets and meet your goals. To identify a placement that is likely to suit you, consider the following.

What type of agency would you prefer?

Information about the agency could include the focus of the work, its size, the number of staff and how bureaucratic it is; it may also indicate the rules and regulations you will have to follow. Obviously, a large bureaucratic setting will offer a different placement experience to a small voluntary agency.

Some types of agencies include:
- government – federal, state and local
- non-government organisations (NGOs)
- not-for-profit organisations, which are often run by community organisations or churches
- private organisations that may make a profit.

How comfortable are you working in a small and more intimate setting in contrast to a larger and less personal workplace? Human service agencies have both strengths and limitations. What could each type of agency offer you? A larger organisation may provide more resources and opportunities for observing different styles of practice. Some students feel more comfortable or familiar with an agency in which guidelines are clear and lines of authority are explicit. A smaller organisation may offer a more intimate relationship with staff members, and you may be required to cover a greater range of tasks because work roles are less regulated.

Consider your previous work experience or perhaps a previous placement. It may be appropriate and important to experience a contrast to this. Do you have any preferences? If so, what are they and why have you reached these conclusions?

What type of clients interest you?

Human service agencies provide services for people from a wide and diverse range of ages and backgrounds. Due to specialisation within the field, most agencies target a particular segment of the population (Kiser 2000). The following list identifies some examples of key target groups:

aged people	offenders
children	people with disabilities
ethnic communities	students
families	unemployed people
general public	veterans
low-income earners	women
men	young people

Do you have particular life or work experiences that make working with any of these groups more or less interesting? Sometimes it is better to avoid areas in which you already have such experiences. At other times, these experiences have a lot to do with why you are doing the course, and you may prefer to do placements in which you work with people to whom you already have a strong commitment.

You might choose to work with groups where you think you can make a difference and you may be less interested if you think their issues are 'permanent' and practice is not going to make their issues 'go away'. You may conclude that, in the latter situation, you would become too frustrated. This conclusion may be in your mind and not accurately reflect reality. You need to acknowledge such beliefs because they will impact on your practice. You may be 'giving' others problems that really belong to you.

What issues interest you?

Human services vary in terms of their major goals and purpose. Some agencies offer a generalist service to people with a range of issues, whereas others will specialise in one type of service. The particular field of practice of an agency tells you about the specialised needs of the clients with whom you will be working.

Use the following list to determine your interest in these different fields of practice. Are there areas you particularly want to avoid at this time? If so, why?

FIELD	LEVEL OF INTEREST
addictions	
ageing (including community care and residential care)	
child protection	
child and family welfare (foster care, parent support, residential care)	
corrections	
crisis support	
disability	
education	
employment assistance	
family violence	
health (hospital and community)	
homelessness (youth, adult and family)	
income security	
information and referral	
legal	
mental health	
rehabilitation	

What skills do you want to gain?

It is important to consider what skills you want to gain from placement. Your learning needs and values, your current level of knowledge and skills, and the type of placement will impact on your skills development. For example, it is unlikely that you could undertake a family therapy placement if you have not studied family therapy in your course or as part of your professional development.

Consider the following list of skills, adapted from the Victorian Combined Schools of Social Work questionnaire. You may want to develop or improve in:

advocacy	information and referral
casework	community development
case management	research
counselling	social policy
emergency assistance	program development
crisis intervention	groupwork

Think about what type of agency would best help you to gain the skills you have identified.

Step 3: Personal interests

Your motivation for and interest in pursuing this course has to be a major consideration in your choice of a placement, although this may not be fulfilled in all of your placements. Your motivation may be based on your future career aspirations, beliefs and passions, or strong feelings about certain fields or approaches or human service issues.

Practical considerations

Your choice of placement may be affected by domestic and personal circumstances such as:

- *Location:* How far are you prepared to travel to the agency?
- *Transport:* Is the agency well-serviced by public transport? If you use your car, does the agency provide a parking bay? In some agencies it is necessary to have a driver's licence, if not a vehicle.
- *Domestic issues:* Do you have flexibility in your working hours, or do you have responsibilities to pick up children, attend to a family member, go to work and so on?
- *Financial considerations:* You may need to consider a local placement to reduce the cost of public transport or using your car. If the agency expects you to use your car, can you afford this? Will the agency reimburse your costs?
- *Police clearance:* Increasingly, students have to provide evidence that they don't have a criminal history of concern to the agency. If in doubt about your own circumstances, it is important to check this out with your training institution or in the interview when you meet your supervisor.
- *Immunisation:* Some agencies now request that students be immunised if they are going to work in settings where they may be exposed to infection. This can be expensive and uncomfortable for some, so it may be important for you to ask.
- *Time or workload constraints:* Do you need a part-time placement? This will be determined largely by your training institution, but it may be a positive option. This may limit what kind of placement you can choose, as many agencies want a full-time placement, but some agencies do prefer a part-time student because of staffing or space considerations. You should ask yourself how a part-time placement might help or hinder your learning.

Step 4: The pre-placement interview

The purpose of the pre-placement interview is to find out whether this placement has the broad potential to meet your learning requirements. You will, therefore, need to be clear about your requirements before you meet with your supervisor. Exercise 2 comprises some useful questions to think about.

Some suggestions about preparing for the pre-placement interview follow Exercise 2.

EXERCISE 2

1 What can you learn from this placement?
2 Is there sufficient scope for you to experience the aspect of practice in which you are interested?
3 What/how can you learn from your supervisor?

What do you need to know about the agency?

Supervisors are busy and would appreciate not having to describe the essential activities of their agency if the information is available on the Internet or in a pamphlet. However, they need to know that you are interested enough to research the field and that you have a broad understanding of the function of the agency, the client group(s) that it serves and, perhaps, some of the types of services it provides. Write a list of relevant questions to help focus the interview.

If the agency is nearby, you can get this information by dropping in to look around and obtain an annual report or pamphlets. Don't expect to chat to your supervisor or other workers at this point. Talk to other students and staff from the training institution. Look up the agency's website, if they have one. Staff at your training institution will usually have information and ideas to help you research the agency or the field of practice.

What do you want to find out at the interview?

Make a list of the practical considerations you want to discuss at the interview. Some considerations may be:
- Will you use an agency car or your own car for work? Does the agency reimburse transport costs?
- Do you require a driver's licence?
- Are you likely to be included in agency meetings?
- Where will you sit? Do you have a computer and telephone and, if not, how can you access one?
- What are the requirements regarding starting times, lunch breaks, finishing times, any out-of-hours work?
- What are the likely tasks of the placement?

Step 5: Applying for a pre-placement meeting

It is becoming more common for supervisors to want more control over the selection process, and so students may be asked to write a letter of introduction or provide a curriculum vitae before a placement interview is offered. This means that you need to be particularly well- prepared and organised to present yourself and your learning needs to a potential supervisor. There may be more than one staff member at the interview and they may want you to present some examples of your work, an academic transcript or perhaps a previous field placement evaluation. A summary of the self-assessment exercises above could be sent or shared.

Step 6: Meeting your supervisor

You will often meet your supervisor for the first time at the pre-placement interview. Your supervisor is critical to the success of your placement, and effective supervision is most likely to occur when there is a match between the learning needs of the student and the approach of the supervisor (Alle-Corliss & Alle-Corliss 1998, p. 65). However, it can be very difficult to assess your personal and academic compatibility with a supervisor in one interview. In addition, your institution may not give you much choice about where you do your placement.

Your expectations are crucial to the success of your placement. It is best to aim for a 'good enough' relationship with your supervisor. Remember that you may have an excellent learning experience with someone who has a very different view of life. The best placements are those in which you have taken some risks and been challenged beyond your comfort zone.

EXERCISE 3

From the list below, select three attributes of an effective supervisor that will be crucial to your learning on placement. Select another two that are desirable but not essential.

ATTRIBUTES	DURING THE PRE-PLACEMENT INTERVIEW
Your supervisor has the time to supervise you.	Your supervisor offers adequate time for the interview, appears prepared and not exhausted, has already thought about some tasks for placement and has prepared information for you.
Your supervisor supervises in a way that is complementary to your style of learning.	Your supervisor discusses the style of supervision, how often it will take place and the expectations for the content of supervision. He or she may use different methods of supervision (for example, process recordings, observations, and so on).
Your supervisor's personality will not clash too much with your own.	For example, does your supervisor have a sense of humour? Is his or her office too tidy or too messy?
Your supervisor has expertise and ability.	Your supervisor has experience in the field and is able to articulate his or her knowledge and skills.
Your supervisor has the ability to share knowledge and skills.	Your supervisor has experience in supervising staff and students and is able to talk about his or her knowledge and skills in an inclusive and accessible way.
Your supervisor is open to your ideas and values difference.	Your supervisor asks questions about your goals and views, does not dominate the discussion, and is respectful of your ability and background.
Your supervisor is willing to allow you to experience a range of practice situations.	Your supervisor is not overprotective of clients, allows you access to staff activities, discusses ways to involve you, and assists you to develop autonomy and self-directed learning as the placement progresses.
Your supervisor has involved the agency and other staff.	The administrative staff respond positively to you. The supervisor involves other staff in the interview or in the placement.
Your supervisor is honest and self-aware.	Your supervisor does not appear defensive about his or her work or knowledge and is able to say what he or she does not know.

After your initial meeting you will have formed impressions of each other and will have some preliminary expectations of supervision: Can you trust your supervisor? Does your supervisor seem interested in you as a person? Are you interested in what motivates your supervisor as a practitioner? Completing Exercise

3, after the pre-placement interview, helps you to decide whether your supervisor can offer you effective supervision.

The important items that you should have answers to at the conclusion of this interview include:

- your field educator's own professional background and experience, including his or her placement supervision and other supervision experiences
- whether your broad learning goals for the placement can be met
- whether your potential supervisor is interested in you and what you bring to the placement
- the frequency, length and availability of the supervisor for formal supervision
- the range of other people who will be involved in supervision
- whether specific learning and/or practical needs have been discussed and resolved.
- the degree of access to other people in the organisation

Be careful of placements that will only allow you to do administrative tasks that will not extend your skills and knowledge. Most agencies require all staff to undertake some administrative activities, such as answering telephones and photocopying, so students should expect to contribute in this way. However, it is important that you have work that is relevant to your learning goals and that you start, maintain and finish a project with or work with individuals, groups or families.

Summary

Taking the time to prepare for placement by thinking about what you *want* and what you *need* will help you to negotiate a successful placement and begin it with realistic and positive expectations. Planning will also help you to make the best use of the initial interview with your supervisor and to set some practical objectives, so that your experience on placement will challenge you to learn new skills and methods or practice without overwhelming you.

2

PREPARING FOR PLACEMENT – SUPERVISOR

Introduction

You are a worker in a busy human service agency. You receive a call from a university, a TAFE or a student to enquire whether you will take a student on placement. Or perhaps your team leader approaches you to supervise a placement, and you have been thinking about supervising a student for some time. A number of factors could be helpful to consider at this point.

- Are you ready to have a student on placement?
- Is your organisation able to support a student placement and, if so, what sort of work would be available for the student?
- How will you determine the right 'fit' between you, the agency and the student?
- What do you know about teaching?
- What would you expect of a supervisor if you were going on placement?
- What characteristics of supervision do you think are important?

In many cases, the only models of supervision that workers have are those they experienced as students or as participants in other training courses. Your experiences of being supervised will play a part in shaping your work as a placement supervisor.

EXERCISE 1

Make a note of three characteristics of supervision that you valued and three things that concerned you as a student in your placement or in a training course. Examine your list. Do you think you will be able to offer the first three characteristics and avoid the second three?

For example, students may value the following characteristics:
- They are given the opportunity to get involved in the work fairly quickly.
- They are given feedback about what they do well, as well as what they do less well.
- They have time and space to try new things.

They may be concerned about the following:
- They are asked to spend a lot of time analysing details when they are already very busy.
- They are left too much to work things out for themselves.
- There is no appropriate time and space for thinking things through.

In this example, the students seem to have a dominant learning style that is focused on learning from doing, and they like it when placement achieves this and struggle when a different learning style is required.

As a worker, you are probably more flexible in how you learn, but you should remember that your student might have a similar learning style to the students in the example at this stage of his or her development. In the example, it helped that the students were interested in getting involved quickly, but this may be more difficult for a student in your agency – it is important to ensure, however, that your student is given some 'doing' things in the early days. You also need to remember that students who seem quite competent should not be taken for granted and asked to do more and more. Students can be asked to do so much that their learning is compromised. It is important for students to have an appropriate space and access to the facilities they need to do a placement in your agency.

Preparing for placement

Is your agency ready?

For students to fully experience the 'flavour' of social work practice in a particular setting, they must have access to resources, personnel and knowledge as if they are a staff member (Ford & Jones 1987, p. 16).

It is difficult to find an agency that does not experience uncertainty and crises, and it is helpful for students to observe how agencies adapt and change as a response. However, students need an environment that is stable enough so that they are not confronted with chaos on a daily basis.

Having a student on placement does make demands on staff time and energy and can interfere with established work patterns, so staff need to be willing to welcome a temporary new member and to spend time with them.

Can your agency offer a good placement?

Students generally report that they learn a great deal from all agency staff and that this is a valuable aspect of being on placement. As the placement supervisor, you are responsible for ensuring that students are given opportunities to interact with other staff, that staff are clear about what they can ask the student to do, and that the student is clear about lines of accountability. You are generally responsible for the student's workload, so you need to know what they are already doing and what others are asking them to do. Information and support on placement comes from many sources both from within and outside your agency. Perhaps it helps to consider that being a placement supervisor is like being a conductor in an orchestra – you bring things together, you know what is happening, you help the student to make sense of their part in the whole process and show them how they can fine-tune their performance, but you can't run around playing all the instruments yourself.

If you are likely to be very busy and unavailable for certain periods, then co-supervise with a colleague. Task supervision by another staff member, or supervision provided by the training institution or a part-time placement may be other ways to offer a viable placement.

Sometimes having more than one student on placement means the students can support each other and solve problems together, instead of relying on the supervisor for ideas and feedback. Group supervision may improve time management, although individual supervision will still need to take place. If support is available from the student's training institution, it is generally a good idea to say, as early as possible, if you think that extra input from the institution would be helpful.

Does your agency have work for a student?

Students need defined tasks for their placement. They need the opportunity to reach agreed objectives in their work with individuals, groups or communities. A range of issues can arise in allocating work: for example, students may be given the work others don't want; they may be kept away from clients who are seen as being too vulnerable or from work that is politically sensitive. Certainly you will want to assess the student's capacity for such work. Some agencies have 'student' cases, those handed from one student to the next. This practice may give clients an opportunity to become skilled in teaching the student, but this often is not explicitly negotiated and is largely exploitative of both students and clients.

With appropriate support, students can do quite complicated and difficult work well, in part because they have more time to work out what they are doing and to follow through on agreed tasks in a timely manner. Agencies tend to provide simple initial tasks – unfortunately, there is no such thing as a simple task and the most routine of tasks can lead to unimagined outcomes.

For the agency, placement may be a great opportunity to get a task done. Indeed, this may be why the agency agreed to offer the placement, and students may enjoy having responsibility for this task as they can see its significance in meeting organisational goals.

Sometimes the work of the agency, by its nature, is too long-term or complex for placement, or it may involve statutory responsibilities for which workers require professional accreditation; hence, it is not suitable for a student on short-term placement. In this case, a project or an evaluation of an agency project may be preferable. If the student requires direct practice and this is not an option in your agency, then co-counselling, with responsible oversight by the supervisor, may offer the learning opportunity for the student.

Have you covered workplace issues?

One of the first issues of concern to many agencies is the level of insurance cover provided by the training institution to cover public liability for any actions of the student, and personal accident insurance for the student. It is important to understand what these provisions are before any need for them arises. The agency insurance policy in relation to the students driving their vehicles should also be explored. Of course, a number of training bodies and agencies will have policies around security checks on potential students that may be required. Many organisations will also have procedural manuals and policies that cover promoting the personal safety of students, and it is important to ensure that students are aware of these.

Students usually obtain a police check prior to the pre-placement interview and could be asked to take the result of the check to the interview to show their prospective supervisor. Many agencies now have stricter policies, and you may need to check if this level of police check meets your agency's requirements.

Students are likely to be required to discuss their experiences on placement in class or in assignments. It is very helpful if you can be clear with students what the agency policy is around ensuring confidentiality. Students may be asked to sign undertakings regarding confidentiality and secrecy, and it is important that field educators consider the implications of these with students, given their status as students who are learning from practice.

Why does your agency want a student on placement?

An agency may see students – particularly students who are finishing their course – as potential locum workers to cover for holidays, or even perhaps as potential employees, in which case they will want students who are as ready for work as possible. An agency may take students to assist in developing a new approach to work, to do a piece of research or to do an integral part of the agency's work – for example, run particular groups – in which case, again, students will need to be highly competent at the beginning of placement. It is reasonable to expect at a minimum that students do the same amount of work you as a field educator can get done in the time it takes to support and educate the student. Nearer to graduation, this balance should shift to be substantially greater.

Students can make you think about what you are doing and how you do it. They also keep you in touch with theoretical developments. Assisting a student to learn is therefore a useful way of pushing yourself to think more about your practice.

Why do you want a student on placement?

Supervisors are essential to successful field placements in their roles as field educators. They link the student, the agency and the school; teach practice knowledge and skills and serve as mentors and role models (Bogo

& Vayda 1998). This important role represents additional work but is rarely institutionalised as a formal part of a worker's role. Research suggests that it is intrinsic factors, such as enjoying teaching, contributing to the profession, and professional development and challenge through teaching, that were the primary motivators. 'The process of teaching inquisitive students stimulated critical reflection and interest in new perspectives for their own practices' (Globerman & Bogo 2003).

Choosing a student

If the agency has taken other students in the past, they may have preferences in regard to a student's age, gender, personality style, year level, and so on. Agencies that take students on a regular basis tend to define a clear role for the student; whether every student fits that role is an important point to consider in making your choice.

EXERCISE 2

Ask your colleagues the following questions.

1 If this agency were to take a student on placement now, what characteristic would you *most* like the student to have?
2 If this agency were to take a student on placement now, what characteristic would you *least* like the student to have?

The general robustness of your agency at this particular time will probably have an impact on how much risk it is possible to take in selecting a student. For example, if the team is cohesive, colleagues are likely to enjoy a challenge and will support a placement, even if you feel that a student may struggle to meet the standards set by you, your agency and the training institution. Overt and covert intolerance of difference by colleagues in regard to characteristics such as gender, age and culture may be issues to consider.

EXERCISE 3

Think about the following questions.

1 Are there any issues in your agency at the moment that might impact on a student?
2 If so, what implications will this have for your choice of student?
3 Would it be better for your agency to have more than one student at this time?
4 Are there any risks for you or your team in having a student on placement at this time?
5 If so, what implications will this have for your choice of student?

How are placements allocated?

Training institutions have different ways of allocating placements to students, but it is important to find the right fit between you, your agency and the student. In most training institutions, supervisors, students, the school and the agency all exercise choice in the selection process. Depending on the institution's requirements, you may be asked to give reasons for making a particular choice so that the school and the student are aware of any issues that need to be dealt with to find an appropriate placement for the student. All parties can experience feelings of rejection as well as acceptance; hence, it is important to think through how you will make your decision.

Are you ready to be a supervisor?

Most of the responsibility in deciding whether you are ready to take a student rests with you. Most training institutions and professional associations define readiness to take a student in terms of the length of time a person has been a practitioner. This is usually two years, based on the assumption that this allows practitioners time to develop enough confidence in their knowledge and skills to be able to teach a student. Reynolds (1965) contended that when people began learning to be practitioners, they moved through a series of stages, the last of which involves the ability to teach others.

It might be worthwhile to consider how often in your current practice you are at the stages outlined by Reynolds (1965):

- acute consciousness of self
- 'sink or swim' adaptation – you jump in and rely on your reactions to either sink or swim
- understanding the situation, but not necessarily being able consciously to direct behaviour
- relative mastery, when the practitioner can both understand the practice situation and purposefully direct behaviour.

Fook, Ryan and Hawkins (2000) analysed the responses of social work and community-development students, as well as new and experienced graduates, to practice vignettes and critical incidents. The responses showed how views of practice changed as the students and graduates became more experienced, and how professional practice is not only about the effective application of knowledge but also is the commitment to and enactment of particular social values and ethical positions.

Their suggested theory of learning offers another way that you might think about your professional development. It could also be helpful in articulating your approach to practice to a student. Consider the following scenario.

> An experienced practitioner, who had supervised many placements, encountered a challenging situation with a student. The student appeared to be competent, but did not seem to want to learn. She was able to discuss the importance of doing a good job, but did not reflect on her practice once it was established that her work was at an acceptable level. The supervisor persisted in trying to engage her in reflective discussions throughout the placement, using a range of strategies to get the student to evaluate her practice, but without success. It was a very frustrating time. After the placement was over, the supervisor decided that she needed to get to the bottom of this situation. She went to the training institution to debrief, and it became clear that, over the course of the placement, the student had come to represent all that the supervisor did not value in practitioners; however, because the quality of the student's work with clients was acceptable, the supervisor did not feel she could legitimately challenge her. The student had made the supervisor feel powerless and had challenged all she held dear. The supervisor applied the knowledge she used in practice to understand how she and the student got caught in this unhelpful cycle. She concluded that in future she would be more explicit that what she valued in practitioners or students was not just their capacity to do the work, but their willingness to learn from it.

Learning to supervise a student is likely to involve you in going through some or all of these developmental stages again. Using the model on page 17, adapted from Fook, Ryan and Hawkins (2000), is a way that you can reflect on your approach to practice.

Describing your approach to practice

One of the key places students learn to link practice and broad ideas is placement. Much of this learning occurs in the context of what is discussed on placement and through supervisors modelling behaviours for their students. As a supervisor, you can best help a student learn if you are able to describe the knowledge, skills and values that underpin your approach to practice. As part of supervision, you will probably ask your student to tell you why something occurred, how they put ideas into practice, and what matters to them as human service workers. Can you articulate these ideas yourself?

DEVELOPMENTAL STAGE MODEL

LEARNING STAGE	CHARACTERISTICS
Individualised approach	The student progresses from looking at social problems in an individualised way to examining the broader context.
Social distancing	The student distances people who are 'different' from them, and experience actually strengthens this bias.
The atheoretical 'agony aunt' syndrome	The student has a tendency to assess and interpret a problem from a simplistic and informal perspective instead of a more formal theoretical perspective.
Problematising and pathologising	The student attributes causes of problems to simple factors, rather than more complex contextual and structural factors that are less easily worked on.
Use of theory	The student progresses from using less theory to using more theory in practice.
Use of community resources	The student moves from having little reliance on community resources to having a greater awareness and use of community resources.
Development of professional identity	The student begins with little identification with the profession, then, with experience, gains more identification.
Perspective on the profession	The student develops from being disillusioned to having increased confidence and a positive orientation to the profession.
Use of authority and dealing with conflict	The student demonstrates a growing comfort with the use of authority and dealing with conflict.

Your approach to practice is made up of a set of beliefs and assumptions about how and why people encounter challenges in contemporary society, how people and communities can change or develop, and what workers can do to assist this change or development. Your approach to practice may comprise several approaches, depending on the demands of the situation, or you may be quite specialised and use one particular approach.

Can you teach others?

In deciding to become a supervisor, you need to think about how you go about teaching others. 'While poor practitioners will not make good supervisors, it does not follow that competent practitioners will automatically make skilful teachers' (Ford & Jones 1987, p. 1).

It is a good idea to have experience in paid employment to give you enough time to be sure of your role as a professional before supervising a student. If you are less experienced or confident, co-supervising with a more experienced worker is a good way to ease you into supervision as you share the responsibility and can discuss issues.

EXERCISE 4

As a starting point, think back over your interview for your current job. What did you tell the interviewers about yourself and your work? What did you suggest that employing you would mean for the organisation?

Think about the following questions.

1 What keeps you coming to work? What matters to you in relation to your contact with the people for whom your workplace provides a service?

You may, for example, believe that providing more opportunities for people, redressing inequalities, giving people a voice and so on is what matters.

2 How do you understand the issues that you deal with in your work?

You might think that these issues are a reflection of a person's innate capacities and limits, you might think people are simply victims of oppressive societal practices or you might believe that both are true. Or is there another way of understanding the issues?

3 What knowledge do you use in your practice and how do you develop and evaluate that knowledge?

Think here of the strains between the constraints on your agency and what you know about the issues which you deal with. Think about what you know about human beings and the society in which they live. How have you developed and tested this knowledge? What does your chosen approach suggest about what matters to you?

4 What skills do you use in putting this knowledge into practice? How did you develop these skills?

Think about the level of skills that you have: some skills are likely to be general and used in a wide range of contexts, others may be very specific. They will relate to work with a wide range of people, including workmates, clients, managers and so on.

5 What ethical positions and values matter to you?

One way of thinking about this is to recall situations you found challenging and try to discern what made you feel happy with the outcomes and what made you feel less happy.

6 How do you characterise your skills, knowledge and values?

For some people, one word, such as feminist or humanist may characterise their approach. For others, it is more complex and may involve balancing conflicting approaches. Can you identify your approach for your students and perhaps relate it to the theory they have studied in their course?

Two main dimensions of helping others to learn are explored here. The first dimension is what motivates you to want to help someone learn about your area of practice and how you conceptualise your practice. The second dimension is your own approach to learning.

In Exercises 1 and 4, you reflected on your experiences of supervision and your current approach to practice. To answer these questions you needed to think about the things that are important to you, what you enjoy about your work, what you like about yourself and what makes you uncomfortable. These factors help to establish your framework for helping someone else to learn. There is often a close correlation between practice frameworks and approaches to teaching that practice. Supervisors don't have different tool kits labelled 'work' and 'teaching practice' – what is different, of course, is their purpose: how they make use of these tools. These ideas are developed further in Part 4.

Gardiner (1989) identified three levels of learning interaction between students and placement supervisors: the focus on the *content* of learning, the focus on the *process* of learning, and the process of *learning to learn*. He argued that supervisors' understanding of the teaching and learning processes determines the level at which they will teach. Since these levels are cumulative, if supervisors' interactions are at the 'learning to learn' level, they will be able to focus on process and content, if that is appropriate for the demands of a particular situation.

This understanding is supported by knowledge about learning processes – a discipline in its own right and grounded in principles derived from educational, social and psychological theories about how people learn. It is important for teachers to draw on these theories (Shardlow & Doel 1996, p. 10)

In making the transition from practitioner to teacher, it is important to understand your own learning style and not assume that others will also learn the same way. Different approaches to learning respond to different approaches to teaching. The incorporation of critical theories in teaching and learning encourages the supervisor to value the student's unique approach to the way that they make sense of the knowledge–practice relationship. This is discussed in more detail in Chapter 6.

When teaching methods correspond with a student's preferred learning strategy, the student's learning achievements will be enhanced (Shardlow & Doel 1996, p. 64). Of course, as placement proceeds, students should be encouraged to develop their approaches to learning in the areas in which they have less facility.

In the pre-placement stage, it can be useful to assess your own learning style, using Exercise 5. This gives you a way to describe your learning style, and hence your favoured approaches to teaching. Your student may have done this exercise or something similar before placement. When he or she begins placement, it may be helpful to compare your learning profiles and identify any commonalities, and then to explore what this comparison suggests about the teaching and learning methods used on placement.

EXERCISE 5

ASSESSING YOUR PREFERRED LEARNING STRATEGIES

The following statements describe different strategies of learning. You are asked to rate each statement from 0 to 4, with 4 representing the statement most accurate for you. Tick one box only for each statement.

No.	Learning strategy	Statement	0	1	2	3	4
1	CE	I prefer to discuss my work with colleagues, because it helps me to think about what I am doing.					
2	RO	I prefer to accurately recall a situation, such as observing someone else's work, but keep an open mind about what I heard or saw.					
3	AC	I prefer to logically reason out the relationship between events and experiences.					
4	AE	I prefer to test out my ideas.					
5	AE	I prefer to participate in group discussion, contribute my ideas, hear the group's reactions, and reach consensus about what to do.					
6	CE	I prefer to develop my ideas through interaction in everyday situations with lots of people, such as colleagues, friends and family.					
7	AC	I prefer to read textbooks or articles and arrive at the meaning for myself, responding to the intellectual challenge.					
8	CE	I prefer to do something concrete, such as conducting an interview, rather than read theory.					
9	RO	I prefer to derive ideas through critical reflection on my past experience: for example, in my career or when I learnt the skills that I now use; or even refer to my past writing.					
10	AC	I prefer to derive my ideas and concepts from experts or use resource books prepared by qualified specialists.					

No.	Learning strategy	Statement	0	1	2	3	4
11	CE	I prefer to rely on my gut reaction to the overall picture (for example, a situation in my agency).					
12	AE	I prefer to learn by experimenting with new methods or ideas about practice.					
13	AC	I prefer to work from a set of principles or recognised theory as guidelines for my own practice and for supervision of students.					
14	RO	I prefer to observe impartially what happens in my own agency.					
15	RO	I prefer to work in groups in which I am expected to throw in ideas that may be creative or imaginative, but may not be strictly logical.					
16	AE	I prefer to be challenged to explore new experiences and ideas or take on new roles despite the uncertainties and the possibility of criticism.					

SCORING

To identify your preferred learning strategy, add the scores that you assigned to each question in the groupings listed below. For example, if you scored 4, 3, 2 and 3 in questions 1, 6, 8 and 11, your result for (CE) Concrete Experience' would be 12 out of a total possible score of 16.

Learning strategy	Total score	Add question	Your results
(CE) Concrete experience	16	1, 6, 8, 11	
(RO) Reflective observation	16	2, 9, 14, 15	
(AC) Abstract conceptualisation	16	3, 7, 10, 13	
(AE) Active experimentation	16	4, 5, 12, 16	

You may find that you have one or two dominant learning styles – the ones with the highest scores. This indicates the processes you are practised at using. It may assist your learning and teaching to start with these approaches, then introduce the styles with which you are less familiar: You will be more effective as a teacher and learner if you can confidently use all styles.

BASIC LEARNING STRATEGIES

This table gives a description of the characteristics of each learning strategy.

Learning strategy	Emphasis	Characteristics
(CE) Concrete experience	Feeling	Uses the senses to actively participate in a situation Develops emotional rapport with others Uses intuition to explore a situation Explores the here-and-now Is concerned with practical outcomes
(RO) Reflective observation	Watching	Accurately recalls observations and perceptions about individuals and transactions Distinguishes between essential and trivial information Keeps an open mind and maintains impartiality in information-gathering Withholds judgements until all possible sources of data are accounted for Emphasises reflection instead of action

Learning strategy	Emphasis	Characteristics
(AC) Abstract conceptualisation	Thinking	Identifies relationships between concepts Draws conclusions from the analysis of data Develops tentative explanations Develops generalisations and principles from the information Develops a plan or proposal to address the identified issues
(AE) Active experimentation	Doing	Tests ideas and concepts already developed Attempts new activities in testing the ideas Tests hypotheses by active experimentation Identifies outcomes that have immediate applications Emphasises practical application instead of reflective understanding

LEARNING MODES, LEARNING ENVIRONMENTS AND EDUCATIONAL METHODS

The following table identifies the ideal learning environment and education methods for each mode of learning.

Mode of learning	Learning environment	Educational method
Concrete experience	Emphasises personal experiences	Prefers: • individualised feedback • sharing feelings about the subject matter • a collegial relationship • self-direction Potential constraint: • theoretical assignments
Reflective observation	Understands concepts	Prefers: • observation and appreciation • expert interpretations • guiding and limiting discussions with others • performance to be judged by external criteria Potential constraint: • task-oriented assignments
Abstract conceptualisation	Prefers logical thinking	Prefers: • case studies • thinking alone • reading and discussing theory Potential constraint: • group interaction and role simulations
Active experimentation	Applies knowledge and skills	Prefers: • small-group discussions • projects • peer feedback • modelling by others Potential constraint: • didactic presentations

Adapted from AASWWE 1991, p. 62

Exercise 5 is based on the work of Kolb (1984), who developed his model of experimental learning in part from an empirical study of social work competencies. Most people's learning style is made up of the four main learning styles described in the exercise. Over time in our practice area, we are likely to develop a relatively balanced approach to learning, because different situations call for different learning strategies. However, when you start out as a supervisor, you might find yourself reverting to type as you tackle a new task. This exercise is useful for supervisors to identify themes in their teaching style as well as their learning style.

Learning styles can be characterised in a range of ways, but this approach to describing learning is a good starting point and will be referred to throughout the text. What is essential is that you and the student discuss your differing understandings and experiences of learning and use these to promote a framework for learning on placement (Shardlow & Doel 1996, p. 74).

People who are concrete (CE) and active (AE) learners will prefer to carry out tasks and work in a team rather than observe others at work. They will learn by reviewing what they have done. People who are abstract (AC) and reflective (RO), on the other hand, may prefer to read a rationale for service delivery, to discuss the program with other workers, and to conceptualise tasks before carrying them out (AASWWE 1991, p. 63).

Exercise 5 also helps you to identify the range of ways students will learn on placement. These can be discussed with students as a way to ensure that there is a reasonable fit between the teaching and learning activities you can provide and the ones students desire.

A simpler version of learning styles, the *Learning Styles Questionnaire*, was developed in 1986 by Honey and Mumford. This model also built upon the work of Kolb and originally was intended to identify the learning styles of managers, so be cautious about applying this framework to the human services.

The four categories defined by Honey and Mumford (1986) are as follows:

- *Activist:* Activists are enthusiastic for new experiences and tend to be dominated by their immediate focus of attention. They welcome new challenges but become bored by implementation and consolidation. They may rush hastily into activities and tend to centre everything on themselves and not consider others.
- *Reflector:* Reflectors observe and evaluate experiences from several different perspectives, collecting as much data as possible and considering many alternatives before deciding on a course of action. They tend to be thoughtful and cautious and may avoid taking action.
- *Theorist:* Theorists mould their observations into complex and logically sound theories. They think problems through in a systematic and analytical way, and their approach may appear detached.
- *Pragmatist:* Pragmatists enjoy experimentation and applying ideas and theories in practice and engaging in active problem-solving. There is a danger that they may cut corners, thereby minimising a proper consideration of facts and feelings (Morrison 2001, p. 93).

Usually one learning style dominates over others and predisposes people to learn best from a particular range of activities. It should not be adhered to rigorously, however, as people are not stuck with one style and using different learning methods should be encouraged. Personal characteristics, such as gender, age and ethnicity, also will influence the way that you teach and how the learning experience is perceived by students (Berg-Weger & Birkenmaier 2000, p. 4).

Meeting the student

First impressions are very important in your assessment about the potential fit between you, your agency and the student. For this reason, some supervisors prefer not to have a great deal of information about the student before they meet them for the first time. For the same reason, other supervisors prefer to know as much as possible so that they can consider how they may best meet the student's needs. The meeting is your opportunity to let the student know what he or she can expect in your agency, as well as to get to know the student.

Some supervisors choose to run the pre-placement meeting like a job interview, using criteria against which they measure the student's responses. Others find it helpful to invite students to spend some time in the agency, so that they can meet a range of people and get an idea of how well they will fit in.

It helps to give the student a brief profile of the agency and some details about the staff, or your agency may have a website that students could be encouraged to explore before their interview. This is a time-efficient way to provide information, especially if you are expecting to interview more than one student. Useful information could include:

- a description of the agency – its mission or goals
- a snapshot of the clients
- an annual report
- a copy of any significant reports, brochures or other information that describes what the agency does and identifies the tasks and learning opportunities that may be available to the student.

You may also want to give the student some information about yourself. The following exercise can help you to identify what information may be useful.

EXERCISE 6

PROFESSIONAL PROFILE

Prepare a simple profile of your professional background and experience. You probably have a curriculum vitae that you could adapt to share with a prospective student. You could include relevant answers from Exercise 4 in which you outlined your practice frameworks.

Clarifying expectations

Doel et al. (1996, pp. 31–2) suggest the following exercises to help you identify your general expectations about student placements and your specific expectations for this placement, as well as to think about issues you might want to raise with prospective students.

EXERCISE 7

GENERAL EXPECTATIONS

Note your responses to the following statements.
1 What I like most about having students on placement is …
2 What I find most difficult is …
3 What is particularly important to me is that a student can …
4 I think the best things a student can get out of placement are …

SPECIFIC EXPECTATIONS FOR THIS PLACEMENT

1 One of my main hopes for this placement is …
2 One of my main concerns about this placement is …

The student could be invited to answer a similar set of questions when you meet to negotiate a placement. Moore (2000, p. 188) suggests some other useful questions to ask in this initial meeting. You could ask why the student is interested in this area of practice. If the student has had a previous field placement, he or she could comment on this experience, in particular the use made of learning opportunities. You could ask the student to identify one or two significant and/or challenging areas of learning for them.

Summary

The supervision experience can be enriching for practitioners and often gives them the opportunity to 'take stock' of their practice and consider their values and ideology. For supervisors to be effective teachers, it is important for them to identify their own learning styles and be aware of other styles so that, in the process of supervision, they can challenge and extend students in a variety of ways.

BEGINNING PLACEMENT

Building a successful placement experience requires thoughtful and attentive planning by both the supervisor and the student. The following three chapters offer ideas to develop a structured placement framework and is a good model for how professionals approach their work with people and communities.

The initial stage of placement includes orientation and the 'multiple beginnings' typical to placement (Kiser 2000, p. 8). As well as exploring the agency and the new environment, students will assess the strengths and limitations of the agency and find out where they can access support and optimum learning. Equally, supervisors will assess the student's strengths and learning needs to begin shaping appropriate tasks.

It will be helpful for students and supervisors to read both Chapters 3 and 4 – they cover the same stage of placement and similar content, but from different perspectives. Both chapters prepare students and supervisors for defining the learning goals and writing learning agreements and other forms of agreements, as discussed in Chapter 5.

2

3

GETTING STARTED – STUDENT

Introduction

By now you have met your supervisor at the initial interview. If you have been placed in a larger agency, you may have been interviewed by one person but assigned to another. If this is the case, it is important to organise a follow-up interview with your actual supervisor, preferably before the placement begins.

It may be apparent from the interview that you and your supervisor have different personality styles, values or interests, but you have agreed that the placement is going to offer you the opportunities you need to meet your important learning goals. You have little control or influence over the supervisor's personality or teaching style, but you can choose to make the most of the positive learning that is possible in the placement. Usually a compromise can be found.

Working in an organisation, like living in a family, is a process of ongoing adjustment and adaptation to change (Alle-Corliss & Alle-Corliss 1998, p. 205). It is unlikely that you will ever work completely on your own, and it is likely that you will spend your professional life in human services in some type of agency. So, learning how to thrive in organisations needs to be part of your long-term learning.

It is easy to be overwhelmed by all the facts, regulations, names, protocols and directions in your first days and weeks. Your supervisor will probably be making adjustments as well to meet the demands of the placement. Placements are relatively short, so it is important not to lose time hoping to 'pick it up'. You need to be a self-directed learner and proactive to ensure that you squeeze every bit of positive learning from this placement.

The first weeks

Remember that you are a student and are not supposed to know everything in your first week, if ever! Experience will give you skills and knowledge, and your supervisor will be aware that yours will be more limited in the beginning. Don't have unrealistic expectations that you will be able to master all possible human service tasks.

1 **Ask for help, directions, advice and names:** Try to use your own resources first – is the information you need contained in your student manual, or would another student know the answer? Most staff will respond positively to a polite question but may be less inclined to help if it is asked repeatedly, at inappropriate times, or if the answer is readily available elsewhere. The following steps will guide you through the first weeks.

2 **Observe and remember:** Link names to faces and positions, roles and departments. Collins, Thomlison and Grinnell (1992) suggest that these observations will not only help you to get to know your colleagues more quickly but will also help you to understand the personal and political nuances of the system in which you must function (p. 87). Later in this chapter the role of formal and informal structures is discussed. These structures help you to recognise early on whom you can trust and learn from and develop a supportive relationship with (Alle-Corliss & Alle-Corliss 1998, p. 42).

You can enhance your experience if you try to stay in the flow of the interaction within the organisation (Kiser 2000, p. 36). This may involve sharing lunch with agency workers, leaving the office door open to hear what banter is exchanged, and attending any scheduled formal or informal meetings.

3 **Read:** You may have become sick of reading during the classroom component of your course, but selective reading is a quick way to become familiar with the regular events occurring in the agency, and to gain essential knowledge about the agency and information about the client group.

4 **Record:** You are likely to be overwhelmed with information in the first few weeks. A diary or a journal can help you to record information and experiences and can also be used to organise the 'content' of your placement into smaller, more manageable parts that make sense to you. A diary is a log of your experiences as they occur. A journal has a number of purposes, including recording important dates and places to be. It can be used to record questions for your supervisor or others; it can contain a list of important information that you need to remember; and it can be a reflective tool to describe your journey through placement – your ideas, issues and concerns as a new professional. It can contain useful notes for discussion in supervision and for completing mid- and final-placement evaluations. Diaries, journals and other reflective tools are covered in more detail in Chapter 8.

5 **Communicate effectively:** The impact on communication of the power imbalance between you and your supervisor can be minimised if you set clear agreements about what you can expect from the other. Open communication helps to avoid misunderstandings and creates a positive working relationship. Most problematic situations can be turned around if you can tolerate shortcomings and concentrate on the positive aspects, thinking creatively of ways to overcome obstacles to your learning goals.

Some of the basic principles of assertive communication to observe during your placement are:
  * Express your fears, needs or concerns as 'I' statements, rather than as the supervisor's or agency's problems.
  * Express preferences as possibilities, not as if they are promised tasks.
  * Explore your reaction to situations and accept responsibility in working through them – share problem-solving possibilities, rather than blame others.
  * Be prepared for the fact that an assertive request does not always result in agreement.

6 **Practice:** Use your skills of engaging, reflective listening and relationship-building with staff, committee members and others you meet in your agency or other agencies you visit as you settle in. Think about what contributed to your success or otherwise in these interactions – name the skills you used and try to identify the processes of the interaction.

7 **Learn to live with the drawbacks:** Learning can occur at many different levels – insignificant tasks such as answering telephones can offer insight into clients' problems and the role of the administrative staff. Conflict with a staff member can teach you strategies to survive a stressful situation, even if it is not immediately obvious. Don't blame or withdraw if you are feeling overwhelmed or left out, and try the communication strategies suggested above.

You may want to get started on 'real' tasks during your orientation program. You are usually asked to observe, read and undertake activities in which your participation is minimal, at this time, but use this to become accustomed to the setting and familiar with the rules and routines of the agency. Make use of the unstructured time to explore, reflect and record thoughts in your journal.

Surviving in a human service agency

As a newcomer to an agency, your understanding of how it works becomes the backdrop and basis for your work. One of the first things to do on placement is to map your agency. The questions in Exercise 1 from O'Connor, Wilson and Setterlund (2003, p. 170) may focus your understanding, or you will find an alternative approach to mapping agencies in Exercise 2 in Chapter 4 (p. 35). Use the most appropriate format for your agency.

Once you have considered the questions, think about the ones that were more difficult to answer. Why is this the case? What does that tell you about the agency, its clients or its workers?

EXERCISE 1

1. What are the agency's goals and missions?
2. What are the current goals?
3. What gives it the right to operate (for example, legislation or a constitution)?
4. What are the sources of its financial, political and professional support?
5. What are its primary areas of concern?
6. How is the agency organised administratively and professionally?
7. What are the formal and informal lines of authority? Who decides who does what?
8. How do staff relate to each other?
9. How do you relate to staff?
10. How do clients perceive the agency?
11. To what extent does the agency define the nature of clients' problems?

To build on the map you have outlined in Exercise 1, try doing Exercises 2 and 3, which have a different perspective.

EXERCISE 2

Learn about your agency through the eyes of a client and perhaps through other services that relate to your agency. One way of doing this is, with permission, to ask other students on placement, or perhaps doing other courses, to visit your agency. Having to answer others' questions can alert you to areas about the agency you need to explore further.

Similarly, visiting other agencies relevant to your placement gives you a chance not only to understand how the activities of the two places do or don't fit together, but also to question the assumptions both agencies make about their client groups. It is useful to develop a list of questions that you can ask on the visit – some pertinent topics are auspice arrangements, funding, the philosophy of the agency, how staff approach service delivery, how the staff respond to current policy issues, and what clients do or don't appreciate about the agency.

Try to remember your first responses to the agency. If you are keeping a journal, read your initial responses. Would clients also respond this way? To what extent does your agency encourage clients to give a broad or narrow view of their situation? How do your answers fit with the map of the agency you outlined in Exercise 1?

EXERCISE 3

Think about a situation you have observed or taken part in – for example, an interaction with colleagues or clients, or a community event – in which you were aware of the impact of your agency's structure, goals, culture and environment on what you or someone else did.

Briefly outline what was done in the situation, and then suggest possible reasons for the way you or the other person responded.

On the basis of this reflection, what have you learned about your placement agency and yourself?

In Exercise 3 we raise the notion of organisational culture, which refers to the 'feel or flavour of organisational life' (Jones & May 1992, p. 229). Organisational culture is made up of the assumptions, values and meanings that give the organisation a sense of identity, defines what it means to be a member of the organisation, and enables us to predict what the organisation is likely to do in certain circumstances. When we arrive at our placement organisation, aspects of the way it presents itself to the rest of the world may strike us as significant, unexpected or even odd. It is important to make notes about our initial experiences, since it is likely that we will quickly become acclimatised, and accept what was 'odd' as 'normal'. Some of the factors we might note here include shared meanings and shared symbols (Jones & May 1992, p. 232). These authors identify some of the shared meanings as: what the organisation assumes about the world and about those who use its services; how they explain why the world is organised this way; and what is the range of acceptable behaviour and action to each other and to those using services. Shared symbols include the stories told about organisational life – official and unofficial; the language and jargon used; and things such as furniture, letterhead, pictures, and the way the organisation is physically structured.

There are inevitable tensions between human service practitioners and the agencies in which they work, for a number of reasons. O'Connor, Wilson and Setterlund (2003, p. 164) outline some of the key tensions.

- Organisations control access to social resources – workers and their organisations compete for resources and ration the distribution of these resources.
- The knowledge and practice of human service practitioners is often contested by other professional groups, the community and clients.
- Organisations are often a target for change by their own workers or workers in other agencies.
- Workers are likely to confront issues of autonomy and to experience challenges to their control over their work.

The following is an outline of some of the problems common to human service agencies in the contemporary environment, as adapted from Berg-Weger and Birkenmaier (2000, p. 90).

- The environment is unstable: funding sources, social policy, accreditation standards and political affiliations are in constant flux and crisis.
- Services lack clear, measurable goals for service delivery. Evaluating the effectiveness of services is difficult without quantifiable performance goals.
- Services experience goal displacement. The shift from the original goal of meeting an identified human need to the goal of organisational survival can alter service delivery.

Do any of these comments apply to your agency? Whatever the structure and functioning of your agency, there are likely to be conflicts and conflicting priorities. Human service agencies have multiple 'masters' and are accountable to a diverse group of organisational and community stakeholders, as illustrated by the figure below.

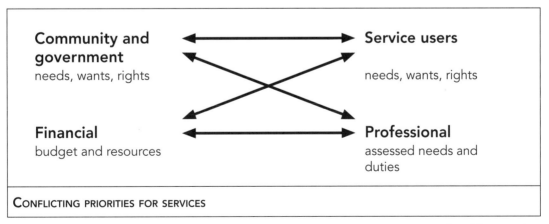

CONFLICTING PRIORITIES FOR SERVICES

Adapted from Morrison 2001, p. 53

Agencies are sometimes conflict-ridden. They may have no shared value system, in spite of the mission statement on the wall. They may have numerous vague goals that are contested by internal as well as external stakeholders. Such pressures may emerge while you are on placement. It may have no effect at all on your placement, or it may mean that your supervisor is distracted and not readily available or that your placement is unable to meet your learning goals.

This pressure can also have an impact on the staff, who may react with anger, confusion and lowered morale. It may result in modification of or reduction to service delivery, increased workload or other changes. It is hard not to be overwhelmed by negativity in these circumstances, so it is important to stay focused on your learning, help out when necessary and be flexible about changes.

There is often room for workers to manoeuvre between these different demands. The nature of human service practice makes it difficult for agencies to prescribe responses to all the issues workers are likely to face, so front-line practitioners often have considerable autonomy. You are likely to see this in your agency. Who do you think is more likely to benefit from this autonomy, and why do you think that is the case?

Organisational work also involves functioning in a team, which may be made up of people with a similar discipline base to yourself, or may consist of workers from different disciplines. Teamwork is covered in Chapter 12. It would be useful to look at that material as you work out how to make the most of this placement.

Summary

Placement can be an exciting and, at times, overwhelming experience. It is important to start your placement with realistic expectations of yourself, you supervisor and the agency. This requires that you are aware of the broader environment in which human service agencies operate and the tensions this causes for workers.

You can use some useful strategies to survive your first weeks and derive maximum benefit from observing what is going on around you.

4

GETTING STARTED – SUPERVISOR

Introduction

Preparation for a student placement should begin some weeks before the date of arrival of the student in the agency. You may need to remind your team leader and other staff of the pending placement, and you may need to prepare material and check office availability. Organising and executing the orientation program will take time and the student is likely to want to consult with you regularly. In the current environment, it is most unlikely that you will be able to reduce your workload during the first few weeks of the placement; however, requesting that you are not given extra duties or making arrangements to minimise time out of the agency will be appreciated by the student as well as by other agency staff.

Little gestures – having a pigeon-hole ready with the student's name on it, or having some stationery items already in their office drawer – will make the student feel welcome. We should not underestimate how students may struggle with the demands of suddenly having professional expectations placed upon them, and also dealing with the feelings that emerge when confronted with people and situations that are difficult, complex and sad.

The first weeks

The following checklist, adapted from Doel et al. (1996, p. 40), outlines points you may need to consider when the student begins placement.

Welcome
- Are there any office traditions to welcome a new face?
- Are there flowers on the student's desk? (It does happen!)
- What introductions are planned?
- What are the lunch arrangements?

Orientation
Where can the student go for ...
- a quiet chat?
- a noisy chat?
- a quiet phone call?
- a cup of tea or coffee?
- lunch?
- exercise?

Where is the ...
- toilet?
- photocopier/fax?
- student's workspace?

Necessary items

The agency should provide …

- a desk and chair
- a telephone
- access to drinks
- access to fresh air
- stationery, diary, pens, identity cards
- a 'starter' pack of relevant policies and procedures.

General issues

Building on the checklist, the following issues should be discussed with the student in the early days of placement.

- What are the student's hours of attendance and lunch breaks?
- Does the student need to sign in and out?
- How will the student be addressed? (It is generally not advisable to encourage students to hide their student status.)
- Where may people smoke?
- May the student make personal phone calls?
- Who should the student contact if he or she is late, sick or unable to come to work?
- What are the occupational health and safety arrangements?
- Are there any security issues? Does the student need a name tag or keys?
- How will issues of equal opportunity and anti-discriminatory practice be addressed in placement? (Students should be directed to the policies of the agency that relate to this.)
- What are the regular meetings or functions that the student must attend?
- Are there any protocols or issues of etiquette that the student may not be aware of, but which are important informal rules (for example, what parking spots should be avoided, the need for tidiness if the student is sharing an office, whether the student will need to pay for coffee and tea, and so on)?
- What decisions may be taken by the student without confirmation by you or another staff member (for example, using the photocopier)?
- Are there any variations to the negotiated placement arrangements?
- What is the timetable for supervision sessions?
- Are there any significant changes to the tasks that were agreed on at the pre-placement meeting? (It may no longer be appropriate for the student to work with a particular group or client or on a specific project, so replacement tasks need to be negotiated.)

Starting work

Learning principles

Other important considerations for the start of placement relate to how you establish the teaching and learning relationship with the student. The first consideration is to start where the student is, moving from the familiar to the unfamiliar (Pettes 1979, p. 65). An assessment of the student's knowledge and confidence in completing a task can be obtained from the self-assessment they did in Chapter 1 (p. 5). For example, previous work experience may have given the student confidence in answering the telephones during a busy lunch hour.

It is important to design an orientation program that covers a range of learning modes: for example, you give the student a list of staff names but they may not be able to retain the names until they meet the staff in person (visual), hear them talk (auditory) or perhaps connect the name with some other piece of information about them.

Information should be presented in stages (Collins, Thomlison & Grinnell 1992, p. 128), moving from the simple to the more complex. It is acknowledged, of course, that work in the human service industry has a high level of uncertainty and the unexpected often happens. Using different methods to teach the same thing, making use of different learning styles, will help reduce any tedium (Collins, Thomlison & Grinnell 1992, p. 128).

When you ask a student to complete a task, the reason for the task needs to be explicit and they should be able to learn from it, rather than it being a time-filler or something that the supervisor decides is required. The student must see that the task is relevant to their learning. For example, if a student is required to routinely document every intervention undertaken with a client or community group, the reason for doing so – that such documentation is the main form of communication between team members and is a legal record of the agency's contact and assessment – should be explained.

With any learning task during the first few weeks of placement, immediate feedback, discussion and positive affirmation will help to reinforce learning. Illustrations from the student's own experience will also reinforce learning. For example, if a student is anxious about working with younger clients, ask the student to recall his or her experiences with a younger person, and then to describe his or her responses. This experience can be used to reinforce that the student already has ideas about how to engage a younger person.

The orientation program

Orientation may begin before the official start of the placement. The student may be invited to an annual general meeting, a staff-development day or another event, or you may send out some preliminary reading so that the student eases into the agency at a pace he or she dictates.

Two basic models for inducting a student into the placement, as suggested by Ford and Jones (1987), are outlined below.

1 *The planned program approach (or deductive or taught approach):* In the first week, most of the time is taken up with a series of sessions in which the emphasis is on giving the student basic knowledge about the agency and its work.

2 *The acquire-it-as-you-go-along approach (or inductive approach):* The student picks up the information in more informal ways through opportunities to experience his or her new role in the agency (p. 51).

Your approach to orientation will depend on the student's learning style, the length of the placement and the nature of the agency. For example, an anxious or inexperienced student may appreciate the carefully planned and slower start of the first approach. A confident and more experienced and motivated student may become bored and disillusioned with this approach, yet, using the second approach, may only acquire superficial and fragmented knowledge. This is a problem if the student is placed in an agency that requires in-depth statutory understanding. Placement in complex agencies, such as large hospitals or statutory organisations, may require the student to have a solid understanding of the place before being able to practise. This may be frustrating but unavoidable for students.

Whatever approach you decide to use – which may, in fact, be a mixture of the two – a guided beginning should give students a balance of direction and elbow room, so that they can find their own way (Doel et al. 1996, p. 43).

Understanding the context of practice

Students need to understand the ecological environment of which the client group is part, as well as gain knowledge of the resources in the environment to provide support and referrals. Understanding the history and strength of relationships between agencies in the community will give the student insight into affiliations between services and the constraints on networking and building ties in the community.

EXERCISE 1

Students can be asked to complete the following activities to develop their understanding of the physical, socioeconomic and cultural systems surrounding them.

1 Locate your agency's resource file for information about other agencies in the vicinity. If your agency doesn't have one, the student could develop one. Organising the data for services by problem types and/or fields of practice will alert students to the links and overlap in service delivery.

2 The student could start a personal resource file filled with information from the local paper, community news, pamphlets, and so on.

3 The student could take a trip to the local supermarket, park or other community space.

4 If appropriate, ask the student to assume the role of a consumer in the placement agency or in another agency. Ask them to wait in a queue for some information or sit in the waiting room for an hour. Get them to keep notes that they can use for reflection later.

5 Ask the student to locate any research, reports, needs studies or program evaluations that analyse the community and its constituents.

6 The student could attend a community meeting about a local social issue or concern.

7 The student could read case notes and community files that offer insights into the profiles of the client group.

8 The student could create an ecomap and include all the organisations with which the placement agency has a relationship. An ecomap is a visual description of the relationships between a person and his or her environment. In this instance, it could be used to show the connection between the agency and the external organisations by using different types of lines (for example, bold lines to depict strong connections, broken lines to depict tenuous relationships).

9 The student may have selected your agency because of his or her interest and previous study in this field of practice. You could ask the student to find relevant research or to undertake an Internet or library search to collect pertinent information about the relevant field.

In the initial supervision sessions, you could ask the student the following questions:

- What have you observed about the agency environment? Is it friendly, alienating, resource-rich?
- How would you describe the demographics of the area and ethnic make-up of the community?
- What social problems could exist as a result of this demographic make-up?
- What resources in the community have you noticed?

You could develop a hypothetical case and ask the student to assess what services your agency or other ones could offer.

Meeting the staff

A student is on placement with the agency as well as with the supervisor (Ford & Jones 1987, p. 16), so it is important to make more than cursory introductions to staff to reinforce that there is a team approach to the student's learning.

Staff should be reminded, perhaps by email or at a staff meeting, of the student's expected date of arrival and what the main focus of placement will be. Enlisting their support is important, as there will be times when they will be asked to back you up or respond to the student's questions. Some staff may take a formal role, such as taking the student on a home visit or being interviewed by the student, during the orientation period. Others, such as senior administrative staff, may be introduced as protocol or a courtesy.

Introduce students gradually to agency staff. Get the student to make appointments with staff members – students will experience the difficulties of trying to fit into other people's schedules. Administrative staff should be included in the introductory sessions as their role and stressors are part of what a student needs to understand.

An organisation chart can help to orient the student to the positions, roles and names of staff, as well as help them to learn about hierarchical structures and authority.

Understanding the agency's services

The student would have gained a simplistic picture of the agency from the initial meeting, but now will require a more comprehensive understanding of its activities in order to carry out learning tasks. Ask the student to undertake one or more of the following activities.

- The student could sit with an intake worker and observe a telephone or face-to-face assessment. The student can be asked to take notes and to complete a genogram from the information discussed. A genogram is a visual description of the relationship between different members of a family.
- The student could sit with the receptionist for a few hours to listen to the types of calls that are received, and to observe the clients who come in and the agencies who make contact and for what purpose.
- The student could read case files selected from the supervisor's caseload. If need be, the cases can be randomly selected from closed files or from among current cases from other program areas.
- The student could read studies or reports completed by the agency.

In a supervision session at the end of the orientation period, you could assess the student's knowledge of the agency's services by asking the following questions: Which agencies refer clients to your agency? To what agencies does your agency refer clients? Can you see any gaps in meeting the needs of your client group?

Understanding the agency structures

Most agencies have developed structures and policies to ensure uniformity and to communicate the lines of accountability. In other agencies, however, it is possible that the lines of authority are ambiguous.

Reading legislation, staff manuals and other regulations governing agency functions can be useful but boring. This task can be enlivened by linking it to a problem-solving exercise, giving students a fictitious or real case study in which they devise interventions and determine the relevance of these resources in solving the problem.

Students could acquire or create an organisation chart and examine the following:

- the formal hierarchy
- the formal relationship between positions
- issues of independence
- areas of potential conflict
- communication and work flow.

An organisational analysis is more than an organisation chart. The following exercise, adapted from the School of Social Work and Social Policy (2003b, pp. 27–8), encourages the student to develop a more in-depth understanding of the agency. An alternative format for analysing organisations is outlined in Exercises 1 to 3 in Chapter 3.

EXERCISE 2

Organisational analysis

1 Briefly describe the auspice arrangement of your placement agency or program (for example, is it government or non-government, community-based, voluntary?).

2 Describe the agency's organisational structure (including its legal basis and decision-making processes), sources of funding, and significant links with other agencies and organisations.

3 Briefly describe the social and community context of your agency or program in terms of where it is located (for example, is it an urban, rural, regional or suburban area?) and the client group or target population serviced (for example, age and gender, economic status, ethnicity, and so on).

4 Identify the goals towards which the program officially works, and comment on how you see them being translated into action.

5 Think about the agency's theoretical approaches.

   a Describe how particular theoretical models or frameworks (for example, the behaviourist, psychosocial, feminist, radical, problem-solving model, and so on) are applied within your agency or program.

   b Critically evaluate how these approaches match, accommodate or come into conflict with social policy, relevant legislation, and agency or program procedures.

   c Critically evaluate how these approaches match, accommodate or come into conflict with professional values, ethics and principles of social work.

6 Think about the agency's practice.

   a Describe how particular practice methods are applied within your agency or program (for example, casework, case management, groupwork, community work, social and political action, community education, direct-service provision, research, advocacy).

   b Critically evaluate how these practice methods match, accommodate or come into conflict with social policy, relevant legislation, and agency or program procedures.

   c Critically evaluate how these practice methods match, accommodate or come into conflict with professional values, ethics and principles of social work.

Understanding the informal structure of the agency and its norms is important, as this is part of the real life of the organisation. The informal structure includes all the policies, rules, relationships and norms that are unspoken and unwritten, yet clearly influence the behaviours of the workers. In fact, it can be considered the 'grease' that allows tasks to be completed.

An example of the difference between explicit and implicit norms and rules, as adapted from Berg-Weger and Birkenmaier (2000, p. 101), follows.

Explicit norms and rules	Implicit norms and rules
Take all concerns to the team leader.	Take concerns elsewhere, because the team leader's door is always closed.
Everybody's voice should be heard.	Don't speak up, because dissenting opinions are not appreciated.
Students are welcome in the agency.	Students create more work for the staff.
The receptionist is employed to do photocopying.	Don't ask the receptionist to do photocopying.
Office hours are from 9 a.m. to 5 p.m.	Staff don't leave the office before 5.30 p.m.

The informal communication has been built up from daily interaction over time, so how can you help the student, who has to operate and function within these structures, learn this information?

EXERCISE 3

Ask the student to observe a typical group activity such as a staff meeting, a planning meeting or even a staff lunch.

1 Which staff members spoke most?

2 Which staff supported or disagreed with each other?

3 Does the organisation chart reflect the decision-making that actually occurred?

4 Which staff member(s) does the student feel more comfortable with? Why?

Recording requirements

Workers in human services are required to record information for a wide range of purposes; therefore, during orientation, students need to be introduced to the particular kinds of reports, case notes, timesheets and other forms of recording the agency employs. Students will probably have a theoretical knowledge of recording requirements, but may not have put it into practice.

Reflective time

Self-awareness and an ongoing willingness to examine feelings and beliefs lies at the core of successful helping (Alle-Corliss & Alle-Corliss 1998, p. 16). Supervisors can promote a positive beginning to this lifelong process by creating time and space during the orientation program for the student to reflect. This discipline can be encouraged by the use of the personal journal and other tools described in Chapter 8.

Most training institutions suggest that students should only be asked to undertake about 50 per cent of the workload of a full-time worker, on the basis that students need to have the time and 'headspace' to reflect on and read about their learning experiences. Some students, especially those who may not feel comfortable with this more 'abstract conceptualising' about their practice (see Chapter 2), may want to resist spending time away from the direct learning tasks, so it will be important to reinforce and encourage this important part of their learning through the use of personal journals and other tools described in Chapter 8, as well as including this expectation in the learning agreement.

Understanding broader structures

Understanding of the agency's activities will be enhanced by knowing about the legislative and social policies that, through funding and programs, influence the agency's functioning. This understanding will also highlight the realities of service delivery and will influence the dreams students have for their placement. Students can learn about this background by reading annual reports, budget papers, staff manuals, mission statements, policy and procedural manuals, by-laws and relevant legislation. Students who have studied social policy in their course can be encouraged to read relevant policy to further enhance this knowledge.

Encourage the student to browse national and daily papers, cutting out editorials and features in which public debates relevant to the placement setting are discussed. This task reflects how theory can be related to practice and highlights the level of political awareness that human service workers must possess.

Evaluating the orientation program

By the end of the orientation program, the student should be able to:
- describe the main legislation affecting the agency's functions
- outline the agency's structure
- know where the funding comes from
- describe the staffing and their main roles
- describe the client group and the main services offered by the agency
- know where to find relevant information, manuals and records
- identify personnel issues and informal norms and rules
- comment on the culture, values and politics of the agency.

It can be useful to devise a brief feedback sheet to evaluate the usefulness of the orientation program. It marks the end of the first stage of the placement and begins the transition to the next stage. Exercise 4 will help you to get this feedback from the student.

EXERCISE 4

Ask students to think about the orientation program and answer the following questions.

1 Name five important things that you have learned.
2 Name five things that you want to learn more about.
3 What was the best part of the orientation program?
4 What are your feelings about being a student in the agency?

At the end of the orientation stage, you should have developed a stronger sense of the level of competency of the student, and the student should have a clearer sense of their learning goals and the opportunities that are available in the agency. Some tasks may have already been started.

Initial tasks should be selected carefully to ensure that students experience early success and don't feel overwhelmed, and to ensure that there is adequate time for debriefing afterwards. This supports and encourages students, but also models to them that professionals need to constantly reflect on their work, however routine or simple the task.

Just as it is irrational to think that you are entirely responsible for your client's progress, it is equally irrational to feel totally responsible for the success of the placement. Be clear from the outset about the limits of your responsibilities (Alle-Corliss & Alle-Corliss 1998, p. 184). The trick is finding the balance between independence and support for students. They should be comfortable and curious about the next step and will demonstrate this by asking to do more complex tasks.

Summary

Students will be on a steep learning curve in the first weeks of placement and how you, as supervisor, construct this experience can influence their confidence and ability to progress to the next stage. Planning your approach to these first weeks will benefit the student and your agency, as everyone will be clear about what to expect and, most importantly, the student will feel welcome. Students will require background knowledge of the agency and client groups, as well as of the broader structures in which the agency operates.

5

CHARTING THE COURSE FOR PLACEMENT – CONTRACTS AND AGREEMENTS

Introduction

Structuring the teaching and learning on placement ensures that it does not drift along without a clear purpose or goals. Although students vary in their learning needs and personalities, there are certain competencies, abilities or skills that they are required to have in any placement. These are incorporated into a learning and teaching framework that supervisors and students can use to plan, review and analyse the progress of the placement. This negotiated learning approach can be adapted to meet the requirements of various courses and the needs of individual students.

The learning agreement

Although there is no universal model for learning on placement, most human service courses require a learning agreement – also called a learning plan, learning contract, curriculum or educational plan – to be formulated. (The term 'learning agreement' is used in this book.) Some training institutions give clear guidelines about what must be covered in such agreements, perhaps even specifying tasks that should be completed. Most will also outline evaluation criteria and these will need to be considered in constructing the learning agreement.

This agreement provides the 'script' for the placement, as it is a statement of what is to happen, why it is to happen and how the parts connect (Collins, Thomlison & Grinnell 1992, p. 111).

Some unhelpful assumptions to be aware of when discussing the content of the learning agreement, as outlined by O'Connor, Wilson and Setterlund (2003, p. 221), are as follows.

- The supervisor can teach the student everything there is to know about practice in a particular agency.
- Social work and welfare work are too messy to provide opportunities for structured learning experiences.
- A placement is solely an opportunity to apply in the field what has been taught in the classroom.

Do you agree with any of these assumptions?

Generally, the learning agreement should reflect the:

- requirements of the training institution and particular course
- opportunities available in the agency
- interests and abilities of the supervisor
- interests and abilities of the student
- teaching and learning style of the supervisor and the student.

The learning agreement should be the result of the combined effort of the student and the supervisor and take into account the academic requirements of the training institution as well as agency requirements. The learning agreement may have evolved from the classroom, the pre-placement meeting, and the student's five-step assessment in Chapter 1. The orientation period and initial supervision sessions will then consolidate the original ideas and create new ones for consideration.

The *what* of students' learning on placement, shaped by the training institution, will generally include core tasks that can apply to working with individuals, families, groups, communities and organisations. The learning agreement should structure the learning content so that it is a developmental and incremental process that occurs over time and becomes increasingly complex and autonomous. Students can usually identify what they want to learn, but may be less clear about the process. Some goals will be both personal and professional, and students may have had them from the outset or perhaps have pointed them out to their teachers during their course. If this is not the first placement, the students' previous experience will inform where they want to start. The learning agreement should reflect individual starting points, as each student has different abilities, capacities and previous experiences.

Supervisors may not find it easy to define the placement's learning goals. The institution may either ask supervisors to reinforce students' classroom learning or expect them to introduce the student to new skills and knowledge. Bearing these factors in mind, it is important for the supervisor to be creative in developing and suggesting a realistic range of possible learning options. Some tasks will reflect the goals of the agency, and others will be based on the student's interests and priorities.

The broad content

The learning experience in human services is distinguished from that in other types of professional training because of its emphasis on principles and processes, rather than routine skills and tasks. Trevithick (2000, p. 13) states that teaching only the 'mechanics' or techniques produces technicians rather than professionals, diminishing students' ability to take a reflective approach to practice and ignoring the importance that process plays in a given interaction.

Rogers and Langevin (2000, p. 217) suggest that the learning necessary to human service practice has four elements: being, knowing, doing and thinking. Thus, the learning agreement and the focus of supervision should be directed at balancing these aspects.

- *Being* refers to the affective qualities and attributes that individuals in the human services need to develop. These include the ability to feel, to value and to empathise with the emotions of other people or indeed of oneself (Ford & Jones 1987, p. 80).
- *Knowing* refers to the theories, concepts, constructs and other information that guide competent practice.
- *Doing* refers to skills and behaviours required for students to demonstrate their ability to act or carry out tasks in a purposeful way.
- *Thinking* refers to cognitive ability to remember, analyse, reason and conceptualise in relation to problems and solutions (Ford & Jones 1987, p. 80). The 'thinking' component of learning needs particular attention as it is often omitted in the development of learning plans (Rogers & Langevin 2000, p. 218).

This model suggests that, whatever the activity, it should be possible to analyse performance using one or more of these four frameworks of understanding. Similarly, if the student has learning difficulties, these will present in one or more of these areas. For example, a student may be able to articulate what is going on for a client (knowing) but can't intervene to help the situation (doing) (Ford & Jones 1987, p. 81).

The specific content

Most human service courses will have varying descriptions about the learning that needs to be covered in their agreements but, in reality, there seems to be remarkable consistency in the core learning areas. In 2006, the six Victorian schools of Social Work began the development of a standardised learning and evaluation document and found common agreement on the following seven core learning areas:

---

1   Values, ethics and professional practice

For example, maintaining an open and respectful perspective towards the values, views and opinions of others, while demonstrating a commitment to enhancing the self-determination of individuals, social units, communities and cultures.

---

2   Processes, skills and relationships

Suggested inclusions:
- interpersonal skills
- teamwork
- report writing
- referral and consultation
- assessment and evaluation.

---

3   Use of knowledge in practice

For example, the ability to apply relevant theory to practice settings, including relevant theories of society and behaviour.

---

4   Self-learning and professional development

For example, the ability to participate proactively in negotiating and developing the supervisory relationship.

---

5   Organisational context

For example, demonstrating an appreciation of the connection between individual problems, public issues and structural disadvantage.

---

6   Research

For example, recognising the research significance of data collection strategies, within agencies and more generally, and an ability to contribute to the development of client- and consumer-sensitive databases.

---

7   Social policy

For example, demonstrating an ability to perceive, analyse and communicate in relation to social and political issues and contexts.

Most human service courses require learning plans to cover four essential areas:
- the main objectives or goals
- the content to be learned and the specific tasks linked to this content
- the method or type of learning experiences to meet the objectives
- the standard for evaluating whether the objectives have been achieved.

You might also want to include a time frame to the agreement. Think about using these four elements to develop the learning plan. Some brief examples follow.

Elements	Questions	Examples
Goals	Where do students want to go? (general, global terms)	Student goals: • I would like to develop my understanding of … • I would like to become familiar with … • I would like to identify the range of …
Tasks	How will the student get there? (the content)	Action: • The student will attend a staff meeting. • The student will participate in a group. • The student will prepare a report.

Elements	Questions	Examples
Methods	How does the student achieve these objectives?	Action: • The student will be observed by his or her supervisor. • The student will discuss his or her findings with the CEO.
Evaluation	How does the student know whether he or she has achieved his or her objectives?	Action: • The student takes increasing responsibility. • The student gives a presentation. The student completes a resource file.

Devising the agreement

Shardlow and Doel (1996, p. 98) offer the following approach to devise the learning agreement.

Step 1 Defining aims

What are all parties attempting to achieve on this placement? The agreement needs to clearly specify the aims and objectives of the placement, framed as both short-term and long-term goals. Remember that some parts of the agreement are course requirements and therefore are not negotiable.

Step 2 Identifying the learning

What will the student learn? If the agency has had previous placements, the supervisor may start by writing down what other students did on placement. Both supervisors and students should refer to the general expectations of the training institution and sample learning agreements the institution may have provided. Once some tasks have been identified, search for themes and group the tasks by category.

Step 3 Putting the tasks in sequence

When will these tasks be undertaken? Should the student approach the tasks in the learning agreement in any particular order? The student may need to complete particular tasks before starting others, so that they gain maximum benefit from the learning. This may relate to the complexity of the work, or mean that the student needs to acquire certain skills or knowledge, or perhaps develop confidence and motivation before proceeding. Other factors, such as the availability of work or timetabling of other activities, may affect the time frame in which tasks will be completed.

Step 4 Devising methods and strategies

How will the student achieve the learning? What methods of learning will be employed in completing the learning agreement? These will become more apparent after considering the student's preferred learning style, the type of learning opportunities available in the agency, and the student's level of comfort and competence in using particular learning methods. For example, making a video of an interview conducted by the student may not be a possible method of learning if there is no equipment or if the agency feels that it will be intimidating to the client. Learning methods or tools, such as supervision, process records and library searches, are discussed in more detail in Chapters 7 and 8.

Step 5 Evaluating the learning

How will the supervisor and the training institution know whether a student is learning? It is better to choose a range of methods to evaluate the student's learning, and, again, these methods should be selected bearing in mind the constraints raised in Step 4. The learning agreement also may identify who will be involved in the evaluation.

Step 6 Presenting the agreement

How should the learning agreement be presented? The format of the agreement is usually set out by the training institution; however, as it is also a tool to monitor the progress of the student, it needs to be presented in a way that is accessible and easy to modify.

Step 7 Reviewing the agreement

How can the learning agreement be modified in light of the progress of the placement? The agreement is a dynamic tool and must be able to be easily revised. Therefore, ways of reviewing the agreement need to be specified. Many courses require a formal assessment of progress midway through the placement, although it may be helpful to build in more regular reviews, perhaps after each month. The purpose of undertaking these reviews is to ensure that the learning agreement is still relevant to the student. For example, if the student develops a skill earlier in the placement than anticipated, this should be acknowledged and the learning agreement changed so that the student gets the opportunity to extend his or her skills.

An example of an agreement

This example of a learning agreement uses Rogers and Langevin's four elements of learning defined previously.

BEING

Main learning goal	Tasks for goal attainment	Methods to meet the goals	Evidence for attainment of goals
To develop an understanding of professional values and ethics.	To attend family meetings to gain an understanding of how my profession is different from other helping professions.	To participate in these meetings and observe the roles of different team members.	Conduct at least two family meetings and demonstrate the role and values of my profession.
	To be able to separate the 'personal' from the 'professional'.	To keep a diary of daily events and my emotional reactions to the events.	Discuss issues in my diary with my supervisor to get feedback on my thoughts and ideas.
	To demonstrate sensitivity and acceptance of diversity when interviewing clients. To attend a workshop on anti-discriminatory practice.	To use process records to document my response to client interviews and my experiences at the workshop.	Receive positive feedback from clients that I have case-managed. By mid-placement, discuss with supervisor at least one new area of learning about myself in relation to working with others who are different from me.

KNOWING

Main learning goal	Tasks for goal attainment	Methods to meet the goals	Evidence for attainment of goals
To become familiar with the current theories and laws relating to mental health and diversity.	To identify the main theoretical frameworks used in this agency. To use my knowledge of the legal rights of mentally ill clients in my work with them.	To undertake a literature search about the incidence of mental-health issues in adolescent boys. To read the Mental Health Act. To go to court with the legal advocate. To do casework with adolescents with mental-health problems.	Become the primary case-manager for three cases and problem-solve using relevant theory. My supervisor to observe my interviews with at least two clients in which I explain their legal rights.
To become more informed about groupwork.	To gather information about the staff's experience of working with young men with mental-health problems.	To attend meetings of the agency's working group whose aim is to develop a life-skills group for young men with mental-health problems.	Complete a protocol manual for the agency that identifies the role of the various team members.

DOING

Main learning goal	Tasks for goal attainment	Methods to meet the goals	Evidence for attainment of goals
To develop skills in working with individuals and groups. To gain skills and practice in recording.	In Week 6 of placement, to plan and facilitate a life-skills group. To develop confidence in writing case assessments. To write appropriate agency records.	To attend a community group session as an observer. To complete a journal entry reflecting on groupwork skills. To attend the scheduled one-day inservice workshop on groupwork with involuntary clients. To read the case files completed by previous students in the student manual. To complete a case plan for at least five clients, using the agency framework.	Discuss with my supervisor my experiences and ideas for running a group. My supervisor to attend a group session with me and give feedback on my groupwork skills. An evaluation form to be completed by community participants, which will include feedback about my role. My supervisor and task supervisor to give feedback on my case notes.

THINKING

Main learning goal	Tasks for goal attainment	Methods to meet the goals	Evidence for attainment of goals
To balance my personal values with the agency's policies and practices.	To identify and manage the conflicting duties within this agency.	To discuss these issues with senior management. To read the policy manual of the agency. To review the literature on organisations that was presented in class. To write a paper outlining my ideas and present it to a staff meeting.	A presentation at a staff meeting about the contested nature of work and some strategies to help staff deal with these conflicts.

Other types of agreements

Some agencies may be interested in negotiating other aspects of how the student and supervisor will work together during placement. These agreements may specify mutual obligations and expectations for the placement and what action will be taken if these obligations and expectations are not met.

Supervision contracts

SUPERVISION CONTRACT

(Supervisor) is responsible for (student)'s work at (agency). It follows that (student) will keep (supervisor) informed about work done and plans for future work and (supervisor) will ensure that (student) understands their roles and responsibilities, carries out work to agency standards, and receives regular, constructive feedback on their progress.

(Supervisor) will facilitate (student) learning by reviewing (student)'s work to assist (student) to generalise learning from specific situations and to critically reflect on their practice. It follows that (student) will provide access to their work with (designated reports, observations).

(Supervisor) and (student) will treat each other with respect. If either has concerns, they will attempt to raise these constructively and will involve (training institution staff member) if outside assistance is required.

Structure for supervision
It is agreed that (student) will receive a minimum of (number) hours of supervision a week and that (supervisor) or (other designated person or persons) will be available for consultation at other times when guidance is required. The structure we have agreed on is:
Times for meetings –

Policy if meetings are to be rescheduled –

The method used to set agendas –

Recording arrangements in relation to material discussed in supervision –

Boundaries about confidentiality of material discussed in supervision –

Content of supervision sessions
Sessions will include:
- A review of work done through reflection, discussion, observation and reports
- A review of (student)'s development as a practitioner
- A planning process to meet emerging needs based on an assessment of the work done
- Regular reviews of progress on items outlined in the learning agreement.

Responsibilities in supervision
The (student) and (supervisor) are responsible for –

The (student) and (supervisor) are willing to contribute –

The ways (training institution's liaison officer) will be involved –

Agreement between .... and ....

Signed and dated: ....

While it may seem that written supervision agreements or contracts are too formal, Morrison (2001, p. 101) offers some compelling reasons for such an approach:

- It reflects the seriousness of the activity.
- It represents a positive modelling of partnership behaviour.
- It ensures that both parties are equally aware of their responsibilities and roles.
- It reduces the chances of the misunderstandings that can occur as a result of a lack of clarity.
- It provides the basis for reviewing and developing the supervisory relationship.
- It spells out what is negotiable and non-negotiable, and the boundaries around confidentiality.

The example, shown on page 45 from O'Connor, Wilson and Setterlund (2003, p. 225), could form the basis of such a contract.

Placement contracts

In addition to what is in the learning agreement, there should be discussion of other roles and responsibilities to clarify mutual expectations. Two suggested formats for placement contracts that cover negotiated obligations and the responsibilities of training institutions and agencies follow. Some courses require the supervisor and student to complete and sign such a placement contract.

PLACEMENT CONTRACT

List of parties to the contract: names and roles

Duration of placement contract: dates, indicate what course and year level the student is undertaking, dates of study days

Description of placement: location, telephone numbers, work undertaken, type of service users, etc.

Practical arrangements: working hours, administrative support, insurance cover, police checks, travel expenses, working conditions

Workload: anticipated range, amount and pace of work

Supervision arrangements: times, frequency, content, record-keeping

Accountability and recording: student's place in line-management structure, types of work where students will need to be with a trained worker, access to records

Roles and responsibilities of parties:

Supervisor's responsibilities
1 To provide a range of work experiences appropriate to the agency and to the level of competence of the student.
2 To discuss with the agency the implications of student placement.
3 To be available and prepared for the student's orientation period.
4 To ensure that the learning agreement is manageable and realistic.
5 To provide structured supervision at least one hour per week.
6 In conjunction with the student, to complete the required assessment documents.
7 To inform the liaison person from the training institution of any circumstances that may affect the quality of placement: for example, unexpected leave, prolonged illness, excessive workloads.
8 To identify occupational health policies in the agency and discuss ways that the student can minimise workplace risk.

More specific responsibilities could include, for example:
9 To provide a back-up supervisor when I will be away on a five-day training course.

Student's responsibilities
1 To discuss with staff from the training institution and the placement supervisor any personal information that may impact on placement (for example, if the student is taking medication that has adverse side effects, or has previous or current personal issues that may affect his or her capacity to perform in placement).

2 To develop and review my learning agreement in consultation with the supervisor and liaison person.

3 To behave in a professional manner in regard to punctuality, dress, respect for clients and staff.

4 To practise within the guidelines of the profession's code of ethics and the agency's processes and protocols.

5 To actively engage in self-evaluation and be open to constructive feedback in supervision sessions.

6 To organise the time, venue and agenda for liaison meetings with the training institution and provide preparatory material.

7 To appropriately terminate with clients, supervisor and agency staff.

More specific responsibilities could include, for example:

8 To be available for reception duties during the lunch period.

9 To be involved in after-hours community meetings once a month.

10 To follow the protocol for marking my whereabouts on the whiteboard.

11 To ensure that any external correspondence is countersigned by the supervisor or task supervisor.

Agency's responsibilities

1 To provide access to phones, computers, desk space and appropriate information about policy and protocol.

2 To reimburse the student for completing work-related tasks away from the office, such as home visits and meetings.

3 To give access to staff meetings and other relevant agency meetings.

4 To provide some administrative support for the completion of learning tasks.

More specific responsibilities could include, for example:

5 To give access to the work car to undertake community consultation.

6 To make sure that student can take time-in-lieu for any out-of-hours work.

Signed .... Date ....
Supervisor

Signed .... Date ....
Student

The framework on pages 46–7, adapted from the School of Social Work and Social Policy (2003b, p. 3) is more specific about the responsibilities of student and supervisor. Most of these responsibilities would be relevant to a range of placements. The points are examples of what could be included.

Summary

A comprehensive and clear learning agreement gives direction to students, supervisors and agencies, and ensures that other requirements – legal, statutory, educational or policy ones, for example – are clearly spelled out.

Ideally, students, supervisors and training institutions should negotiate the learning agreement so that the objectives are relevant and achievable and students feel a sense of control over their learning.

Although there are different types of agreement, which vary in their degree of detail, some common areas that should be covered are: aims, tasks, sequence of tasks, methods, evaluation, presentation and review.

TEACHING AND LEARNING ON PLACEMENT

Placement offers students a continuous opportunity for formal and informal learning. Initiatives in field education have encouraged a shift away from both apprenticeship and therapeutic approaches towards reflective and facilitative teaching (Beddoe 2000). The latter approach recognises that not all the expertise lies with the supervisor; the student is also a contributor to teaching and learning processes and the supervisor should also examine how their own cultural experience might influence their interpretation of events. This approach emphasises students' strengths instead of their shortcomings and involves listening to students' stories and identifying areas in which they show competency or have had past successes. Meaningful learning is not just based on positive experiences: skills and knowledge can be gained from interactions with supervisors, other staff or clients that are problematic, and are, in fact, difficult and challenging (Berg-Weger & Birkenmaier 2000).

In Part 3, a framework for enhancing learning is outlined, and the foundations of good supervision are discussed. A range of tools that can be used in teaching and learning are described. The last chapter provides a model to encourage the linking of students' learning from specific situations to broader theories and contexts.

3

6

CRITICAL REFLECTION FOR TEACHING AND LEARNING

Introduction

This chapter focuses on the educational approaches framing supervision methods that can be utilised by both supervisors and students within contemporary training of human service practitioners. In particular, this chapter will explore the 'what and why' of the student's experiences as he or she becomes involved in the practice tasks of the agency.

Educational approaches

Educational theories are concerned with the acquisition of knowledge and the transformation of the way in which we experience and interact with the world. Early educational models applied to training human service workers were derived from industry. Supervision was viewed as 'overseeing' and was characterised by an apprenticeship style that assumes the supervisor is the expert and the student needs to observe and listen to his or her supervisor and then incorporate this approach into his or her own work.

Other traditional models utilised psychodynamic concepts, which diagnosed certain behaviours and learning 'blocks' associated with anxiety, uncertainty and sometimes conflict within both the supervisor and the student.

Since the 1980s, there has been more evidence to suggest that, for supervision to be more effective, it needs to be understood more broadly than as simply monitoring performance. Supervision needs to be seen as a partnership between the student and the supervisor, when the student is proactive in the supervision process and there is an opportunity to mutually explore, reflect and learn (Irwin 2000). At the same time, as outlined elsewhere here, a balance has to be struck between being supportive of the student, meeting the administrative needs of the organisation, and offering those who use the organisation's resources the best service possible.

The adult learning model outlined by Schön (1983) focuses on the skills and experience adults bring to the learning situation, together with their experience in solving problems in the past and their motivation to solve problems as a way of learning (Bucknell 2000). This shift clearly requires a change to the perception of who is entitled to 'produce' knowledge and challenges the teaching of technologies and competency-based criteria as the predominant means for acquiring professional knowledge and skills (Noble 2001).

The emergence of a critical reflective paradigm in human service education has a number of strands to it. Increasingly, it is being regarded as an important way of exploring the knowledge–practice relationship in social work activity (Noble 2001). Second, the notion of reflective practice helps to steer us away from taking an anti-intellectual approach which rejects theory and relies on common sense or an over-reliance on the use of theory to solve problems (Thompson 2005, p. 147). Finally, the push for a more critically reflective approach comes from the belief that the supervision should be linked to an emancipatory and empowering process that maximises a working partnership. A reflective approach to learning provides the key to narrowing the gap between theory and practice and recognises the active role that a practitioner plays in this integration. When applied to a placement context, it provides a framework that helps both the supervisor and the student to learn from each other in a systematic manner.

A critical reflective approach is linked here to a solution-, rather than problem-, focused approach to learning. Attention is paid to the learner's strengths and to engaging with the learner in finding the most appropriate way forward wherever possible. Supervisors can apply this approach to their own learning about supervision, as well as to assisting students to learn from their work. Students can apply this approach to their own learning about practice, and perhaps to their learning about how to make the best use of supervision.

Solution-focused approach

A range of solution-focused approaches incorporates elements of adult learning. It identifies experiences in the student's past that have provided a base for the development of the core competencies. This process helps to build the student's confidence and lessen the de-skilling that students often feel when required to demonstrate competence (Bucknell 2000). Established strengths in terms of knowledge, skills or values are identified, and goals in relation to their further development are identified. In particular, this approach:

- recognises the student as the 'expert' in his or her own learning
- views supervision as a mutual learning experience
- seeks to depersonalise any problems faced by the student and to focus on the capacities of the student
- is oriented towards exploration of future possibilities rather than past issues.

The style of talk a supervisor may use with this approach (or a student may use in preparing for supervision) is illustrated below:

- What works, even for a short time?
- What is happening when things seem to be going well?
- What are you learning about you in relation to this work situation?
- Is there anyone who seems to be able to cope with this situation? What are they doing?

The goal is to be able to generalise learning from familiar to less familiar situations. This topic is covered in Chapter 9 in some detail.

The diagram below is a modified version of the Kolb learning cycle outlined in Chapter 2.

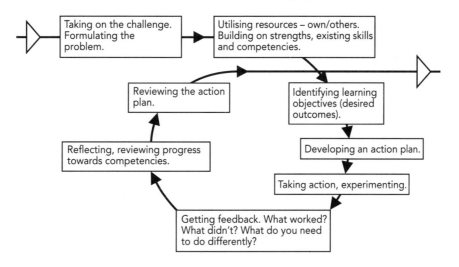

Source: D. Bucknell (2000), 'Practice teaching: Problem to solution', *Social Work Education*, vol. 19, no. 2, p. 130.

As you can see, most of these ideas are not new. Following the solutions-based principles, supervision starts from the identification of the solution, rather than an analysis of the problem, and the student uses supervision to receive feedback and guidance. Critical reflection provides a process by which this approach can be implemented.

Critical reflection

Over recent years, critical reflection and reflective practice have gained in popularity in all types of professional education, including nursing, teaching and the human services broadly. Napier (2006) says that it is commonplace to hear that the helping professions should be 'reflective practitioners and that reflective practice is integral' to our work, yet it is occurring at a time when there is less and less time for pausing and thinking about our practice (p. 7).

Reflective practice is much indebted to the work of Schön (1983, 1987), who introduced the key concepts of 'knowing-in-action' and 'reflection-in-action'. 'Knowing-in-action' refers to the tacit knowledge and developing knowledge that we have in doing things which is not related to any theoretical framework. Schön (1983) outlines this knowing as: 'actions, recognitions, and judgements which we know how to carry out spontaneously' (p. 54). Often we are unaware of the origin of this knowledge and are usually unable to describe the 'knowing' behind the action we have chosen.

Intuition is seen as an invaluable element of best practice. 'Reflection-in-action' is an extension of this knowing to include a practitioner's ability to reflect on how they approached a situation and develop new responses through 'trial and error' (Healy 2005). The practitioner becomes a researcher through this process of reflection. They are 'not dependent on the categories of established theory and technique, but construct a new theory of the unique case' (Schön 1983, p. 68). Essentially, reflective practice encourages practitioners to take time to think about the work they are doing, and to recognise and draw upon formal knowledge, as well as their lived experiences, as the basis for practice.

The 'critical' element adds an expectation of exploring practice in the context of the social system in which it operates (Gardner 2006) and hence explores issues of power, the political context, and how to work *with*, rather than *for*, others to achieve desired objectives.

Like solution-focused work, critical reflection is based on 'constructivist' tradition where the person's construction of reality is central; so, it follows that all practice, good or bad, is based on particular assumptions or theories about a whole assortment of knowledge and value areas, such as human behaviour, good parenting, social responsibility, and so forth. Sometimes these assumptions are deeply hidden, and sometimes they are explicitly stated. Professional practice may become outdated or ineffective when the unquestioned assumptions hidden in our taken-for-granted practices don't match our stated beliefs. In short, there may be large gaps between our desired theory and our actual practice. Often our practice may be based on deep-seated ideas about gender, age, disability, culture, sexual orientation and class that may limit our ability to work effectively. Often we are capable of fooling ourselves into believing that because our stated beliefs are acceptable, then our practice must be of quality (Fook & Gardner 2004).

The critical reflective approach is a way of improving practice, by exposing it to ongoing scrutiny and development. It is critical in that it provides the potential to delve quite deeply into previously unexamined areas of our thinking and practice. In this sense it potentially provides a different capacity for change than more 'objective' evaluation measures, which can be more superficial. While all types of evaluation are necessary, the critical reflection process can successfully bring about different kinds of changes, for two reasons. First, it has the capacity to take us beyond our 'comfort zones', and is therefore particularly useful for long-experienced practitioners who may feel they have little left to learn. Second, it creates the capacity for self-evaluation. People are in some ways more likely to accept and integrate the insights developed through this process precisely because they are not imposed externally. Some broad points to keep in mind when reflecting critically on what is happening are as follows:

- Identify situations of openness and uncertainty as opportunities for creative practice.
- Be alert to the use of language that frames problems and issues.
- Examine the content of and methods for making judgements and assessments.
- Question the ideology underlying particular services and decisions.
- Pay attention to different perspectives and contexts.

Bogo (2006, p. 57) discusses the use of reflective evaluation and suggests a number of questions that can be used in this process. These include the following:

- In what ways is the situation changing?
- Am I focusing on those changes, understanding them, putting them into words and using them as a base for future change?
- What does the other person think will work to address the issues that have been identified? How am I taking this into account?

A useful approach to critical reflection is the use of the critical incident technique. Taylor (2004) summarises critical incidents as 'the times where we have to take some action and whatever we do has important consequences' (p. 104). These incidents are triggers for reflection and can, Taylor (2004) suggests, be considered under three formats:

- Technical reflection, where particular procedures or evidence are considered, and the processes of assessing and planning, implementing and evaluating are commonly used.
- Practical reflection, which focuses on internalised knowledge, reactions and feelings; the processes of outlining the experience, interpreting why and what happened, and identifying learning for the future are used.
- Emancipatory reflection, which focuses on structures and power within situations. The challenge for the learner using this form of reflection is to start with a detailed construction of the event and then to deconstruct it, leading to looking at the constraints on practice and ways to challenge them.

In these processes, Taylor (2004, pp. 105–6) argues that the listener needs to listen more than talk, to challenge attitudes, and to encourage the other to make sense of the situation under review. Process reports, outlined in Chapter 8, will be helpful here.

With these ideas in mind, how can we use this approach in supervision? Educationalists have found that reflection is the most difficult aspect of learning, particularly if student practitioners are not encouraged to develop this skill (Ellis 2000). At the same time, emerging practitioners need to learn ways of fitting a critical reflective model of learning with the employer's expectations that education will produce graduates with competencies and technical skills.

A critical reflective approach does not negate the requirement for students to accept responsibility for their learning and the need to demonstrate an acceptable level of competency in a range of areas. What it does do is to move the balance of power to a form of student-centred learning that can offer a more empowering approach to the learning process.

EXERCISE 1

Ben is a 45-year-old student who was employed as a teacher before commencing social work studies. He is a second-generation Italian who is married with two children. He is committed to social work as a career change and had exposure to many complex social situations in his last position at the local high school. He is confident that he wants to work in the area of child protection when he graduates, and is very committed to what he describes as 'needy children'. A few weeks into his first placement, supervision has raised issues about Ben's approach to his cases. His manner is rigid and inflexible; he has 'tunnel-vision' about what he thinks is useful to learn and what is not, and is defensive about any critical feedback. He also appears to be judgemental about people and their deficiencies, tending to blame the victim.

- From a critical theory perspective, what are some of the significant elements in this case?
- How might a supervisor apply a critical reflective perspective?

Fook (2002) suggests a process of critical reflection that includes deconstruction, resistance and challenge, and reconstruction. The deconstruction would look at issues of diversity such as age, gender and culture, and at how Ben's perception of the world and his role as a helper could be influenced by these structures. The inequality inherent in the supervisory relationship may also be fuelling Ben's resistant behaviour, especially if there is an age or experience discrepancy. The challenge is to acknowledge the unfair language that has been used to describe Ben's behaviour, as well as his strengths and abilities. Identifying where you are coming from in terms of your own assumptions and ideas is part of this consideration. The reconstruction process would include having a 'reflective conversation' (Schön 1987) about the different views, values and beliefs to create a new discourse and gain a more useful sense of the different world-views of Ben and his supervisor. Supervision would be used as a way to enquire about and affirm Ben's experiences, but also to encourage him to explore how his assumptions may impact on his work.

The specific teaching and learning tools that use a critical reflective approach include journals, the critical incident format, think sheets and narratives (see Chapter 8).

The following list summarises the advantages of critical reflection in field supervision.

ADVANTAGES OF CRITICAL REFLECTION IN FIELD SUPERVISION

- improved supervisory practice
  – more creative and aware of more options through avoiding routine approaches to problems
- reduction of oppressive practice
  – awareness of possible discriminatory and stereotyping behaviour or of inappropriate use of power
- better teamwork
  – more collegiate ways of working and ensuring that our practice is not abusive
- increased accountability
  – better ability to evaluate and self-evaluate
- capacity for personal growth
  – 'recognising that the personal is political'
- increased confidence
  – more open and better learning through a non-judgemental environment

Summary

Following a brief summary of a range of approaches to learning in supervision, this chapter has outlined a solution-focused approach combined with the use of critical reflection. Stages in the critical reflective approach are outlined and illustrated with a case example, and links are made to teaching and learning tools outlined in Chapter 8.

7

DEVELOPING GOOD SUPERVISORY PRACTICES

Introduction

Good supervisory practices result from understanding the different functions and clarifying expectations of supervision, building the supervisory relationship, monitoring what is discussed in supervision, structuring supervision sessions, keeping records and giving feedback.

All situations on placement are opportunities for teaching and learning. In this chapter, the focus is on formal supervision sessions; yet we recognise that many of the issues discussed apply to chats in the corridor and in the car, and so on. Informal supervision is one way that students or supervisors can deal with an immediate need for checking procedures: gaining important information or receiving support to handle a crisis, for instance. It essentially is responsive rather than planned supervision, and it occurs more frequently at the beginning of a placement. The behaviours of both students and supervisors in both formal and informal contexts will have an impact on the supervisory relationship and can have a profound effect on students' learning. Whatever the context and type of supervision, it should involve two interlocking functions: learning about the tasks and learning about the learning.

The functions of supervision

The literature takes a number of approaches to describing what processes are needed for effective supervision and the roles supervisors may choose to play. Different functions and roles may be dominant at different phases of the supervision process over time, and in relation to different issues that the student or the organisation faces. Some student learning styles may also suggest different roles to the supervisor.

There is broad agreement that the supervisory process in fieldwork commonly has three principal functions – administrative, educational and supportive – that may complement or be in conflict with each other (Kadushin 1976). For example, if a student's standard of work is a problem, the supervisor can be caught between the requirement to protect a client or community and the need to allow the student the opportunity to work on tasks so that he or she can learn (administrative and educational). The supervisor may want to reassure the student (supportive), yet also may have to judge the student's standard of work (administrative and educational). The student must meet his or her obligations by telling the supervisor what he or she has been doing, even if the student suspects that his or her work might be criticised. A healthy supervisory relationship will comprise all three functions and will manage the inherent conflict between them. If the relationship is based on sufficient levels of trust and respect, these tensions can be managed to minimise the harm to all concerned. Within these broad functions, others provide some expansion by combining aspects of these three functions. Davys (1999), for example, adds the following:

* *Enabling:* a mix of the field educator's supporting and empowering students, achieved by reliability, encouragement, approachability, respect for difference and intolerance of any marginalisation of the student by others in the organisation.

- *Assessing:* a mix of the broad education and administrative functions, addresses the issue of evaluating whether or not the student's work reaches the required standard, and indeed, the extent to which it exceeds this base line.
- *Being accountable for student work:* an aspect of the administrative and education functions that needs to be clear to all parties and which requires that field educators have access to student work; it also includes accountability to the educational program for the student's learning and assessment.

The three main functions of supervision, and an example of each, follow.

- *Educational* (students are assisted to develop their professional competence): The supervisory relationship should help students learn from their practice, identify the principles that underpin their practice, and make links to the theoretical material taught by the training institution. It aims to promote professional competence, and to reinforce formal theoretical and on-the-job knowledge and skills. Example: 'What signs or indications did you observe that led you to take this action?'
- *Administrative* (students are assisted to improve the quality of their work and are guided to do an appropriate amount of work): Supervisors are accountable to their agencies and to the people with whom students work. They are responsible for directing and assessing students' work and for ensuring that the legal, safety, professional and ethical responsibilities are covered. Example: 'It would be important to record this information in the client's file and to inform the case manager of your contact.'
- *Supportive* (the impact of the work on students is considered): Supervisors offer reassurance and encouragement to students, validating them as people and as new practitioners. Supervisors monitor the levels of stress experienced by students, reassuring them about the emotional demands the work makes on them, assisting them to resolve conflicts, and advising them, when necessary, to seek external counselling. Example: 'You handled that difficult case with great sensitivity.'

Students ideally need to experience all of these approaches. The weight given to each will depend on the particular tasks at hand and perhaps on the stage of placement. The three functions are rarely carried out in isolation: for example, debriefing a student after an event is both educational and supportive (Kadushin 1976, p. 86). A common danger is that supervisors concentrate on case management instead of incorporating a developmental and educational focus. If they focus solely on the support function, supervision may come to resemble therapy.

Expectations of supervision

As discussed in Chapters 1 and 2, it is essential that there is negotiation early in placement to clarify the parameters and expectations of the supervisory relationship. Making a contract is a useful way to record the specific expectations of supervision as well as the practical requirements of the training institution. (See Chapter 5 for more detailed information.) Examples of such an approach follow.

> ***Supervisor:***
> *I generally take a problem-oriented approach, where I can be fairly directive. I am looking for your ability to explain a situation.*

Or, perhaps:

> ***Supervisor:***
> *I generally take a process-oriented approach in which I am more interested in exploring your responses to a situation.*

> ***Student:***
> *How would you suggest that we address any concerns or differences of opinion that might arise during my placement?*

Exercise 1, adapted from Morrison (2001, pp. 37–43), helps to clarify the degree to which supervisors and students have shared expectations about supervision and the different functions outlined earlier, and draws attention to any areas that are not being addressed. It is a good idea for students and supervisors to do this exercise at the beginning of placement, perhaps as part of the negotiation for the supervision agreement (see Chapter 5), as well as before the halfway point.

EXERCISE 1

FOR THE STUDENT AND SUPERVISOR

The tasks outlined in the following lists relate to the different functions of supervision. Make a photocopy of these lists so that you both have a copy. Tick the tasks that you feel are appropriate to be supervised. Compare your lists and discuss any items that are not shared.

Repeat the exercise before the halfway point of placement, ticking what you still feel are appropriate tasks for supervision. Then tick the tasks in the second column that you feel are being carried out in supervision.

THE SUPPORT FUNCTION CHECKLIST

Tasks	Before placement	During placement
To validate the student both as a developing professional and as a person		
To create a safe environment for the student to reflect on his or her practice and its impact on him or her as a person		
To clarify the boundaries between support and counselling and the issue of confidentiality in supervision		
To debrief the student and give him or her permission to talk about feelings raised by his or her work		
To help the student explore any emotional blocks to his or her work		
To explore issues of difference and discrimination that may be experienced by the student		
To monitor the overall health and emotional functioning of the student		
To clarify when the student should be advised to seek professional help		
Other (*specify*)		

THE EDUCATIONAL FUNCTION CHECKLIST

Tasks	Before placement	During placement
To assist the development of the student's professional competence		
To appreciate and assess the student's theoretical base, skills, knowledge and personal abilities		
To understand the student's preferred learning style and blocks to learning		

To discuss the student's value base and its impact on his or her work		
To give regular and constructive feedback to the student on his or her work		
To help the student to be self-reflective about his or her work and interaction with clients and other staff		
To give the student access to opportunities to develop further knowledge and skills		
Other (*specify*)		

THE ADMINISTRATIVE FUNCTION CHECKLIST

Tasks	Before placement	During placement
To ensure that the student understands his or her role and responsibilities		
To ensure the student's work is reviewed regularly		
To ensure that the student has an appropriate workload		
To ensure that student activities are properly documented and carried out according to agency policies and procedures		
To ensure that the student knows when the supervisor needs to be consulted		
Other (*specify*)		

The following exercise, adapted from Collins, Thomlison and Grinnell (1992), is another way to acknowledge and define expectations of supervision.

EXERCISE 2

FOR THE SUPERVISOR

Complete a preliminary assessment of the student's placement using the following headings:
- adjustment to the setting and learning activities
- developing strengths
- emerging concerns
- other comments.

FOR THE STUDENT

Complete a self-evaluation using the same or similar headings. You can also include responses to the following questions.

1 Do you feel supported?
2 Are you happy with the supervision arrangements?
3 How well do you think you work with your supervisor?
4 What issues do you tend to focus on most in supervision?
5 Are there any areas on which you would like to spend more time?

This exercise should not be seen as a formal evaluation. It facilitates the process of an open dialogue between student and supervisor, limits the possibility of misunderstanding and disappointment, and lays a good basis for the supervisory relationship.

Developing the supervisory relationship

The most exciting tasks and learning environment are no substitute for a good supervisory relationship. As in all human service practice, teamwork is often the way work gets done. In a good relationship, shortcomings on either side are forgiven; in a poor one, very few are forgotten or forgiven. A good supervisory relationship does not occur by chance. A number of factors can be influenced by the development of the supervisory relationship, including the use of power, personal differences, styles of supervision, responses to difficulties, and the balance of the different functions of supervision. You may have an opportunity to have some choice in selecting a student or supervisor, but more often than not the training institution and/or the agency controls the allocation process. But despite any organisational constraints, both student and supervisor can negotiate and develop a professional and respectful working alliance, even if it is characterised by some anxiety and conflict on either side. The relationship can elicit a range of responses from the student. On the more negative side, it might be characterised by dependency, perceived threats to autonomy, failure to engage, and submissiveness; and, on the positive side, by autonomy, success, independence and pleasure. For the supervisor, emotions can include anxiety, competitiveness or the desire to nurture the student.

Use of power

Supervisors can feel uncomfortable with the authority and power vested in their role and they may seek to side-step it, which will only confuse the student, who is only too aware of the power imbalance (Kadushin 1976, p. 98). The power inherent in the supervisory role may be amplified or minimised by differences and similarities in age, gender, culture, experience or (dis)ability.

The supervisory relationship is almost always affected if supervisors abdicate authority because they are worried about upsetting students or fear students will not accept their authority. If, on the other hand, supervisors abuse their authority and are overly critical and judgemental, the supervisory relationship also may become dysfunctional. It is recommended that the following principles are discussed in initial supervision sessions in order to develop a positive supervisory relationship.

- Students and supervisors recognise the legitimate power of supervisors inherent in their formal role and position.
- This power is to be exercised constructively in a two-way relationship between people of equal status and worth as human beings.
- Students and supervisors recognise the informal power that derives both from their professional and personal attributes, and from identities based on gender, age, class, ethnicity, sexual orientation, ideology or (dis)ability (Brown & Bourne 1996, p. 34).

Difference

The impact of difference is a reality in supervision. When perceived differences are linked to the need to raise issues with the other party, it can make students and supervisors anxious, fearing they will make things worse or perhaps be accused of discrimination. Differences between the student and supervisor need to be openly recognised. If differences are ignored and the supervisor maintains that he or she treats everyone the same, others may be forced to assume the beliefs of the dominant individual or group. If difference is confused with disagreement, it can mean that issues, such as those about performance, are avoided. This is discussed in more detail in Chapters 14 and 15.

Issues of diversity and difference between student and supervisor need to be addressed in the supervisory relationship. The following examples illustrate this.

A Greek female worker supervising a Greek female student in Australia may share strong, empowering feelings of mutual identification of gender and culture. However, a collusive alliance may be formed that denies the formal power of the supervisor. If the student fails to complete some tasks satisfactorily, the supervisor may protect her rather than confronting her about her learning difficulty. An Anglo-Saxon female worker supervising an Asian female student may use her membership of the dominant culture to undermine the student's cultural identity by negating her knowledge of 'normal' family values. Conversely, the supervisor may feel uncomfortable about giving critical feedback because she fears it will be perceived as discriminatory or because the student will not respect her authority. A supervisor might negate a male student's skills in working with oppressed female clients; conversely, the supervisor could defer to the power and status of the student's gender and feel uncomfortable about being critical of his work. If a supervisor is a feminist, the student may find it difficult to express different values because the student is in a position of less power. If the student is a feminist, the supervisor, if he or she has a different ideology, may try to undermine that of the student; conversely, the supervisor may be anxious not to appear to be anti-feminist and may become defensive about sharing his or her ideological position during supervision.

Styles of supervisory relationships

The way power is exercised or avoided will have an impact on your style of relationship as supervisors and students. Supervisory styles can be broadly categorised as authoritative and facilitative (Heron 1990). Authoritative styles are:

- *prescriptive:* supervisors give advice and explicit direction to the student
- *informative:* supervisors impart knowledge and information to the student
- *confrontational:* supervisors give clear, direct feedback about behaviour and challenge beliefs and attitudes.

Facilitative styles are:

- *cathartic:* supervisor enables the student to release tensions and emotions
- *reflective:* supervisor encourages the student to be reflective and self-directive
- *supportive:* supervisor confirms and validates the student's values and worth.

Exercise 3 consists of questions to help supervisors and students consider supervisory styles and expectations of supervision.

EXERCISE 3

FOR THE STUDENT AND SUPERVISOR

1 How much will you disclose of yourself in terms of how your life has shaped who you are now?
2 How do you cope with making mistakes?
3 What do you do if you are feeling under pressure?
4 How do you let people know you don't approve of what they are doing?
5 How do you let people know you like the way you are being treated?
6 How do you cope with being assessed or assessing others?
7 What expectations do you have of a supervisory relationship?
8 What previous experiences have you had that might impact on how a supervisory relationship develops and works?

The style of the supervisory relationship may change over time. There are different opportunities, tasks and issues, depending on the stage of development of the relationship. Using a journal or diary, as discussed in Chapter 8, may help you to chart any changes in the style of the relationship over time.

Balancing the functions of supervision

It is important to review supervision at regular intervals throughout placement in terms of which functions – administrative, educational or supportive – are getting most 'air play'. If, as a student, you think that your supervisory relationship is not balanced in these functions, it may be for one or more of the following reasons.

- Your supervisor lacks time to devote to each function.
- Your supervisor experiences conflict between the need to support you and the requirement to point out inadequate work.
- You are not clear about supervisory goals.
- Your supervisor lacks skills and knowledge in supervision.
- Tensions in your agency limit your opportunities to learn.

One way to ensure you are keeping as good a balance as possible is to consider the tasks you are focusing on and the skills you are using. Use the checklists from Exercise 1 to help you do this. Once you can categorise the tasks and skills, you are in a stronger position to make conscious decisions about how you will use supervision time.

Techniques and content of sessions

Describing what is talked about and how it is talked about will help you to monitor what is happening in supervision sessions more precisely. Of course, much communication is non-verbal and you will also need to pay attention to this important part of what is transacted in supervision. Supervision that relies heavily on just one style of talk, or ignores students' learning styles, is unlikely to be responsive to most students' needs. Wilson (2000) offers some other communication techniques to use in supervision (p. 36).

Technique	Description	Examples	Limitation
Linear questions	investigative assume that phenomena are connected in a linear way	'Could you tell me what that was about?' 'What problems are you having with that report?'	Students may not feel supported to explore underlying learning issues.
Circular questions	explore the relationship between different elements	'What happens when you try to raise that issue with your colleague?'	It can be time-consuming to explore issues.
Strategic questions	challenge the student's view raise specific expectations about future action	'Do you think that you are ready to take on this type of case?' 'How long will it take you to finish that report?'	Students may feel directed and confronted.
Reflexive questions	assume circular connections between the issues faced look for ways to move forward	'If you were able to raise these ideas with the manager, how do you think she would react?'	It can be time-consuming to challenge students to problem-solve.

Technique	Description	Examples	Limitation
Reflecting	Supervisors paraphrase what students have said to check that they have understood what students wished to convey.	'When Mr V. kept wandering around the room you got pretty frustrated with him.'	It is more time-consuming than supervisors telling students what they think is happening.
Interpreting	Supervisors suggest ways in which two matters might be linked – this may be expressed as a question or statement.	'Perhaps Mr V. kept moving around because he did not want to hear what you had to say.'	The supervisor may do the thinking and it may be hard for students to challenge his or her interpretations.
Giving directives	Supervisors provide explicit directions to students.	'You will need to finish that report by tomorrow.'	The supervisor can do all the thinking about the task.
Giving information	Supervisors pass on knowledge about practice issues – this may be practice wisdom or be from policy documents, theoretical material, etc.	'Our service is funded by a variety of government sources.'	Supervisors may do all the talking, which can be boring for students.
Encouraging and reassuring	Supervisors are explicit about what has been done well or is to be done in the future.	'You handled that situation in a courageous manner.'	This feedback may not be useful if it is too general and too repetitive.

These techniques can be used to focus on the student's thinking, feeling or action. When these means of processing information are balanced, students are most likely to benefit from the learning. This is explored further in Exercise 4. You can use the table to list what you currently do and identify other things to try in supervision.

EXERCISE 4

FOR THE SUPERVISOR

If possible, tape your supervision sessions. Count the number of times you use each technique in a half-hour session. Alternatively, you could number the sequence of behaviours you use in covering a particular issue. Start again with a different coloured pen when you move to a new topic. Do you tend to follow the same sequences? Is this a good thing?

	Student's		
	thinking	feeling	action
Questions – linear			
Questions – circular			
Questions – strategic			
Questions – reflexive			
Reflecting			
Interpreting			
Giving directives			
Giving information			
Encouraging and reassuring			

The following example shows the record of the activities of two different supervisors. The first is represented by letters, the second by numbers. The first is a typical pattern for busy supervisors. The style of supervision is administrative – supervisors satisfy themselves that they know enough about the situation, then issue directions about what to do next. The second record using numbers shows a supervisory style that is more focused on facilitating the student's thinking about the task and assisting the student to come to some conclusions about what to do next.

	Student's		
	thinking	feeling	action
Questions – linear		1	A, C
Questions – circular	B, D 2		3
Questions – strategic			7
Questions – reflexive		4	9
Reflecting	5		E 6
Interpreting			
Giving directives			
Giving information	8		6
Encouraging and reassuring	10		

The pattern of techniques used by supervisors will vary with the stage of placement and the issue under discussion. Nevertheless, if you find that you consistently ignore certain aspects, think about what this means for your supervisory style. In broad terms, the more boxes you use – with the exception of directives about feelings! – the more comprehensive the learning opportunity offered to the student.

Another method you can use is to measure in minutes the time spent in discussion of particular content in a session using the following table. Four key areas are divided into specific facts and the broader issues that underpin them. If the discussion in supervision is all above the line, you are unlikely to be generalising the learning. If the discussion is all below the line, individual tasks may not be receiving enough attention. While the specific task and the stage of placement will impact on how time is spent, in general there needs to be a balance across the four areas and above and below the line.

	Task	Student as learner	Agency matters	Human service field
Facts				
Issues				

In the following example, the content areas have been filled out for two interactions marking the minutes with forward slashes. The second interaction is in bold. The first interaction was slightly quicker, but concentrated on the specifics of the situation in the agency context. It would be difficult to discern what the student learned from interaction, because the supervisor did not check the student's understanding. In the second interaction, there is more linking of the specific issues to the broader issues and there is more chance that the student has been helped to learn in more depth about the specific task.

	Task	Student as learner	Agency matters	Human service field
Facts	//		//	/
	/	**/**	**/**	
Issues	/			
	/	**/**	**/**	**/**

Supervision sessions

Structuring sessions

Although informal contact, feedback and information-sharing are part of the learning process, supervision sessions are planned, regular times in which students and supervisors discuss students' work and review their progress. As such, supervision is different from consultation or briefing or debriefing activities (Ford & Jones 1987, p. 63). The norm for supervision in most placements is about one hour per week.

A supervision session, like other formal interactions at work, should be planned, purposive and goal-directed. Planned contact ensures that supervision is a priority and doesn't just occur 'whenever things slow down', because most human service agencies almost never slow down (Kiser 2000, p. 89). The frequency, timing and duration can be negotiated when the supervision contract is set up at the beginning of placement (see Chapter 5). Supervision time is valuable and often difficult to arrange, so you will want to use the time well. Setting an agenda and preparing material to be discussed will help you to focus on the learning objectives and any concerns and questions. The following strategies ensure that both parties can prepare and that issues are not being avoided or discussed because of lack of time.

- Students propose an agenda and give it to their supervisors two days before the session.
- Students give their journal, process records and other relevant material to the supervisor two days beforehand, so that key issues and concerns can be highlighted.
- Students and supervisors use the last five minutes of each supervision session to set an agenda for the next session. The following questions will help you to set this agenda.
    1 Why is this meeting occurring?
    2 What is its purpose?
    3 What would you like to cover?
    4 What are your desired outcomes?
    5 What questions do you wish to ask?

Supervision sessions should also include planning for future learning activities. The following strategies will help you to plan such activities.
- Allow some time before the end of each session to review how the time was spent.
- Review the processes as well as the content of the session. Ford and Jones (1987) suggest that the style of supervision can get 'fixed'; using a variety of methods and tools can make the process more interesting (p. 68). These methods are covered in more detail in Chapter 8.
- Supervision is usually focused entirely on the student, but you can use the sessions to do other things such as reviewing a journal article or preparing a joint piece of work.

Recording sessions

Keeping a record of student activities, including a summary of each supervision session, can be onerous, but clarifying what will be recorded and planning how to use summaries from the outset of placement can make this job easier. Recording sessions has the following advantages:
- It means that everyone is clear about feedback, especially if the notes are shared.
- It ensures transparency and reduces students' concerns.
- It models the process of keeping careful records of contact (as a worker would do with a client or project).
- It collates examples and concrete evidence that can be used in required evaluation documentation.

A useful format for recording supervision sessions follows. The possible content areas are given a number. A record sheet is then filled in for each session, identifying the topics for that session by number. It is easy to use and the activities can be changed to reflect the context of your placement.

RECORD OF SUPERVISION SESSION/MEETING

Student's name:		Supervisor's name:	
1	Reviewing case notes, diary, process records, journal	7	Supervisor provides educational input
2	Reflecting about practice (student)	8	Student provides educational input
3	Problem-solving about practice issues	9	Reviewing learning agreement
4	Discussing additional skills or strategies	10	Feedback about student's progress
5	Demonstrating skill or strategy (supervisor)	11	Discussing evaluation documents
6	Demonstrating skill or strategy (student)	12	Other (specify)

Date of meeting	Time spent	Material covered (Select number from list)	Comments		Initials (student)	Initials (supervisor)

Here is another format for recording supervision sessions that could be adapted for use in any placement setting.

NOTES ON SUPERVISION SESSION

Between .... and ....

Date ....

Topic	Discussion	Agreed action, timeline, who has responsibility

Agenda items for next session: Preparation required:

....

....

Signed ....

Date.....................................

Giving feedback

Feedback is a key component of learning and teaching during supervision as it promotes open communication and ensures that information is understood correctly. By offering or inviting feedback, students show that they are prepared to accept criticism, and supervisors invite feedback on their own teaching style. However, giving and receiving feedback can be difficult for both supervisors and students because it requires being able to deal with the feelings that this brings up (Trevithick 2000, p. 98). As a result, it has been found that supervisors make very few assessment comments during supervision, even though it has also been found that students are usually worried about some aspect of their performance (Hughes & Heycox 2000, p. 93).

Feedback is the process of relaying observations, impressions, feelings or other evaluative information about people's behaviour for their own use or learning (Ford & Jones 1987, p. 74). Egan (2000) describes three purposes of feedback in the context of working with clients, and these are just as relevant to the placement context:
- *Confirmatory:* It lets clients (or students) know when they are on course.
- *Corrective:* It provides clients (or students) with information they need to get back on course.
- *Motivating and challenging:* It shows the consequences of both adequate and inadequate performance (p. 389).

Giving feedback is primarily the responsibility of supervisors, but students can also take some action to find out how they are progressing. Either the student or the supervisor could raise the subject using cues such as 'It would be good to spend some time talking about that last interview' or 'Could we talk about the interview I did yesterday?' Feedback should contain some judgements about whether the student is meeting his or her learning objectives (AASWWE 1991, p. 115).

Exercise 5 is a useful means for students and supervisors to evaluate whether they are giving or receiving adequate feedback.

EXERCISE 5

FOR THE STUDENT

Think over your supervision sessions.

1 If feedback or constructive comments on your work are not a regular part of supervision sessions, do any of the following reasons explain why?

- You are achieving but your supervisor is not aware that positive feedback is required for your confidence.
- You are not achieving and your supervisor does not know how to give you constructive criticism.
- You may be giving cues that you are vulnerable and your supervisor feels uneasy about your reaction.

2 What can you do to change this?

FOR THE SUPERVISOR

Think about the feedback you have given to the student recently.

1 Is the feedback evaluative as well as descriptive?

2 Is your feedback encouraging as well as honest and direct?

3 Does the student know what you think about his or her progress?

4 Do you find it easier to give feedback to certain people (for example, people who may be younger, subordinates, women)?

Finding the balance between being honest and being facilitative can be difficult (Trevithick 2000, p. 98). The following guidelines should help you find this balance when giving feedback. Note that the term 'receiver' is used instead of 'student' or 'supervisor', as either one may need to give the feedback. When you give feedback, try to remember the following points.

1 *Be concrete:* Describe specific behaviours and give reasons or examples: for example, instead of saying 'I thought that the interview went well', it would be more helpful to say: 'I really liked the way you started the interview by quickly introducing yourself and putting the client at ease.'

2 *Be timely:* Try not to have a delay between the activity and giving the feedback, and have sufficient information. Some receivers may require more time and preparation to receive feedback.

3 *Be careful about language:* Instead of using the term 'criticism', use terms like 'coaching', 'critical appraisal', 'critical feedback'.

4 *Be consultative:* It can be irritating for the receiver to hear something he or she already knows about his or her work. Doel et al. (1996) suggest it is preferable to say, 'As we agreed, I'm going to give you some feedback about your court report, but I thought it only fair to ask you what you thought about it first' (p. 76).

5 *Be balanced:* Recognise both strengths and weaknesses. Doel et al. (1996) recommend giving feedback in terms of 'what I would keep' and 'what I would change'.

6 *Be objective:* Focus on the behaviour, rather than on personal attributes: for example, 'It was a good idea to focus on the issue of his gambling, but I don't know if he appreciated you bringing it up in

front of his wife. Maybe you could have waited to see if his wife brought it up first', rather than 'You were too confronting with him.'

7 *Be supportive:* Focus on sharing ideas and information, rather than on giving advice; and explore alternatives, rather than offering answers and solutions. This leaves receivers free to decide for themselves how to use these ideas (Shardlow & Doel 1996, p. 111): for example, 'I was interested in how you decided to handle the disagreement during the committee meeting' or 'I would have thought that some of the members would have liked to be given an opportunity to speak' or 'What were you thinking could be achieved by choosing to change the agenda?'

8 *Be creative:* Most feedback tends to be given verbally and thus is open to misinterpretation or misunderstanding, or may not be heard at all. Demonstration, direct observation and process recording will promote understanding and self-evaluation. Written feedback can provide a useful record for students and contribute to the evaluation process.

9 *Be informed:* Incorporate literature from the classroom and other research to support feedback and to encourage the expectation that critical feedback is part of human service education and is essential for practice development (Abbott & Lyster 1998, p. 54).

Receiving feedback

Doel et al. (1996) offer some strategies to help you receive feedback. It is important to be aware of your own responses when receiving feedback. Do you seek feedback or do you avoid it? Do different situations or different people make a difference to how you react?

1 *Ask for feedback:* Both students and supervisors need feedback so that they can develop their practice skills. It can be particularly hard for students because supervisors have more power, status and experience. If supervisors show themselves willing to receive feedback, the student can practise giving it and it helps to equalise the relationship.

2 *Try not to become defensive:* Challenging feedback is often delivered as criticism and can trigger defensiveness. Treating feedback as one source of information about yourself, rather than as personal criticism, is a way of discovering more about yourself.

3 *Respond to unfair feedback:* If feedback is not given appropriately or makes you feel overly vulnerable, it is important not to deny the other person's perception, but let it be known that you have a different view: for example, 'I hear that you have not been happy about [X]; however, I see that situation a bit differently.'

Other types of supervision

Although one-to-one supervision sessions contribute significantly to students' learning, they can be time-consuming and limit students' exposure to different practice styles and theories (Cleak, Hawkins & Hess 2000, p. 165). Possible alternative arrangements for supervision include task supervision, collective supervision and group supervision.

Task supervision

Another worker in an agency may contribute to a student's learning by supervising the student in a specific project, program or task, and taking responsibility for the educational function of supervision in this context. The task supervisor may come from a different occupational background to the student. A student is increasingly likely to be supervised by a task supervisor on a day-to-day basis on placement, and the designated supervisor may be located in a different section or agency.

Using a task supervisor can expand the opportunities for the student to undertake different learning tasks and can dilute dependency on a single supervisor and provide a different perspective on the student's performance (Cleak, Hawkins & Hess 2000, p. 165). However, it is especially important that lines of accountability are clarified, especially about feedback and assessment responsibilities, and the role of the primary supervisor.

Collective supervision

This model is possible in agencies that operate on non-bureaucratic principles with shared processes. No single person is solely responsible for any area. It is a flexible and creative approach to supervision and uses expertise from workers in different sites or agencies. For example, a student might be placed in a community organisation and receive day-to-day task supervision by workers in two programs, with formal supervision provided by the training institution. The following example reflects creativity in the supervisor roles and involvement across three organisational structures.

> Simone's perception of the tripartite student–supervisors relationship was as a 'collaborative peer relationship'. The consumer advocate provided ongoing task supervision, complemented by fortnightly educational sessions with a human service worker from the network employed by one of the psychiatric service units.

Group supervision

The traditional structure of face-to-face and one-to-one supervision provides a highly individualised approach to teaching and learning. Group supervision can offer some creative additional learning opportunities for students, as it shares the responsibility for teaching and can avoid some of the potential difficulties of the dyad structure.

Group supervision of students is characterised by a regular pattern of focused discussion between supervisor(s) and two or more students (Ford & Jones 1987, p. 94). It can be used in any settings, such as community-work agencies, hospitals or larger statutory organisations, in which a group of students are undertaking their placement at the same time. There are a variety of models of group supervision:

- A group of students receive individual supervision, but also meet in a group with one or more supervisors for mainly educational and supportive functions.
- A group of students meet with a supervisor, who conducts all aspects of supervision in the group, including individual evaluations. Student units often use this model.
- A student has an individual supervisor but co-works with other students or workers on a particular project or program.

The potential benefits of group supervision are that it can save time for an agency and allow it to support a number of students on placement at the same time. When group supervision is properly structured and planned, it has a number of distinct advantages over individual supervision, as outlined below. Group supervision:

- allows students and supervisors to observe and learn from each other
- encourages use of different learning methods, such as group discussion, structured exercises, working in pairs or triads
- provides new insights for students because of the diversity of perspectives of group members
- exposes students to a range of values and supervision approaches, minimises issues of power, and allows students more freedom to differ with supervisors (Ford & Jones 1987, p. 96)
- encourages students to develop supportive relationships with other students and workers
- gives students the chance to experience group activities and explore their responses to group processes.

However, group supervision should not be considered a substitute for, or a cost-saving alternative to, individual supervision. It doesn't suit all learning situations and placements (Morrison 2001, p. 201). The disadvantages of group supervision are similar to those of any group process:

- The group can be derailed by members who are very vocal or needy or vulnerable or disruptive, so that learning needs of individuals are subjugated.
- Scrutiny by peers and assessment by the group may diminish a student's capacity to share honestly. The student may lack trust, or may fear that they will look bad.
- An inexperienced or unskilled facilitator may not be able to handle the dynamics of the group.
- Students can become frustrated by a group agenda that may not be appropriate for the varying levels of competence and learning needs of group members.

Group supervision is an approach with enormous potential and one that may become more common in the future as workers find it harder to juggle work and the demands of supervising placements (Brown & Bourne 1996, p. 163). For group supervision to be effective, it needs to be planned and organised in the same way as individual supervision. Group members should develop a contract to decide on aims, tasks, methods, expectations and regular reviews. The following list of questions and issues will help you to develop a group contract.

Clear structure	**Lack of structure**
How often and for how long do we meet?	The agenda is not made clear at the beginning of sessions and there is no time to discuss the focus of the following week's session.
Who can join?	
Is attendance voluntary or compulsory?	
Are sessions only for students or can other people join in?	The group often runs over time and some members miss out on presenting their work or ideas.
How will the time be structured?	
Clear purpose	**Diffuse purpose**
Is the group aimed at providing support, education, self-discovery?	Members often introduce irrelevant issues that are not part of the group contract.
What activities will be undertaken?	Members give long descriptive accounts of a case without any clear purpose for doing so.
Clear rules	**Unclear rules**
How does the group handle confidentiality and sensitive issues?	Members are unclear about whether they have permission to bring up an organisational issue.
How does the content and outcome of group activities relate to individual supervision?	Some members miss sessions and are not required to participate in the exercises, which leaves it to a few 'regulars' to contribute.
What are the rules about attendance and participation?	
How are decisions recorded?	
Clear role for facilitator	**Unclear role for facilitator**
Should the supervisor be responsible for guiding and balancing the content and process, or should the group have this control?	The facilitator is unable to control members who play out their antagonistic relationship within the group.
	Presenters often feel that they are being criticised by other members and this is not challenged by the facilitator.
	The facilitator does not encourage participation.
Methods are negotiated	**Methods are not negotiated**
What can students expect to be involved in (for example, role plays, case discussions, student presentations, small-group exercises)?	Facilitator plays the expert and does not introduce opportunities for members to share their own views.
Who decides what the group will do?	Group members take a conservative approach and rely on discussion rather than try out other more creative methods.

Morrison (2001, pp. 229–30) suggests the following group exercise that is useful in developing the interviewing skills of group members. It is based on Kolb's experiential learning cycle, described in more detail in Chapter 2.

EXERCISE 6

FOR THE STUDENT AND SUPERVISOR

In the group, identify someone (the presenter) who is willing to bring a case or issue to share with the group. The presenter gives a brief outline of the case or issue (no more than five minutes).

Other members (the interviewers) are allocated one part of the Kolb cycle: one person focuses on 'experiencing', one on 'reflecting', one on 'analysing' and one on 'action planning'. The task of each interviewer is to explore the case or issue using questions and ideas from their part of the cycle. For example, the reflector will ask 'feeling' questions, the experiencer will ask the presenter to describe the event, the analyser will hypothesise about the situation, and the planner might suggest ideas to help.

The interviewers should spend five to ten minutes preparing their questions. Use the ideas on questioning suggested in the previous section on techniques and content. Discuss the case or issue for about 30 minutes, starting with the first interviewer in the cycle and going around the group, remembering that you may go around a number of times and not always in order. Try to stay within your designated role. You could coach another interviewer to add something relevant to their role, if appropriate. At the end of 30 minutes, the interviewers should summarise what they have heard: for instance, the reflector summarises what was heard in terms of feelings, the analyser focuses on the explanations, and so on. Finally, the presenter identifies:

- what has become clearer
- what has become more complex or confusing
- the ideas they now have for taking the case or issue forward
- what further help may be needed.

The task of the facilitator is to ensure that the guidelines for the exercise and the timelines are followed and to identify any follow-up action and support.

Supervision of student units

An agency and training institution may provide a placement for a small unit of students – usually a work group with a particular set of obligations to the host agency. For example, in a hospital the unit may be responsible for work in particular wards, or in a community centre the unit may work on a specific project. The supervisor may be an employee of the agency, or sometimes is an employee of the training institution.

It is an efficient way of providing training: placements can still be offered even if there is an insufficient number of qualified supervisors, and it can provide a labour force for agencies to carry out an innovative form of practice. Teaching and learning in student units is similar to that experienced in supervision in all placements; however, one key difference is that the students are developing relationships with each other, as well as with the supervisor and other workers. It is important that attention is paid to the process of group formation, group rules are clear and the supervisor treats all students fairly. A mix of individual and group supervision is appropriate for student units. It is not unusual for students to be somewhat competitive in terms of the level of difficulty of the work they are allocated, how well they are going and how they are regarded by the supervisor. It is important for the supervisor to monitor the group's development, to set tasks that encourage cooperation rather than competition, and perhaps to draw students' attention to how they are functioning as a group. A functional unit can provide students with a great deal of support and peer learning.

Summary

The supervision relationship – whether it is individual, group, collective or in student units – is the crux of placement for students and can influence how much or how little learning takes place for supervisors and students. A planned approach, in which there is a balance of the three key functions of supervision, will establish a solid basis for a healthy and constructive supervisory relationship.

8

TEACHING AND LEARNING TOOLS

Introduction

You need to grasp the opportunities for learning that are all around you on placement – whether it is spending time with your supervisor while driving to meetings, having a chat with workers in the tea room, debriefing after something has happened, watching other practitioners at work or participating in workplace meetings.

Strategies are needed to assist students to retrieve, sift and sort significant learning experiences (Ellis 2000). Formal learning opportunities should be carefully chosen to contribute to the overall placement goals. It is the responsibility of the student to negotiate and use these opportunities for learning, and it is the responsibility of the supervisor to facilitate and extend the student's learning. To assess your learning opportunities, do Exercise 1 part-way through your placement.

EXERCISE 1

FOR THE STUDENT AND SUPERVISOR

Consider a particular time period, say a week, of placement and note all learning opportunities from that week in the following table. Compare notes with each other. You might find that you have different experiences of learning.

1 If there are differences, what does it suggest about your placement?
2 Consider any differences between the first and second row. What do these suggest about teaching and learning on this placement?

	Student's views of opportunities	Supervisor's views of opportunities
Opportunities to observe and discuss work issues (include names and positions of those involved)		
Opportunities to practise		

Shardlow and Doel (1996) suggest that a successful and balanced placement should comprise a significant range of different methods to optimise students' development of knowledge, skills and values (p. 117). Ford and Jones (1987) argue that using a range of methods also models to students how they can use a variety of interventions in their own practice, as well as it being a fairer way to make more aspects of a student's performance available for evaluation (pp. 79–81).

Other important reasons for using different teaching and learning tools include:
- to ensure that the learning from practice is maximised – successful practice does not necessarily indicate that learning has taken place
- to enable the quality of work and learning to be evaluated
- to provide written documentation on the student's progress and a record of any issues
- to cover the four aspects of learning – feeling, watching, thinking and doing – outlined in Exercise 5, Chapter 2 (Ford & Jones 1987).

Are there other factors that might guide your selection of particular teaching and learning tools in your agency?

The teaching and learning approach

The following principles can be used to determine the approach most appropriate for teaching and learning in a particular student–supervisor dyad in a particular agency (Shardlow & Doel 1996, p. 114).
- The specific learning and administrative goals of students should be linked to a particular method of keeping track of their work and their learning from that work.
- The progress of learning should be monitored by regularly reviewing the effects or outcomes of the learning methods used.
- Different methods for teaching and learning should be negotiated when the learning agreement is being developed. If the agency or supervisor requires these methods to be used without adequate negotiation, it may lead to resentment and non-compliance from the student.
- Methods of learning must be efficient. Teaching on placement is frequently one-to-one, which can be time-consuming and a luxury for many agencies. Supervisors should think carefully about how to use the time available for promoting learning.
- As many techniques require observation of clients or staff, consent must be obtained, usually in writing. Agreement is usually obtained if students explain that, as students in training, such observation helps to improve their practice and will be used by supervisors to guide students.
- Prepare any equipment beforehand to minimise the intrusion on observation time.
- Learning can be maximised if students retain control of how the learning method will be used for reflection. For example, students might prepare a summary of learning issues to discuss after taping an interview.
- Take a constructive approach to reviewing students' work; 'Hair-splitting and over-concern with detail is usually best avoided' (Ford & Jones 1987, p. 92).
- Supervisors should prepare students about what they are looking for, so that students can focus their efforts and not feel overwhelmed by the prospect of being assessed on too wide a range of skills.

The main teaching and learning tools fit into three categories: discussion tools, observation tools, and activities. Students and supervisors should try to include as many as possible over the course of the placement.

Teaching and learning tools		
Discussion tools	Observation tools	Activities
process records care plans diaries intake summaries minutes of meetings journals think sheets log sheets critical-incident reports agency records: including intake summaries, care plans, and minutes of meetings organisational analyses concept maps internet material films articles books journals policy documents	modelling direct observation videotaping audiotaping one-way screens	role plays games simulation skills training presentations co-working reading agency visits court and tribunal visits consultations committee meetings contact with individuals and groups

EXERCISE 2

FOR THE STUDENT AND SUPERVISOR

Think about a particular practice issue you are dealing with at present.

1 Which of these tools are you currently using?

2 Can you identify others that might be useful?

3 What stops you using a wider range of tools than may be the case at the moment?

Discussion tools

The dominant and most enduring vehicle for teaching is discussion. Through discussion, information is exchanged and there is opportunity for an event or experience to be conveyed in an open and unstructured way. Discussion is both an event and a process (Brown & Bourne 1996, p. 11). The process of discussion in supervision is covered in more detail in Chapter 7.

A great deal of information can be conveyed in a short time, as people communicate more quickly by talking than any other method of communication. Also, it is the least 'edited' of the non-direct methods available. However, there is usually no record of the work or learning by either the student or the supervisor (Ford & Jones 1987, p. 83).

Process records

Process recording has been used for many years as a reflective tool, but has been criticised as 'old-fashioned, time consuming and frustrating for both student and supervisor' (Fox & Gutheil 2000, p. 41).

Process records are highly detailed written accounts of practice after it has happened, which include some analysis and interpretation. Most process records use direct quotes and include a description of what happened – as well as students can recall. In truth, it may not reflect what students or other people actually experienced or what actually took place. If, after the event, students think that their intervention could have been better, they may change the process record to reflect this insight. While this may not improve the accuracy of the record, it does indicate that it facilitated learning because students were able to critically reflect on their practice (Collins, Thomlison & Grinnell 1992, p. 162).

Generally, individual clients are the subjects of these records, but they can be used to record family interviews or meetings between staff and clients, staff or committee meetings, and so on.

Process records are practical and easily accessible, and are a useful reflective tool for students. They are also a useful means for supervisors to gain insight into the thoughts and feelings of the student without relying on the more common retrospective student self-report (Shardlow & Doel 1996, p. 142).

The disadvantage of this method is that it may be considered laborious and time-consuming for students who are not used to examining their thoughts and feelings, or who dislike writing (Ford & Jones 1987, p. 91). It also requires the supervisor to spend time reading and reflecting on the content.

The following format aims to increase the student's self-awareness and differentiate between facts and feelings.

Name of student ....

Client's name ....

Date of interview .... (second interview)

Content dialogue	Student's feelings	Client's feelings	Knowledge used/skills demonstrated	Comments – student/supervisor
Client (C): 'I think I will be well enough to go home soon.'	I felt guilty because I knew that the client's family had other plans for her.	The client was making a stand about her wishes – she may have been fearful or angry about what might be planned for her.	I was taken aback by her assertive statement. My question was not a good thing to say as I made the client defensive.	
Student (S): 'Who told you that?'	I was pleased that I resisted the urge to reassure her, as that would have been untruthful.			
C: 'I don't care what they say. I am feeling stronger and know I can manage at home. Don't you agree?'		The client was feeling scared and powerless and perhaps wanting support from me.		Student: It would have been better to show empathy, such as 'I'm glad that you feel better', and then probe to explore her understanding about the practicalities of her going home. Supervisor: That's a good idea, but you managed to do this with your next response.

S: 'I'm glad to hear that you are getting better. Can you tell me more about what your family has said about the situation?'			I showed empathy here and then asked an open question to gain more information about what the client knows. It also engaged the client to talk more about herself.	Student: I was happy about this response, but it was a bit clumsy. Supervisor: Yes, it was a good response. Perhaps ask a more concrete question that gets to the client's feelings rather than her experiences, such as 'How do you feel about what your family is hoping for you?'

The following example of a process report uses the Fox and Gutheil structure. This is only the start of the report – a typical report would be more detailed.

Step 1: Preparation and the purpose of the intervention

Booked the interview room but there was a crisis case, so I had to ask Mrs B. to wait for 10 minutes, which she didn't like as she appeared anxious and wouldn't sit down in the waiting room. Reviewed Mrs B.'s file and checked what I wrote from our first interview last week.

Step 2: The process of the intervention and other relevant information (observation)

Mrs B. begins to cry.

Long pause.

Step 3: Student's thoughts and analyses (knowledge)

I knew her anxiety levels were high and the delay may have made her feel she was not important.

Step 4: Interventions (skills)

I maintained eye contact with her, offered her the tissues and waited until she seemed ready to talk.

Step 5: Next steps (planning)

I started to get a bit impatient, even though I knew this would not help. I decided that I need to engage with her and explore what her crying was about.

Step 6: Questions (questioning)

I panicked a bit and asked myself if I could cope – was she crying at me, or just crying? Was I uncomfortable about her distress, or because I was worried about my reaction to her crying (feeling inadequate).

Diaries and journals

A diary is an opportunity to record events and personal reactions during the placement. The use of and access to students' diaries and journals needs to be discussed and agreed to at the outset of placement. Some supervisors encourage students to keep a personal reflective account of the placement experience, which will remain private. However, students may choose to share part or all of such journals. Other supervisors see the journal as a summary of the progress of the placement that will be shared, so the content needs to be more objective and less emotive. A diary may just be a log of daily events, appointments and important dates to remember. A journal records the content and significance of learning tasks – it is not, therefore, necessary for students to record every activity but only significant ones that contributed to their learning.

Students should be encouraged to be reflective and to express a range of emotions, as this can be a good way for them to own their feelings and be assertive in expressing them.

Collins, Thomlison and Grinnell (1992) suggest that learning has two initial stages: collecting information and making sense of the information. A journal should be organised to fulfil both functions. In the example below, the format of the journal encourages students to record events and reflect on them by focusing on their reactions and how they make sense of the broader issues. Over time, these three aspects may integrate more naturally.

Summary of information (date and event)	Reflection and personal reaction	Broader issues
Interview with Mrs B. Recently separated and unsure of her entitlements. Very distressed and cried during the interview and wanted to talk about her marriage and why she felt worthless.	I was uncomfortable about Mrs B. crying and had trouble focusing on explaining the benefits and was unable to gather enough information to assess her entitlement.	Realised that I did not cope when the client did not go in the direction that I had planned. Why do women take the blame when marriages fail?

A fourth column called 'Action' could be added, in which students record ideas for follow-up action. In the example above, action points in a fourth column might include:

- Talk about this experience in supervision.
- Do a process record on the next interview.
- Obtain ideas about handling emotions from the supervisor.
- Read about feminist theory.

Bolio, Keogh and Walker (1985, p. 56) offer practical suggestions to the student on initiating and developing an individual portfolio (their term for a journal).

- It is meant to be a personal document; there is no right or wrong way to keep it. Use a method that suits you, as its usefulness will be in proportion to the extent to which it is your own.
- Be frank and honest in your entries: write it as it is, not as you would like it to be, nor as you think it should be.
- Have a positive approach to the portfolio: treat it as a close friend, not as an enemy. The key is to write, write, write. The more you plan, the less spontaneous it will be.
- Feel free to express yourself in diagrams and pictures and with cuttings and cartoons. Sometimes a picture can express what you are trying to say better than you can in writing.
- The portfolio is meant to be a workbook; therefore, use underlining, circling, different coloured inks, and anything else that will draw out significant elements. It may be a good idea to leave some space after each entry for recording later reflections.
- Follow up issues that surface when you are working with your portfolio. Don't let other things take your attention.
- Be faithful to it: persevere in the face of initial difficulties in keeping the portfolio.
- Record experiences as soon as possible after they happen, and as fully as possible. Students have found it helpful to carry a little notebook with them, so that they can jot down notes on their feelings, behaviours or thoughts, then write them up in their portfolios.
- Have a regular time to write in the portfolio, and a fixed time each week to reflect back on it.
- Although it may be a private portfolio, talking about ideas, thoughts and reflections will bring feedback that can help to deepen them.
- Be selective. Students have reported that in the beginning they wrote a great deal more than was necessary.

Writing in journals

Self-reflection is a core part of professional competence in most helping professions, but it is seen as more difficult to teach or assess effectively (Ixer 1999, p. 521). Journals and diaries are reflective tools to help you advance your understanding of yourself, both personally and professionally. A journal encourages you to:

- notice and put into words the ideas, perceptions, hunches, practice wisdom, joys, hardships, frustrations, and failings and successes you experience
- gain experience of how reflective writing can significantly extend your capacity for reflective practice
- maintain a personal record of significant events and important ideas, resources, theories, hypotheses and critiques of issues
- recognise that unexamined practice is a practice hardly worth doing!

Your journal will reveal your actions, feelings, values and beliefs, and your taken-for-granted assumptions about practice and the sociocultural world.

The guidelines by Western (2003, p. 7) for 'journalling' with clients can be adapted for use with students:

- As a supervisor, it is important to have some idea of what it is like to keep a journal before you ask students to do it.
- Consider when and how journalling could be effective. At what stage might you introduce the technique? How can it be used in supervision or to explore particular issues or feelings?
- Students should be given time to think about what they have written and allow their thoughts and ideas to be felt and understood.
- Unstructured journalling may not be appropriate for students with a history of recent trauma or who are emotionally vulnerable in some way.
- Different techniques can be used:
    - *Open:* Write whatever comes into your mind.
    - *Focused:* Write about …
    - *Guided:* Write about a particular aspect of …

Here are some basic questions that can help students to focus on and extend the content of their reflection.

- *Setting:* Where was I? What could I see, hear and feel in this setting?
- *Personnel:* Who was I involved with? Who else was in the interaction?
- *Account of the activity:* What did I do/say first? How might this be perceived by others?
- *Thoughts:* What was I thinking at the time? What happened next?

Some questions to extend students' self-awareness are:

- How can I focus on what is happening for me?
- What am I experiencing in my inner world?
- What feelings and emotions are aroused?
- If I stay with the dominant feeling, where does it lead me?
- What other experiences come to mind when I think about what is happening for me?

Some questions to extend students' critique are:

- What are my assumptions, values and beliefs?
- Where do these come from?
- What is it that causes me to maintain these?
- What view of power do they imply?
- Whose interests are served by my beliefs and corresponding action?
- What competing views are apparent?
- What constrains or encourages my view that change might be possible?

Think sheets

Think sheets were developed by Regan in 1977 but continue to be a useful way to discuss and conceptualise interactions on placement in a structured way. Completing a think sheet is a more structured exercise than writing in a journal and encourages students to reflect on both the behaviour and the emotional responses to a learning task.

Identifying data
(with whom, where, significant issues, events)

Practical assistance
(to distinguish between concrete and other kinds of help)

Feeling component
(to look at own feelings and the different levels of emotions of others)
Student
Client/other
Feeling level

What student learned
(the content of what has been learnt)

How student learned
(focus on the process of learning and strengthening the learning)

Learning blocks
(identifying any issues that impact on learning in this situation)

Reflection on critical incidents

You will be aware of those specific points in interactions in which your choice of action has a greater than normal impact on the way the interaction proceeds. You may be able to use this awareness at the time to process what is happening, to consider the available choices and the consequences of each choice. However, it is usually after the event that this awareness develops.

The questions in Exercise 3 explore, in some depth, what a critical incident meant to you, what contributed to your action or inaction at the time, and what this might mean for future work.

EXERCISE 3

FOR THE STUDENT

Consider a critical incident that occurred on placement and reflect on why it happened and why it was critical.

1 What images do you recall?
2 What sounds, smells and tactile sensations do you recall?
3 Which people or comments or practice stand out in your mind?

Next consider the affective domain – reflect on how you felt.

4 What was the high or low spot of the incident?
5 Were you surprised, angered, elated, curious, confused or depressed by anything in the experience? Describe your mood and feelings.
6 What do you think others were feeling?

Now interpret the events.

7 What have you learned from this incident?

8 From this experience, what can you conclude about your understanding of and skills in assessment or analysis?

9 What was your key insight or learning?

10 How does this relate to your framework for practice?

Finally, consider your decisions.

11 What skills and areas of understanding do you need to develop further as a result of your reflection?

12 What would this require?

13 What methods does this experience reinforce as valuable for future practice?

Narratives

Noble (2001) developed the use of narratives, or storytelling, as a critical reflective tool that offers the student important insights and links between their personal and professional selves. By writing creatively, students are encouraged to be spontaneous and to make explicit their experiences, feelings and thoughts during placement while exploring the elusive theory and practice link (p. 351).

The narrative is a particular form of student-centred learning that encourages a process of reflection about the way that people define themselves and their environments and may include the following techniques.

• The student writes a narration of an experience or event, which is shared in an individual supervision or group session. The student is then asked a number of questions or invited to discuss the following ideas:
    – Could they write the story with a different ending?
    – Could the story be reworked from a different position (e.g. from the point of view of a child, or a person of the opposite sex or from a different cultural background)?
    – Identify what is missing, or what is undesirable.
    – Work with the key words or particular emotions identified, and explore the implications for this and other practice situations.
    – Draw out the structural elements of power, gender, discrimination and socioeconomic elements

Noble (2001), however, cautions that this process does not begin and end with just affirming and 'idealising' the narrative. To become a critically reflective tool, the student and supervisor need to engage in a theory-building exercise that brings the critical dimension into the reflection.

Agency records

It is important that students are competent in producing all forms of organisation reporting relevant to the tasks they do, and that they understand the principles of good report writing and the role of report writing in organisational life. These records vary significantly between organisations – in some they reflect what has been done, while in others reporting requirements play a significant role in determining what work is done and indeed, how it is done – for example, in child protection or corrections. In some of these contexts, records are centralised and managed electronically. In others it may appear that records are the personal property of workers (Bateman 1995, p. 72), although in law they are the property of the employer and, in many settings, clients have access to them. It is important that students and field educators understand the complexity of the use of agency records when reading and using them, as well as writing them. In some contexts, field educators will need to countersign reports – a recognition that they, not the student, are ultimately responsible for what is written. It is a good principle to keep in mind that you only write what you would be prepared for the person(s) written about to read.

Agency staff write reports for many reasons, and hence they take many forms: letters, minutes of meetings, reports, file notes, submissions, diaries. O'Connor, Wilson and Setterlund (2003, p. 187) suggest that four broad types of information are presented in many reports:

- Subjective data: what those concerned see as the situation and the issues to be addressed.
- Objective data: those aspects of the situation that can be observed or measured.
- Assessment: the conclusions that have been formed from the available information.
- Plan: what action is proposed based on the assessment.

It is an important skill to learn how to write competent, clear and informative reports of work done efficiently. Some of the skills developed at training institutions may be helpful here – how to present a logical argument in a critical essay, the use of topic and concluding sentences for paragraphs, the use of the literature to highlight the areas that need to be explored (but generally not referenced in the same way!) will all help here. Some forms of reports require a particular approach: Bateman (1995) presents a helpful framework for writing for advocacy purposes, Coley and Scheinberg (1990) have a very useful guide for writing proposals, and Watson (1999) gives a useful framework for writing minutes.

Supervisors can assist students to develop these skills by working with students to identify the principles behind good report writing in their organisation context, and giving students a range of report writing tasks to enable them to see points of similarity and difference in good reports for a range of purposes.

Organisational analysis

Conducting an organisational analysis is an essential part of a student's learning experience and a supervisor's teaching experience. There is a range of useful models of analysis, and the student's training institution may have requirements about what model is chosen. Refer to Exercise 1 in Chapter 3 (p. 28) and Exercise 2 in Chapter 4 (p. 35) for two models for mapping organisations.

Concept maps

Concept maps are a useful way of organising what you know about a particular topic. Concept maps comprise a selection of concepts or topics (usually nouns), connected by words (usually verbs) that say how these concepts are related. They help you to identify links between particular topics or tasks and can suggest links you may not have imagined or that you make but have trouble naming. Some topics that might be relevant for concept mapping in your placement are: gender, human behaviour, age, change, disability, control and conflict.

One suggestion for early in the placement is to make a concept map of your framework for practice. This helps you to organise what you currently know, and to examine how this knowledge is useful to you in a specific agency. You could use 'post-it' notes or small pieces of paper you can move around to explore the links between the concepts. It can take quite a while to develop a map that is both succinct and thorough enough to be useful. The example on page 83 uses a simple flowchart to outline a practice framework.

This can be a useful tool in supervision. By asking the student to identify the main concepts underpinning his or her thoughts about a particular task, the student and the supervisor can see what the student is emphasising, and perhaps what is being ignored.

To check that your concept map is complete, consider the following issues.

- Does your map have linking words? Omitting words on a line linking two concepts can occur quite often.
- Does your map use linking sentences instead of linking words? Try to isolate the concepts in the sentence and only include these concepts in the map.

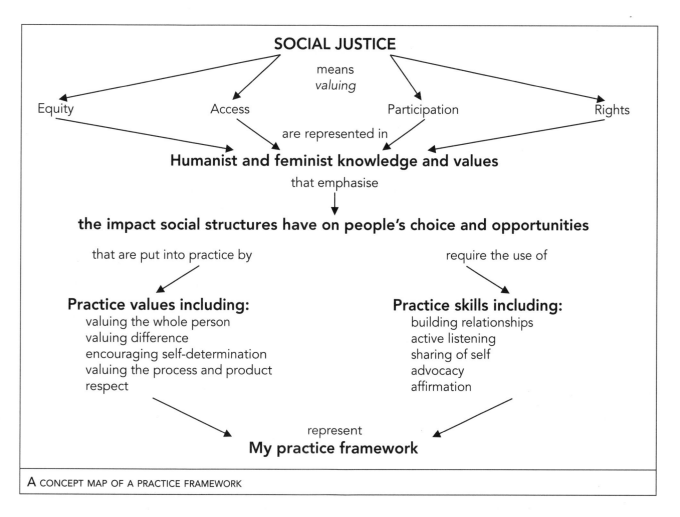

A CONCEPT MAP OF A PRACTICE FRAMEWORK

- Does your map only have straight lines? (That is, there are no cross-links between concepts.) Think about how concepts on the two side edges and the top and bottom of the page may be related. Draw in possible links and perhaps identify other concepts that link these ideas.

Your map can assist you to identify misconceptions and misunderstandings. Not being able to fit a concept meaningfully on the map may indicate a lack of understanding of the concept. It is a good idea to list the concepts you think might be important, but are currently unable to place, for future consideration. Where appropriate, include feelings and value beliefs to add meaning to your map and give it more depth.

Observation tools

There are two common methods of observation on placement: the supervisor models practice for the student and the supervisor observes the student completing a practice task, through direct observation, tapes and videos, and co-working.

Modelling

Modelling has its origins in traditional apprenticeships in which supervisors demonstrated skills for students to observe and then try for themselves. Modelling is not always a conscious process, either on the part of the 'modeller' or the 'observer' (AASWWE 1991, p. 75). Students will often learn from supervisors' ideas and values and from the way in which these are manifested in their behaviour, even in the tea room!

Some supervisors are reluctant to use modelling as it 'focuses on behaviours and strategies, but omits reflective and conceptual activities' (Shardlow & Doel 1996, p. 41). However, it is a powerful method for instructing about and demystifying an aspect of professional practice in a way that cannot be easily done by reading or listening. It is preferable to introduce the method as *one* way, rather than *the* way, to learn.

What is the process for helping the student to learn from this method? The traditional method for direct observation is for the student to sit quietly in the room where an interview or meeting is taking place and to observe the interaction and the supervisor's practice (Shardlow & Doel 1996, p. 119). However, other methods include the student observing from behind a one-way screen, the interaction being audiotaped or videotaped, or the student co-working with the supervisor.

If the student is observing a meeting or an interview, it is essential that he or she has a task to complete or a theme to observe and analyse, rather than just being asked to respond to general questions, such as: 'What did you think of that?' To give the student confidence and security about the process, discuss the student's role, as well as any sensitive issues that may arise, before the session. Have a contingency plan if problems do arise.

Shardlow and Doel (1996) also suggest that the student and supervisor should discuss and agree on criteria for good practice so that the student can use these criteria to make judgements about the quality of practice observed (p. 120).

Students could be asked to observe and record the practice on a summary form. Exercise 4 comprises questions that will get students to focus on the process, content and skills, and related theories of interaction.

EXERCISE 4

FOR THE STUDENT

Questions about process
1 Who was present?
2 Who took charge (for example, client, family member or workers)?
3 How did you know who took charge?
4 What roles did you see being played out?
5 How did you think the clients, family members or community members felt?
6 What did you observe about their body language and affective behaviour?

Questions about content
1 What are the facts and important details of the case?
2 What information do you think is important to know but was not discussed?
3 What information appeared to be most relevant to the purpose of the meeting or interview?

Questions about skills or theory
1 What skills were observed (for example, open questions, reflections, use of empathy)?
2 Did you pick up any conflict, disagreements or tensions? How were they enacted?

When students are observing other practitioners' work, they should be respectful of their practice – an approach that focuses on strengths makes this easier. For instance, a student may criticise a worker who takes notes during an interview with a client. The student could be encouraged to think about why the worker did this. It may have been important to record accurate information to ensure that the client was advised correctly. The worker may have showed other attending skills to ensure that the client felt heard. What other strategies can the student suggest? Did the worker inform the client that he or she would take notes, and, if so, how did he or she do this?

Observing students' work

The supervisor observes the student, sitting in the same room or behind a one-way screen, in a non-participative or minor participatory role (Ford & Jones 1987, p. 86). This method is used in many placements and is often a requirement of human service courses. Maidment (2000) notes that structured observations 'are memorable events for students so supervisors need to accord these events the priority they deserve' (p. 208).

Unfortunately, it is not unusual for students to miss out on valuable learning because the following steps to make direct observation 'memorable' are not followed.

- Introduce direct observation when the student is feeling comfortable in his or her role and trusting of the supervisor, otherwise it may make the student feel exposed or threatened.
- Establish the criteria for which skills and processes are to be demonstrated. The supervisor should record these on an observation checklist, which will be used as the basis of discussion afterwards.
- Debriefing immediately after observation will help the student deal with any anxiety, even if the content cannot be discussed.

Direct observation is an excellent opportunity for learning and teaching by both parties. The supervisor is able to view the student's work directly and to compare this with what the supervisor believes the student is learning from other methods. However, it is difficult to coordinate times and appropriate situations for observation. Also, it can confront supervisors with aspects of their own practice – do you say one thing, but do another? For students, it can be an anxiety-provoking exercise that may misrepresent their real abilities.

Audio and video recording

Audio and video recording, although widely recognised for their value in teaching, are not frequently used during placements (Maidment 2000, p. 209). Recording is hard to organise and may not be available or appropriate in a setting where interpersonal practice and development is not a primary learning goal. It is more commonly used in traditional casework and counselling agencies, but could also be useful for students working in teams and running committees and meetings.

It also appears that there is considerable resistance by students and supervisors to this method of observation, yet, if used appropriately, it has some clear advantages.

It is useful to video record an interaction and then view, freeze and review segments to observe in detail aspects of the student's work, especially the non-verbal aspects, such as body language, voice intonation and facial expressions. Cournoyer (2000, p. 117) suggests that it can be enlightening to view the videotape with the sound turned off to evaluate the non-verbal dimension of a student's communication. Try the following exercise.

EXERCISE 5

FOR THE STUDENT

Watch a videotape of your chosen interaction and respond to the following questions.

1 How confident and comfortable do you appear?

2 What gestures (such as hand movements) convey how you may be feeling and thinking?

3 Could these be interpreted positively or negatively by other people?

The video also offers the opportunity for observation of the other parties in the interaction.

4 What is your impression of how they may be feeling?

5 What verbal and non-verbal cues inform your impression?

Like direct observation, the advantage of this method is that it gives detailed and accurate feedback on the student's performance, but it has added value as it is a record that can be used again for review and comparison at a later date or as evidence for evaluation.

It can be difficult, however, to obtain and use the equipment, and for supervisors and students to find the time to watch and discuss it. It may engender 'performance anxiety', but most human service courses now include video recording so students should feel reasonably comfortable about using this method. Ford and Jones (1987, p. 91) caution that video recording tends to 'flatten out' the emotions and the subtleties of communication, and it may constrain spontaneity because of the technical procedures that need to be followed.

Audio tape-recording provides an honest account of a student task and enables the student and supervisor to hear their practice and to note the patterns of interaction (AASWWE 1991). It may make it difficult for students to concentrate on what the client is saying because they are so concerned with what they themselves are saying (Fox & Gutheil 2000, p. 42). As a method of observation, it has the same advantages as video recording, but tape-recorders are usually easier to access and use and take to other locations.

The main disadvantage is that supervisors cannot see the non-verbal aspects of the interaction, but students can brief them with the details, such as who was present, the seating arrangements, and body language used by students and other parties.

Co-working

This method involves the supervisor and student intentionally working together on a case or project (Ford & Jones 1987, p. 103). Sometimes it is necessary to work together for clinical, safety or legal reasons, such as in residential settings, in groupwork, or in child protection and mental health teams. In other agencies, it may not be the norm, but it can be negotiated if it will benefit the student and does not compromise clients. It has the advantages and disadvantages of direct observation, but it can be a time-efficient means for supervisors to gain direct access to students' work. Co-working is discussed in more detail in Chapter 10.

Teaching and learning activities

Role plays

Practising skills by role-playing or simulation is usually resisted by students, but often becomes the most positively regarded aspect of human service courses. Role-playing enables students to learn by experiencing interactions that replicate reality and the experience of others: clients, staff members or community members, for example. It is different from acting because students or supervisors attempt to portray a situation as if it was real, using their own frame of reference to convey the behaviour, rather than following a set script.

In particular, role-playing enables the student to:

- prepare for unfamiliar situations that may generate anxiety
- identify with how the other person may be feeling and experiencing a situation
- recognise and try out different responses to difficult situations that involve high emotion, conflict and aggression.

Supervisors can demonstrate different strategies and be involved in a mutual learning method, and it is an opportunity for them to assess students' readiness to undertake a task.

As with any method that involves direct observation of students, strategies – such as clear briefing and allowing for students' input to the exercise – will defuse some of the anxiety about this method. Typically, the situations to be role-played are ones that arouse powerful emotions in students, so 'de-roling' afterwards for all involved is crucial in order to deal with any feelings that arise.

The advantage of role-playing is that it allows students who need confidence to practise in a safe environment. It can happen spontaneously and doesn't require equipment. However, it can be threatening initially and will be unhelpful if a student identifies too strongly with the material.

In the following example, the student anticipates a tricky situation.

Student: *I am concerned about presenting my findings at the committee meeting tomorrow. I know that the 'Y faction' has opposed the study from the beginning and they are going to give me a hard time.*

Supervisor: *Yes, that could occur. How about we do a role play together about what might happen tomorrow at the meeting?*

Student: *Okay, but what do I do?*

Supervisor: *First, we need to decide what role might be most helpful for you. Would you rather be yourself and I will be a member of the 'Y faction', or should I be you and you act how you think a member of the 'Y faction' will behave?*

Student: *I think I would like to see how you handle potential conflict and I will try to imagine the sort of objections that the 'Y faction' will have.*

Supervisor: *All right. Now, we first need to discuss the details of the role play a little more, such as the setting, who is likely to be there and what your role is supposed to be.*

Student: *Well, I know some of that information, but it's a good idea to know who else will be there, as they might give me some support.*

Supervisor: *Yes, you could ring a few of the committee members before tomorrow to find out. The next thing is for you to prepare me a little about the kinds of objections that you expect there will be. I expect we should role play for about 15 to 20 minutes. We may not have time now, as we will need to have time to prepare as well as debrief afterwards. I will reschedule one of my meetings so we can do it before tomorrow.*

The supervisor decides not to use a discussion method to help the student with the anxiety-provoking task; instead, the supervisor encourages the student to experience what the situation might be like and find out how she may respond. The preparation before this role play helps to structure the 'script' to resemble the real-life situation.

Skills training

This particular form of training focuses on specific behaviours or issues that have emerged from practice. Sessions are structured so that there is time for discussion of skills, modelling by the supervisor, rehearsal by the student (often in role play), reflection and feedback, perhaps further practice, and discussion about how the skills will be used before the next supervision session.

Let's assume that, in the previous example, it becomes clear that the student is not confident about handling conflict and the core issue is that he or she finds it difficult to identify the issues underpinning the conflict and gets caught up in the personal nature of the discussion. The skill that needs developing in this context is the student's ability to reflect on content. The following example shows one way of running a skills-training session.

Supervisor: *Well, it seems that one of the issues making it more difficult for you to cope with the conflict at the committee meeting is that you are finding it difficult to stick to the issues and not feel personally attacked. This is very natural and it is hurtful. Have you had previous situations where this has happened?*

Student: *Well, yes, I guess in my family we were always hassled about being polite and people avoided getting into conflict. I suppose I am trying to avoid conflict, but I can see it won't work.*

Supervisor:	*No, but it is a strategy like many others and maybe if we see it in those terms, you will be able to put more of an emotional distance between you and those you feel are attacking you personally.*
Student:	*I guess so. I know what reflection is – I just don't seem to be able to use it when I feel stressed.*
Supervisor:	*In this situation I think you should try hurling some abuse at me, and I'll try to model some strategies that are designed to get the discussion back to the issues at hand, then you can have a go. Is that okay?*
Student:	*We'll give it a go – no hard feelings! Now, let's see, I think Mr X. might say something like 'I'm sick of sitting here listening to you going on and on about the fairest way to deal with this issue – there's nothing fair in this world, and the sooner you jumped-up idiots from uni get that, the better!'*
Supervisor:	*You're frustrated with how long it is taking to get a decision.*
Student:	*Too right I am. And I'm tired of you trying to run the show.*
Supervisor:	*You have put a lot of effort into this project and it would be good to see it finished.*
Student:	*Of course I want to see it finished!*
Supervisor:	*That's what everyone wants. What needs to be done to get to that point?*
Student:	*Well, it was certainly hard to keep my anger at you on the boil. Maybe I should have a go.*

After the role play, the student and supervisor discuss how it felt and what pressures they experienced. The student may, for example, conclude that the situation was challenging because when he or she felt under attack it was hard to listen, which made it difficult to use reflection appropriately.

Having identified the necessary skills and potential barriers to using them, then practising them and discussing situations in which the student might use these skills, the groundwork is laid for evaluating the effectiveness of this teaching in later sessions.

Student presentations

Students need to know how to advocate for their clients and agencies in public settings, facilitate group and family meetings, contribute to team discussions and training sessions, and run community meetings. These tasks all require sound presentation skills (Maidment 2000, p. 212). Most placement settings provide opportunities for students to gain confidence speaking at public forums and can be planned to match individual levels of confidence and ability.

Reading

Reading to inform practice takes on a new dimension for students on placement as they begin to see the relevance of literature to their practice. Textbooks, agency manuals, case files and legal documents are all useful, but the materials don't have to be factual; novels and poetry also can be useful to aid learning (Shardlow & Doel 1996, p. 133).

Supervisors can guide students about what reading is most helpful and can reinforce its importance by building reading time into the placement. However, unstructured reading time without an apparent purpose will remind students of class time and may be resisted.

Visits to agencies

An important part of learning about the placement agency and the work that it does is to compare it with agencies that offer similar services. Agency visits can also give students the opportunity to look at other workplaces in which they may wish to undertake subsequent placements or work after graduation.

Discuss the options with your supervisor and coordinate visits with other interested staff or students to minimise the workload for these agencies. Always prepare a list of questions to ask, perhaps using the outline offered in the section on orientation in Chapter 4 (p. 33), or use some of the questions from the formats for organisational analysis in Chapters 3 and 4.

Agency visits conducted by students can be a useful way for agency staff to update their resources and information about new services or changes to existing services. Students should inform staff about any planned visits so that staff can ask for any specific information that may be useful to them.

Summary

Using a variety of teaching methods and learning opportunities will reinforce students' existing knowledge and stimulate them to try new things with confidence and openness. Planned learning experiences, such as modelling, direct observation, agency visits, writing and reading, will be more successful if they are structured so that both students and supervisors have input and time to reflect on the experience. The informal and spontaneous learning opportunities that placement presents to students are equally valuable – sometimes the chat in the tea room can help another piece of the puzzle fall into place.

9

LINKING LEARNING AND PRACTICE IN PLACEMENT

Introduction

Placement requires students to integrate theory and practice – that is, to apply general principles to specific situations. In all aspects of our lives, our actions reflect our framework of personal theories – the way we make sense of particular situations. Quite often we are not conscious of these frameworks, yet they can filter out or highlight the knowledge we need to be competent human service practitioners.

One of the key challenges for students is to develop this consciousness of how theoretical frameworks influence their practice. The three-dimensional model below illustrates how the skills that students use in practice are explicitly connected to theories and phases of the work in a range of methods such as community, group or individual work.

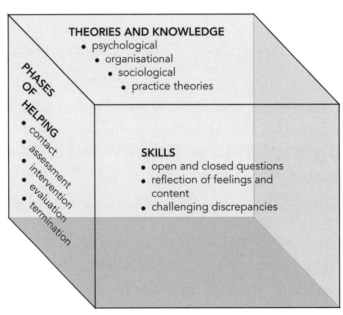

Placement enriches students' frameworks with knowledge that has been articulated and tested by others. Being an effective professional requires students to have a theoretical base to inform their decision-making.

Supervisors may feel apprehensive and uncertain about how much the training institution will require them to make explicit links between theory and practice. Responsibility for ensuring that this occurs rests with all parties – students, supervisors and the training institution. It is certainly not the sole responsibility of the supervisor. What is generally required of the supervisor, however, is to assist students to grapple with the intersection of their knowledge and direct practice (Shardlow & Doel 1996, p. 46). In order to do this, students and supervisors need to think about what theories are and how they are used, the terminology and knowledge of the human service field, and the integration of theory and practice.

In this chapter, different ways of conceptualising and integrating theories and some models for teaching and learning are explored. Each model can be applied to understanding a range of practice experiences.

What are theories?

Theories attempt to bring together a range of explanations that may have a bearing on the strategies or interventions that are chosen (Trevithick 2000, p. 10). Howe (1987) suggests that theory helps us to understand people and their circumstances in five keys areas (p. 171):

1 *Observation:* Theory tells us what we see and what to look out for.
2 *Description:* Theory provides a conceptual vocabulary and framework within which observations can be arranged and organised.
3 *Explanation:* Theory suggests how different observations may be linked; it offers possible causal relationships between one event and another.
4 *Prediction:* Theory indicates what happens next.
5 *Intervention:* Theory suggests what might be done to bring about change.

Postmodernists repudiate grand theories and, instead, prefer small-scale theorising, building upon the unique experiences of individuals to incorporate different realities (Trevithick 2000, p. 32).

Understanding the terms

The integration of theory and practice is made more difficult because of the way terms such as theory, hypothesis, method, model, approach and perspective are used in the human service field. Trevithick (2000, p. 15) offers the following definitions of these terms.

- *Theory:* Every attempt to try to make sense of the world constitutes a theory – a characteristic of informal theory is that it goes beyond description to include explanation about why things happen. Formal theories tend to be based on scientific criteria that can be empirically tested. Finally, grand theories, such as those of psychoanalysis or Marxism, attempt to explain large-scale phenomena.
- *Hypothesis:* A hypothesis attempts to define, explain and predict certain events to increase our understanding. The hypothesis is tested against evidence that either confirms or refutes it.
- *Method:* This term can refer to general forms of practice, such as groupwork, family work or community work, or to specific types of interventions, such as crisis intervention, task-centred approaches.
- *Model:* A model offers a description rather than an explanation and is generally a lower-order attempt to describe phenomena.
- *Approach:* An approach is a way of ordering our minds about particular issues or problems. Approaches are less precisely conceptualised than theories. Trevithick (2000) uses the term 'practice approach' to describe a systematic approach to practice that draws on theory (p. 18). This could include some practices that are described as methods, such as crisis intervention or cognitive therapy.
- *Perspective:* A perspective is a partial, but important, way of thinking about, observing and ordering phenomena. It generally reflects a person's value framework, such as anti-discriminatory, anti-oppressive, feminist or radical perspectives. Some agencies, for example, describe their workplaces as feminist because they have minimal hierarchy and open decision-making processes and their documentation is written in a gender-neutral way.

Types of knowledge

Drury Hudson (1997) argues that the professional knowledge of human service practitioners has been largely influenced by the social sciences – psychology, sociology, social policy and organisational theory – as well as being influenced by historical trends. Social sciences, in turn, have been influenced by empirical and scientific measurements that account for human behaviour. Postmodernism, however, has challenged the notion that reality is independent of the thoughts, beliefs and values of the practitioner and considers all experience to be subjective and socially constructed (p. 36).

The following model of professional knowledge, adapted from Drury Hudson (1997, pp. 35–44), identifies five principal forms of knowledge – each overlapping the other areas.

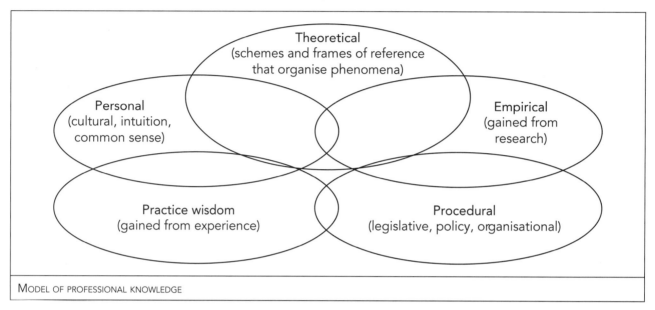

MODEL OF PROFESSIONAL KNOWLEDGE

Drury Hudson (1997, p. 43)

Theoretical knowledge is expressed as concepts, schemes or frames of reference that present an organised view of phenomena and enable the profession to explain, describe, predict and control the world. They should not be confused with facts or truth and remain essentially guesses or hypotheses. As such, professionals should continue to reflect on and be aware of the assumptions underlying their choice of theory for practice. Psychology's three main theories – humanism, behaviourism and psychoanalysis – are examples of well-known theoretical knowledge.

Empirical knowledge is derived from research, involving the systematic gathering and interpretation of data in order to document and describe experiences, explain events, predict future states or evaluate outcomes. Professional practice based on intuition or common sense can easily be coloured by an individual's perception. Incorporating empirical knowledge into practice helps to reduce the possibility of bias, enables workers to examine alternative explanations and makes them more accountable in their practice. For example, many agencies undertake research by collecting data about who uses their services and the types of problems that are dealt with, as a way to ensure that their service is relevant.

Personal knowledge is developed through an inherent or spontaneous process outside a person's immediate consciousness and is largely based on instinct or feeling. Such knowledge includes intuition, cultural knowledge and common sense. Because this knowledge is developed as a product of socially accepted order and reason, it can be problematic in that what makes sense to one person may not necessarily make sense to another. Agencies working with diverse ethnic groups usually employ workers from these groups because their personal knowledge of the culture is very valuable to developing appropriate services.

Practice wisdom is knowledge gained from the conduct of professional practice by working on different problems and issues. Often practice wisdom is not formalised and recorded in writing. It may be largely inaccessible to many who could benefit from it. Practitioners who rely heavily on practice wisdom may not easily be able to explain why they intervened in a certain way. Many human service workers have specific knowledge in particular fields of practice – child protection or homelessness, for example – because of their accumulated experience in their area.

Procedural wisdom is reflected in the policy, legislation and organisational rules or guidelines within which a profession must function. Such guidelines require a great deal of discretion and judgement in their application to a practice situation. Practitioners who rely too heavily on this form of knowledge may have a rigid and insensitive adherence to policy and regulations.

Understanding the different kinds of knowledge can be helpful in identifying and explaining the basis of your judgements and decision-making. Drury Hudson (1997) found that social workers are inclined to rely largely on practice wisdom, and personal and procedural knowledge, and are less likely to consciously apply theoretical and empirical knowledge.

Integrating theory and practice

Praxis, or the integration of theory and practice, does not result from the simple addition of theory to practice, or vice versa. Rather, integration is experienced as a conceptual leap: a particular event can be seen as an example of a broader principle or a specific direction can be discerned from a general principle. Integration results when you can make new sense of what were previously seen as unrelated events (O'Connor, Wilson & Setterlund 2003, p. 217). Schön (1995) noted that the practitioner has to transform theory in the light of learning from practice (reflection-on-action) and through improvisation during the course of tackling a task (reflection-in-action). It is clear that the reflective process is an integral part of learning how broad ideas and specific issues might be connected: that is, learning how to learn.

Reflection during an interaction or in hindsight gives students an opportunity to articulate the theories that applied to a particular situation. Deductive learning (reasoning) requires students to master the theories that underpin complex social situations. Supervisors and training institutions often assume that students will bring this type of knowledge to placement.

Students may find that on placement theoretical knowledge from their course or subjects comes together at last with practice. The theories finally make sense. Students may also panic as they realise that the effort put into studying to get through assessment has not left them with confidence in their ability to use this theory.

Inductive (inferential) learning comes from practising and drawing ideas from one experience to apply to other situations. For some, the shift between inductive and deductive reasoning is natural, but for others it requires a conscious effort of will. This will reflect students' personal learning style, as well as how far they are along the track of understanding theory. Their learning style is likely to determine at which end of the specific–general continuum they prefer to start. As was noted in Chapter 3, students need to concentrate on developing flexibility in their approaches to learning. To maximise learning, strategies that extend their capacity to generalise from specific situations and to develop a specific approach from broad principles should be employed.

Through reflection, students will often make links between the ideal they planned or hoped for and the reality of what occurred. Indeed, successful integration of theory and practice depends on being able to put words around their real world and their ideal world. Through this process, relevant knowledge, values and skills for understanding a situation and what it is possible to achieve in their agency context are identified. This is likely to be expressed in cause-and-effect statements such as: 'When I rush ahead of where people are at they eventually ignore me.' Over time, students will become more aware of such statements and then can look for patterns in what they know and how they use that knowledge.

EXERCISE 1

FOR THE STUDENT

1 Think of two practice experiences in which you were happy with the outcome. State the outcomes as cause-and-effect statements.

2 Think of two practice experiences in which you were not happy with the outcome. State the outcomes as cause-and-effect statements.

3 Is there any overlap in these statements?

4 What underlying theoretical, value and skill assumptions are important in your statements?

5 To which broader body of knowledge or values do the statements link?

Bogo and Vayda (1998) adapted Kolb's work on learning cycles and devised a loop of integration of theory and practice to conceptualise a reflective approach to learning. The stages of the loop are as follows.

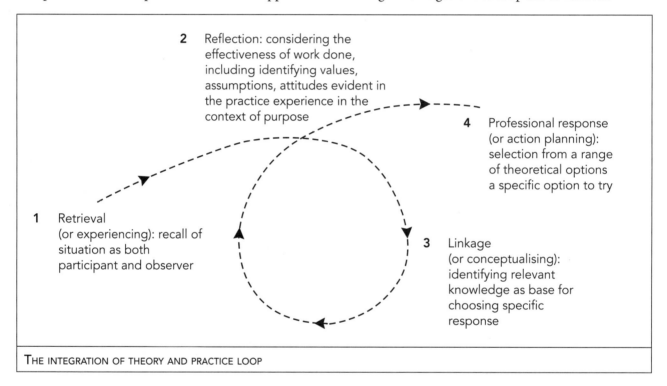

2 Reflection: considering the effectiveness of work done, including identifying values, assumptions, attitudes evident in the practice experience in the context of purpose

4 Professional response (or action planning): selection from a range of theoretical options a specific option to try

1 Retrieval (or experiencing): recall of situation as both participant and observer

3 Linkage (or conceptualising): identifying relevant knowledge as base for choosing specific response

THE INTEGRATION OF THEORY AND PRACTICE LOOP

- *Experiencing* (descriptive stage): The supervisor listens and attempts to understand the situation as experienced by the student. It is important that any observations are as accurate as possible. (The learning and teaching tools described in Chapter 8, such as taped records, journals, or shared experiences with the supervisor, would be helpful.) Encouragement, not criticism, is important at this stage.
- *Reflecting* (clarification stage): The supervisor and student explore the issues raised by a situation. The student becomes aware of their emotional and cognitive responses to the situation. Through reflection the student 'explores feelings, patterns, and connections arising from the experience' (Morrison 2001, p. 138). During this stage, the learning from this situation can be linked to other learning from previous supervision sessions. It is also important to clarify what responses relate to the situation under review and what might be imported from personal or organisational issues (Morrison 2001).
- *Conceptualising* (analysis and evaluative stage): The student and supervisor analyse and seek to understand the situation by hypothesising, identifying relevant theory and asking why. They move from the specifics of this situation to generalisations based on research, theories, professional values, or cultural

and political perspectives. During this stage of the cycle, a set of statements is developed about the causes of a problematic situation and how it might be managed.

- *Action planning* (implementation and review stage): Translating his or her analysis into a plan enables the student to progress with the task once the areas of concern have been discussed and resolved. The analysis and learning are tested out in action – theory and practice are linked and evaluated in a further reflective cycle.

Kolb's experiential learning cycle has been adapted by other authors to describe supervision as a cycle of experience, reflection, conceptualisation and, finally, active experimentation (Davys 2000, p. 90).

It is suggested that the supervisor, or the student in preparation for supervision, follows these cycles in general terms. It is possible to identify in the cycles the different functions of supervision – administration, education and support – outlined in Chapter 7. For instance, if the supervisor discusses a particular practice situation and then directly develops a plan of action, the administrative function is dominant. If the supervisor focuses on the impact of the work on the student, rather than on the outcomes of the work, the supportive function is dominant.

It is not necessary or desirable in all situations to follow through the whole cycle, but if this form of reflection is not used in some of the work on a regular basis by both students and supervisors, the learning may not be maximised. Educationalists suggest that reflection is the most neglected part of the learning process, even though it is recognised as critical for the professional development of human service practitioners. It is likely that students and supervisors will gain most from using time in this way if both have had an opportunity to prepare for supervision.

Questions and activities can be selected by supervisors from the following list to facilitate the reflective learning of students. The questions have been adapted from Morrison (2001, pp. 143–8). It is not suggested that these questions be used all of the time, or that there are not other useful questions for each stage of the cycle. Supervisors could consider which of the questions they currently use, whether the questions vary with different students and, if so, why they vary. They could expand the range of questions they use to suit themselves and the students.

Experiencing

1 What was your role in the situation?
2 What was your aim? What planning did you do?
3 What did you expect to happen?
4 What happened? Identify the different perceptions of other parties.
5 What did you do or say?
6 What reactions did you notice to what you said and did?
7 What surprised or puzzled you?
8 What did you notice about yourself/the client/your co-worker/a community member?
9 What went according to plan? What didn't?

These questions can be enhanced by using methods such as process records, think sheets, journals, video recording, co-working and direct observation.

Reflecting

1 What did you feel at the start of the situation? What feelings did you bring to the situation?
2 What did the situation or your feelings remind you of?
3 Describe a time when you last experienced those feelings.
4 What do you think the client/group member/worker was feeling? How do you know this?
5 Where and when did you feel most or least comfortable?
6 What ideas came to you during the situation?

7   What feelings were you left with? Does this always happen after seeing this kind of case/meeting/event?

These questions can be enhanced by using methods such as role play, think sheets, genograms and ecograms.

Analysing

1   List three assumptions that you/the client/group member/other worker brought to the situation.
2   How would you explain or understand what happened in that situation?
3   How would the situation be different if …? (For example, if the client had been a female, or you were older than the board member, or this was not your first situation.)
4   How else can you explain what happened?
5   How might the other party explain what happened?
6   Did the power relations shift during the situation? If so, why?
7   How else might you have managed the situation?
8   What is not known?

These questions can be enhanced by using methods such as reading articles and case presentations, training, doing literature searches.

Action planning

1   In the light of the reflection and analysis we have done, what is your overall summary of where things are at and what needs to be done next?
2   What information, ideas and/or support do you need before proceeding?
3   What is urgent and essential?
4   From your perspective, what would be a successful outcome for the next situation?
5   What would be a successful outcome for the next situation for the client/group member/community?
6   What might be your strategy for the next situation?
7   Who else needs to be involved?
8   What can I do as a supervisor that would be helpful at this stage?

These questions can be enhanced by using methods such as role play, developing a case plan, and referring to other practitioners for advice and information.

The processes students might engage in at different stages of the learning cycle, as outlined by Morrison (2001, p. 141), are shown in the diagram on the opposite page.

The essence of the reflective learning model is that individuals make sense of problematic situations in different ways depending on influences such as education, life history, cultural heritage, and political and economic perspectives. Formal or theoretical knowledge can be inadequate for some situations and there is not always one right answer for every situation. Students' participation in this active reflection process reshapes their understanding of events and helps them to question personal assumptions, which can result in a shift of attitude and values (Maidment 2000, p. 214). You need to be supportive rather than confrontational as a supervisor when you use this method, encouraging the student to take risks and explore concepts and issues for themselves (AASWWE 1991, p. 67).

EXPERIENCING

- Supervisors invite you to give detailed observations of people you are working with (context, environment, feelings, views, interactions, words and actions) to understand how these people experience a situation (or intervention, service, and so on).
- Students consciously notice their own responses (feelings, attitudes, words, behaviours) and try to develop an awareness of things they have missed to this point.

ACTION PLANNING

- Students test options to identify the possible pros and cons of different actions for the needs of people they work with and those of stakeholders.
- Plans are generated based on analysis.
- Students' needs for resources and support are identified.
- Risks and innovations are explored, limitations are acknowledged and contingencies considered.

REFLECTING

- Students explore their feelings and use this to deepen observations of practice.
- Students are able to acknowledge the source of their own feelings and separate what belongs to them and what belongs to others.
- Students seek to link the current situation with previous experience and knowledge.
- Students are willing to address what they find challenging.

ANALYSING AND UNDERSTANDING

- The students' work is analysed, in conjunction with supervisors, with reference to values, research, policy and role requirements.
- Issues of power, difference and perception are explored by students and supervisors.
- Students are willing to consider alternative explanations or hypotheses.

THE SUPERVISION CYCLE

Summary

An understanding of the theoretical frameworks and terminology of the human service field gives students the language to describe their practice and the ability to analyse it from a broader perspective. Supervisors can encourage students to develop these skills at all stages of the learning cycle using open-ended questions that focus on experience, reflection, analysis and action planning.

METHODS AND CONTEXTS OF PRACTICE

Some examples of the different methods of practice in human services are interpersonal work or casework, family work, groupwork, community work, policy practice, research and administration. Each method is underpinned by a range of theoretical bases and has its own practical requirements. The different methods will create specific learning challenges and opportunities for students on placement in regard to their work with others and the skills in assessment and practice they will need. Ideologies or knowledge about how change occurs and the style of work will vary with different methods.

Of course, the different methods of practice have in common core knowledge, skills and values, and organisational issues. Much of the discussion to date has assumed work with an individual focus as the basic unit of practice. In Part 4, the particular issues for placement in agencies that do community work, policy, project and research work are explored. Some of the specific implications of rural placements and overseas are also discussed. It will be interesting for students and supervisors to observe whether their approach to teaching and learning is changed by the demands and opportunities inherent in these methods of practice.

4

10

COMMUNITY WORK

Introduction

The term 'community work' is often used to refer to intervention in communities, while the term 'community development' is used to refer to the process of change and development that takes place in communities (Henderson & Thomas 2002, p. 3). In this book, 'community work' refers to both processes. Community work is a form of practice in which people are brought together to determine a direction for change and to mobilise the necessary resources to achieve that change. It is linked to all the other practice methods; however, a student will need to develop some specific skills and knowledge in a community work placement.

EXERCISE 1

FOR THE STUDENT

In preparation for this chapter, take some time to answer the following questions.
1. What are the core principles and skills of community work?
2. What knowledge underpins these principles and skills in the context of this placement?
3. What are the similarities between these principles and knowledge and the practice of community work in your placement?

The following brief overview illustrates the link between community work and learning about it on placement.

How does change occur?

Community workers can resource people who share a community identity to change their situation by building their capacity to act together. When people are disadvantaged, they are often living at the limits of their capacity and feel caught or stuck. Community work aims to enhance people's capacity to move past this 'stuck-ness'. Core values in community work reflect a preference for a society based on cooperation and solidarity, rather than on individualism and competition. Often the work begins in a one-dimensional way, in that it focuses specifically on a defined need and tries to reinforce people's ability to cope with that need. It does not require the worker to address all the needs of a person or group of people. There is a strong emphasis on ensuring that the processes are democratic, that strong relationships are developed between the participants, and that people develop confidence in their ability to take charge and develop and use their skills. Community workers may focus on an analysis of injustice and inequality in society, or they may take a less politically motivated view of why the community functions the way it does. Either way, workers need to look for links between individual and social issues.

To define your approach, think about the extent to which your approach to change is 'top down' or 'bottom up'.

Bottom-up practice aims to enable people who are experiencing some form of exploitation to take more control. The practitioner does this by facilitating links between people who share common issues and increasing their influence by developing their skills to work together to change the situation. Top-down practice – often called social planning or inter-agency work – establishes links between different services or policy-makers and the people using these services, with the aim of informing the services or policy-makers about the needs of specific communities. It does this by working with those involved to alter policies or improve services (O'Connor, Wilson & Setterlund 2003, pp. 137–8).

When community members come together they are required to make group decisions. This process can build the group's capacities in a potent way. It is also the point at which many groups' difficulties occur. Workers need to be knowledgeable and skilled in supporting groups to develop appropriate decision-making structures and processes. Group structures may be informal, auspiced, constituted associations, companies (profit and non-profit), cooperatives and trusts, for example. The decision-making processes used in groups may include chairing meetings, setting agendas, establishing consensus or majority rule, minute-taking, conflict resolution and facilitating the participation of all members. These are all quite public activities: they focus on what people can do rather than on their problems, and they certainly require that students and practitioners work *with*, not *for*, others. This might make students feel more vulnerable. It will also assist them in their role as beginning community workers.

EXERCISE 2

FOR THE STUDENT

Think about three things that make you feel threatened about working with community groups. Think about three things that make you feel empowered.

For example, students might feel anxious that people will challenge them and they won't know how to respond at the time. At the same time, they might think that one of the advantages of groupwork in communities is that they won't have all the responsibility and, if they get stuck, there will be others to help out. In exploring their fears and hopes about practice, students often find that they have the resources to cope.

In the following scenario, the decision-making processes used by a community centre are complicated by tensions between members in different program areas and competing needs and interests. The student is aware of the limitations of his role and is assisted by his supervisor to complete the process of working with the committee as a group. In many instances, community work involves working to management committees.

Ben was on placement in a community agency that was hoping to set up services for older people. Some capital was potentially available to help the centre acquire more suitable premises. However, there was also tension about this as the staff in the community centre who provided child care felt that there would be competition with older people for the current space and for the space in a new community centre. Sara, Ben's supervisor, had a long-term commitment to the needs of older people. She was concerned about the impact the gentrification process was having on older residents, the lack of a meaningful role for this group as the suburb changed, and the lack of appropriate services to enable them to stay in their homes in the inner-city community. Sara was well established in the centre and had a successful track record in bottom-up work with a number of community groups. She had managed to avoid outright conflict over the proposal to apply for funds for the aged-care program, but she recognised that there would be difficulties. When Ben started placement he knew that this work would be a core part of his practice, but he was quickly overwhelmed by the resistance from other influential community centre members. The notes below reflect his experiences in a planning meeting, for which he had been asked to prepare a brief for the group on the prospective funding body's expectations of the centre.

'I presented my report, which had been cleared with Sara. It almost sounded too good to be true at first, because the health funding seemed so much more generous than the welfare funding they were all used to dealing with. The health department wanted clear links between the funds spent and the outcomes for older people, which was an issue for a number of reasons. Some members thought this would stifle innovation and would not assist older people to determine what they wanted, since the auspicing agency predetermined "good" outcomes. Others wondered how the centre's current accounting measures would cope. I think it was generally threatening in a culture in which people were used to working quite autonomously. The chair of the meeting, the centre president, was obviously keen to go ahead because it solved the problem of future space but not because she was committed to aged care. As we had discussed, Sara took over at this point to try to get some of the issues out in the open. It would not have been appropriate for me to challenge staff. I thought Sara did a good job of naming the agendas people had, finding some common ground and encouraging people to work together to find a solution. It was difficult, though, to really process members' concerns in the available time. It seemed that if the group managed to identify some issues they could make a decision about, someone would feel put on the spot and would hold things up so they could go back to other workers in their areas to get direction. I learned that you just can't hurry some things and, if you do, it is likely there will be more problems down the road.'

EXERCISE 3

FOR THE STUDENT

Think about the committee of management in your agency.

1 What do you think the committee expects you to achieve? Does this raise issues for you?

FOR THE SUPERVISOR

1 What issues are likely to be seen as critical in relation to having a student in your organisation?
2 What level of commitment to providing student placements does the management committee, or other hierarchies in your organisation, have?

Students need to learn to make connections between broader social issues and individual experiences, to build understanding of the issues and to identify the opportunities to act. Supervisors need to find a balance between their attention to day-to-day practice and finding time to consider and describe what community work is in their agency and appropriately share that work with students. They may also need to consider what social policies, legislation or set of beliefs they are either challenging or supporting by their actions.

The political realities

Many of the agencies that employ community workers are stand-alone community-based organisations. In some, people who live in the community form part of the committee that employs the worker. Other community workers may be employed by governments – a complex situation because governments also represent the community, but often are perceived to be removed from the day-to-day realities of its life. However, community work typically takes place in an organisational structure that gives the people who use the services fairly direct control of the work. This is also quite a complex situation. To work in an empowering way, the worker, as much as possible, transfers decision-making, knowledge and skills to the people who use the service. Yet these same people are also the worker's employers.

Community workers must be able to empower others, including their committees of management, so that the committee has an informed say in determining the priority areas for the worker's practice. Community work is a very public activity and if a student upsets community members the supervisor will hear about it quickly. In some cases, the supervisor may have to choose the needs of the community or committee over the needs of the student.

Students or supervisors may have other connections in the community, and this is another political dimension of practice. They may be community members, and hence have an additional set of rights and responsibilities. This issue is discussed further in Chapter 13. As a student, if you are an 'insider' in the community in which you do your placement, it is important to be clear about the impact this may have. In this context, it is particularly important that you consider using some form of agreement for placement, as discussed in Chapter 5.

If you are an 'outsider', you will have to negotiate entry to the community. As an outsider, you normally won't have established relationships with the people in the community and you won't know their situation. If you can develop a genuine understanding of people's situations – by being with people, listening to them, hearing and responding to what they are saying about their situation – you can move closer to gaining the status of insider.

Knowledge and practice skills

Knowledge about how practice is carried out may be formalised in agency policy, or it may be more or less left to the worker to decide what to do. One way of identifying the knowledge and skills needed by community workers and the assumptions they make about society is to examine what they are trying to do. The skills used by community workers or community-work students can be enhanced by knowledge about the community and the particular issue about which people are organising.

Imagine you begin work in a suburb, town or rural area. You know none of the people with whom you will work. You then meet a potential client who talks about their child's involvement in chroming. This is one relationship – a private matter between you and this parent. You meet a second parent with the same issue. This is also one relationship – again, a private matter between you and this parent. You might try to link the two parents and then link other people in the community who have an interest in this issue, making private issues public and moving from individual to collective response. This ability to make links is a core community-work skill (Kelly & Sewell 1988).

Other skills are involved in forming these relationships. The worker must hear the person's story, which involves observation, listening, different forms of questioning and research into the issue. Picking the commonalities and bringing individual parties together to make a group are yet other necessary skills. The worker may have a commitment to a particular group and will locate themselves alongside members of the group so they can hear their story. These stories may not be expressed as requests for help; rather, they may be observations or emotional reactions. This is a 'going out' process different from many other forms of human service practice in which people, voluntarily or otherwise, 'bring in' their issues to a worker.

A community-based organisation may focus on change at different levels of the social system. Issues raised by individuals are shared by others, or people working collectively on an issue may feel comfortable about raising other issues with workers. The worker needs to be aware of the potentials for change at all levels and be prepared to work at different levels of the system.

The supervisor may assume in this context that change occurs when people are given the opportunity to try new things, that people can be more in charge of their own destiny when they have choices, and that everyone is a learner. Their practice base is generic and is strongly underpinned by a structural analysis of society, rather than by any one approach to practice or a theoretical approach.

If the organisation is involved in work that is politically sensitive, or the work depends on existing relationships, the student may observe what is happening but not be given any responsibility in these areas. The agency may wish to limit the student somewhat if he or she wants to set up programs that require resources the agency won't have once the placement finishes. You can see from this example that the methods adopted, the style of the work and the politics of practice interact to determine the opportunities and limitations for the student on placement.

EXERCISE 4

FOR THE STUDENT

Think about individuals you have met on placement or issues you have some experience of, then answer these questions.

1　What do you know about these people or these issues?
2　What themes, stories and issues are you hearing from individuals that might reflect a common issue?
3　How would you move from focusing on the individual issue to the common problem?
4　Who do you need to talk to?
5　How do you achieve this move?

Now think about a particular group you have been involved with on placement.

6　How can I best locate myself to hear the stories of this group? (For example, am I an expert, a facilitator, an explorer or something else?)
7　Why am I committed to hearing their story?

FOR THE SUPERVISOR

Think about community-work practice in your agency.

1　Is it easier for you to talk about this practice or to demonstrate it? Why?
2　What makes it more or less difficult in your agency to ensure students learn the skills of how to connect people?
3　How would you know that a student was competent at doing this?

Ideas are powerful. Often hearing what someone else has done motivates and directs change. Workers and students can bring information and knowledge, or information about how to get knowledge, to a group – for example, workers may know how another group addressed a similar issue. They should be able to help groups seek out those who can best assist the group on a range of issues – legal, financial, political, social and procedural. It is also important that workers and groups don't blindly seek to replicate what happens elsewhere. They need to be able to identify and use core knowledge and principles that are useful for their situation.

Using knowledge in supervision

Teaching and learning about community work focuses on identifying what in the system constrains or facilitates movement towards desired outcomes. It is also important to understand what constrains and facilitates each student's learning while on placement.

To empower students and build their capacities means that supervisors, as far as possible, must transfer decision-making and knowledge to students. However, this must be done in the context of an inherently unequal relationship between student and supervisor, mirroring, to some extent, the tension experienced by the community worker in practice. It can be a challenge to set up appropriate boundaries for the roles of student and supervisor in community-based organisations, for reasons already outlined. Generally speaking, it is best to address this matter explicitly at the beginning of placement and not wait for an issue to arise.

Supervisors may adopt a reflective style to help students draw their own conclusions – this form of consciousness-raising underpins teaching and learning. It is important for students to be able to articulate how social systems can constrain those with whom they work, then test this out by reflecting on their placement experiences and being prepared to modify their understanding.

Supervisors in community work, like most practitioners, also tend to tell stories about their own or others' practice in order to understand a situation and explore what is effective practice in a particular context – a more top-down approach. In this sense, community workers tend to rely on an oral rather than a written tradition. It will be helpful for supervisors to check how well their natural styles of instruction and approach to the work fit individual students' learning styles and approaches to practice.

Co-working

Students and supervisors may be able to take advantage of co-working to enhance students' learning. Ideally, the learning experience in a co-working situation has three stages:

1 *Planning:* It is useful to develop some learning objectives before sessions, as well as identify the outcomes of the work itself. This can be done by students outlining their concerns, needs and hopes in relation to their work with a specific person or issue. The planning phase could follow a period in which students reflect on the tensions between the *real* and the *ideal* in practice, and focus on the abilities that will help them to build new skills. In this session it helps to:

   - suggest and perhaps practise new skills to move closer to the ideal
   - discuss how students will know that they are moving closer to the ideal
   - agree on a method for collecting information during the co-working session.

2 *Observation:* Both parties should have agreed on what specifically will be observed in both students' and supervisors' practice. For example, the student may observe how the supervisor introduces a new idea to a community meeting and the supervisor may observe how the student makes introductions. If the student usually works alongside the supervisor, this process of observation should not be intrusive for either the community members or the student. In other contexts, the supervisor's or student's presence may mark the occasion as quite different, and the feelings of community members and the issues raised will need to be negotiated with community members.

   As far as possible, the normal protocols for co-working need to be observed: Who is responsible for what? How will the student and supervisor communicate during a session? When does the supervisor step in and be more directive?

   Deciding what to observe – and therefore to focus on – in supervision is important. Work practice and any associated issues should be discussed. Limit the number of issues for discussion – time and energy may be limited, and it is important to focus on understanding reasons for practice, and developing strategies and techniques to work on issues that are considered significant. Some general principles are important here.

   - Any issues must have been clearly observed in the co-working session.
   - The student is likely to accept feedback focused on, specific elements of behaviour.
   - The emotional significance of the issue to the student will impact on the number of issues that can be effectively raised.

   As far as possible, the student should be involved in making any decisions that arise from supervision sessions.

3 *Feedback:* Information collected by both parties needs to be reviewed and evaluated, as part of the reflective practice discussed earlier. Successful patterns of working should be identified and reinforced as a way of attending to perceived gaps.

Documentation

Unlike other forms of human service practice, community work does not usually require workers to maintain case files. The written documentation that relates to the community-work process inevitably becomes the property of the group: minutes of meetings, reports of workers on their activities, letters, submissions, strategic plans, and so on. There is often debate about the extent to which community workers should be expected to keep notes of the work they have done and, also, about how much the records should be linked to discrete projects and how much they should be 'owned' by the worker. The questions in Exercise 5 will help students to identify their agency's approach to record-keeping.

EXERCISE 5

FOR THE STUDENT AND SUPERVISOR

1 What is your agency's policy about keeping records on work done with community groups?
2 How did this policy develop?
3 What are the advantages and limitations of this policy?

Work diaries

Community workers are likely to rely on a work diary, both to jog their memory about what has happened and to ensure that their time is used constructively. Details of the day's achievements, who was contacted, what still needs to happen, high points, and issues where further work is needed can be recorded in a diary. Students can use their diaries to record issues for discussion in supervision.

Process reports and log sheets

It is helpful to use devices such as process reports and log sheets to record specific interactions. These have been detailed more fully in Chapter 8. They give students the opportunity to learn from what has happened and they provide supervisors with information on events that they may not have witnessed.

In community work, a process report need not be confined to one-to-one interactions. It may be useful to record meetings and group discussions. Log sheets can be useful in processing specific incidents.

Skills in documenting what happens in a group need to be developed, and a framework to record the information, such as the following one, will be helpful.

1 Outline the purpose of the meeting and the student's role.
2 Organise the 'content' of the group meetings:
   - Describe how the meeting started.
   - Note any decisions reached, the reasons for these decisions and the responses of group members to these decisions.
   - Describe the dominant feelings within the group and how these might have changed over time.
   - As the recorder, be aware of your own feelings and try to make links between what you feel and what was happening in the group.
   - Note how the meeting ended, paying attention to whether this will have any implications for future work with the group.
3 Summarise your roles (or those of your supervisor) in the interactions and suggest what the impact of these roles or behaviours may be on the eventual outcomes. Compare what *actually* happened with

your *ideal* of what might have happened and think of ways in which you could practise in the future to move closer to the ideal.

An example of a student's assessment of a critical incident, and of what might have been done, follows.

I realised that through the process of discussing what might be done to improve the facilities for the play group, A. was feeling more and more excluded and almost victimised. She is the one who puts a lot of energy into the group but her efforts to take on leadership roles are not always appreciated. B., who generally has the ideas that the rest of the group accept but is not available to do much of the work, was directing the agenda. I felt bad for not having seen this happening earlier and realised that A. also makes me feel inadequate at times and I also want to push her to one side … I had to quickly try to make sense of these jumbled feelings and to try to avoid fuelling the group processes that were excluding A. I decided that the best thing I could do was to be honest about what I saw happening and try to get the group to discuss their issues more openly.

The student's role in this group was to facilitate discussion and resource the group, which was deciding how to operate in the current situation. This record was about the second meeting of the group, following a supervision session in which it had been suggested that the student was being too task-focused and needed to pay more attention to how the group operated. Her notes reflect her awareness of the gap between what she saw happening and what she felt were good processes. Her feelings as well as her cognitive capacities helped her make sense of what happened and she reverted to the basic principle of honesty as a way of moving forward.

Diaries and process records are useful to organise time, review the use of time and learn for the future. However, diaries tend to be private documents, not readily available to those who are discussed in them. Sometimes, then, it is necessary to have records that relate to specific projects. They might offer a broad outline of the issues the project is to address, the agreed aims of the project and the approach that will be taken. Do you see examples of these records in your agency?

Community profiles

Community profiles are a way of summarising the history, resources and challenges facing a community about a particular issue. Students are often asked to prepare community profiles. Such documents should be accessible to any interested party, so students need to be as objective as possible in the information that is presented. Students can find a range of outlines for community profiles in the literature (see, for example, the chapter 'Getting to know your community' in Henderson and Thomas 2002). Profiles may be focused on a particular issue, or they may pull together a wide range of information that will help decide future strategies. Students may need to make use of official statistics and other studies, or they may include a survey as part of their information-gathering activities. Additional notes on community assessment are in Chapter 13.

Completing a profile relies on observation – students could walk or drive around slowly, or sit and watch people as they go about their business. In addition, it is always a good idea for the student to check the assumptions they have made from their observations against any available data or with other workers and community members. It is very easy to see only what confirms our first impressions. Berg-Weger and Birkenmaier (2000, pp. 197–8) suggest the following structure for analysing a community.

- Outline the geographical features of the community and what physically defines the boundaries of the community. Pay attention to issues of access between this community and others.
- Identify the economic characteristics suggested by patterns of employment or unemployment, the job opportunities that exist within the community and the distances people travel out of the community.

Estimate income levels and the range of income levels, and describe the availability of transport and who uses it.

- Note the social characteristics (for example, age, gender, class, ethnicity, family types, sexual orientation) of the people who live in the community. Who is left in the community during the day? What sub-communities exist in the larger community? (To help students identify sub-communities, they could look at differences in housing stock; any boundaries, such as main roads, railway lines, rivers, valleys and hills, within the community; and the people they see out and about.) What facilities in the community (for example, places of worship, halls, shopping centres, clubs, libraries and societies, parks and recreational areas or buildings) facilitate people meeting together? What type of housing is available? (Is housing owned or rented? What is the general age and condition of the housing? Is housing oriented to families, single people or couples? Is there much stock for sale or rent, and is this housing clustered in some areas or is it dispersed?) Finally, how do community members react to students and perhaps to other strangers?
- Examine the political characteristics of the community. At election times, these may be quite overt, and the party politics of residents may be evident. More covert evidence of the political clout of the community can be gathered from the overall state of roads, footpaths and parks, street lighting and traffic flows. Political offices for elected representatives and who uses them may also indicate something about the political activity of residents.

Other forms of recording

A range of other forms of recording is used in community work. Students will need to develop specific skills to produce such documents as minutes of meetings, funding submissions, and letters and reports to committees or other bodies.

Appropriate content and structures for each of these documents need to be selected. Different agencies will require different styles of writing, and discerning what style of report is required is an important skill. These reports must be written clearly and be appropriate for the audience – particularly when there are numerous people with whom good communication needs to be maintained for effective community work.

Finishing placement

At the beginning of placement it is important for the student and the supervisor to think about how the student will finish the placement, particularly in the context of the student's work with community members. As a student, you have to consider what, if any, commitment you will maintain with the community once placement is over. It is important not to promise what you cannot deliver. It can be easier at the time to say that you will still be around, rather than deal with your own feelings and the feelings of others if you are leaving the community as well as finishing placement. If you are doing placement in your own community, finishing placement may simply mean that you will have less time and therefore a different level of involvement with the issues. Chapter 19 contains general information about finishing placement.

Summary

Community-work practice is an integral part of the delivery of human services, and students will benefit from learning the skills associated with working as part of a team, group or community. While many community-work skills and methods are used in other types of human services, particular challenges and concerns for students and supervisors are inherent in organisations in which the person that uses the service may also be the boss!

11

RESEARCH AND POLICY

Introduction

Many placements will involve aspects of research and policy practice, but the implications of this for teaching and learning on placement are rarely explored in the literature. In some placements, the chief aim is to produce policy documents or research material. Policy practice and research practice are interrelated – it is difficult to develop policy without doing research, and most research in human service agencies has policy implications.

Examples of policy and research practice include:
- formulating legislation through research, lobbying, responding to discussion documents
- researching social policy: for example, the impact on family members of legislation that relates to decision-making for people with impaired capacity
- finding evidence to support a particular approach to practice or the evaluation of a program
- doing action research with a group of residents to decide on the most effective way to resolve a local issue
- developing agency policy on emerging issues
- implementing policy that has been formulated as part of a change-management process.

Placements vary in the extent to which the work is entirely focused on direct practice with individuals or families, or developing opportunities for community members (see Chapter 10), or understanding issues relevant to the agency in a systematic way (research), or refining organisational responses to practice (developing policy), or changing legislation or policy. In some agencies, project work may predominate and at times it can be difficult for students to see the connection between this form of practice and what has been covered in their course.

Most human services courses focus initially on interpersonal work as the cornerstone of practice. This is valid, but the purpose of interpersonal work can vary. A worker in human services will interact with people who may wear one of many labels: fellow worker or student, community member, citizen, politician, director, constituent, consumer and client. One of the key learning tasks in relation to project work is to learn about both the range of ways in which we can interact with others and the common base that helps to establish our identity as human services workers.

If you are a student planning to undertake a placement to develop your research and policy skills, or you are an agency that conducts policy and research work, entirely or in part, the following questions are a useful starting point.

EXERCISE 1

FOR THE SUPERVISOR

1 What is the mix of work usually given to students on placement?
2 Does this represent the full range of work done in the agency?
3 Is some work reserved specifically for students?

This chapter needs to be read in conjunction with Chapter 10 on community work, as, in some agencies, community work may be regarded as a type of project.

While policy and research practice share many points, there are also important differences, which will be explored in this chapter.

Research practice

Research may involve getting information together for a community profile or for policy material; or it may describe a practice model or the work done to put in a funding submission. Sometimes research focuses on determining the effectiveness of existing programs or collating information to guide the development of new programs.

An agency may believe that research will be useful in discerning future directions or providing evidence to support ideas that have emerged from practice. In these situations, research is an adjunct to the core business – delivering a range of services – but it is a way of achieving these desired outcomes.

The need for such research may motivate an agency to request a student on placement, and students will be aware that, in taking this placement, they will conduct research.

Students may do placement in agencies in which a research project is already established: a good example is that of students on placement in an aged-care facility in which the work focused on enhancing the participation of residents in the life of the facility. The students were asked to work with a research team to design survey instruments, administer questionnaires, and work on interventions designed to enhance participation. In some ways the work was no different from that of a typical placement in a residential facility, but in other ways it was quite different. The research team were interested in measuring issues before and after intervention, and the measured differences were shared publicly. The team had no ongoing commitment to the facility once the research program was concluded. The work was similar to a time-limited intervention, but, because it was conducted within a research rather than a practice paradigm, it seemed to the students to be more public and political – it was closely linked to the life of the facility and also stood outside it.

Research work on placement raises particular issues for the placement agency and students and needs to be carefully thought through before students begin the work. Exercise 2 identifies some considerations for supervisors and students.

EXERCISE 2

FOR THE SUPERVISOR

Consider the following questions.
1 What outcomes does the agency want from the research?
2 What issues in terms of ethics, knowledge and skills are inherent in the research and how will these be dealt with?
3 Does the agency need to get additional assistance to carry out the research?
4 Is this research likely to raise expectations that can't be met in the future?

In any research work, it is common for the following steps to be taken:
1 Identify the issue.
2 Identify what is already known about the issue from literature and in practice.
3 Decide what question(s) will be answered.
4 Identify an appropriate way to go about answering the question(s), given what is known about this issue.
5 Identify the resources that will be needed to carry out the research.
6 Gather the information.
7 Analyse the information and share it with the stakeholders.
8 Arrive at a set of conclusions.
9 Publish the results.

Many of the issues associated with research on placement overlap with those outlined in Chapter 10 about community work placements and those explored in the following discussion of policy practice.

Policy practice

You are surrounded by the results of policy-making in almost all areas of your life – from informal policies in your families or living groups, to formal social policies, such as those that determine your access to income support. Your placement agency will have policies on a range of matters, from the legislation or constitution that establishes it as a legal entity to how staff access the photocopier.

EXERCISE 3

The following brief guide is one approach to social-policy development. If you have another approach, try using the broad headings in this section to further explore your knowledge of policy practice.

How change occurs

In policy, structural solutions to difficulties that clients or organisations have in common can be identified. It is one form of planned approach to change and involves understanding the following:
- the interrelationships between political and economic processes within and without your agency
- the processes by which power is distributed within organisations
- the existing constraints and control mechanisms
- the worker's experience of these issues in his or her everyday working life (Rees 1991, p. 104).

The development of policy involves recognising the political dimensions of the issues individuals or organisations face and thinking strategically about the solution to these issues. This analysis may be carried out by workers and other experts or with those who experience the issues. A decision about who should be involved in this stage of policy development is often based on an assessment of what strategies are likely to be effective. Some strategies that can be employed are:

- policy analysis
- policy development and implementation
- legislative advocacy
- reform through litigation
- social action.

There are a number of approaches to this form of planned social change. The following approach, as outlined by O'Connor, Wilson and Setterlund (2003, pp. 196–7), identifies the elements of developing policy. You will need to relate this to the context of your placement agency.

What outcomes do you want to achieve? What type of change is sought?

What is the focus for change? Who or what needs to be targeted to achieve the desired change? To answer this question, you need to determine which organisations promulgate the current policy and understand the content of relevant policies. Who has the power to influence outcomes and how are they influenced? What is right as well as wrong with current policy, and how ready are the relevant authorities to change?

Who should be involved? What combination of individuals, interest groups or organisations should be involved to determine the direction change should take? It is always a good idea to involve those whose lives are affected by the policy, because they will have to live with the outcome.

Any group developing policy should have the following skills:

- the ability to think clearly and to critically analyse information
- the ability to use empirical and demographic information (including literature reviews), as well as subjective knowledge, to clarify issues and assess alternatives
- the ability to use rational arguments to develop a case and to engage in rational decision-making
- the ability to communicate and negotiate with people from different backgrounds and with different views
- the ability to reflect on how personal values affect how a problem or issue is understood.

These skills are an extension of those used in interpersonal work; however, policy work is sometimes more visible and open to scrutiny than interpersonal work and you might feel that you are less in charge of the process.

Once the group has established the necessary skill base, it will then need to select strategies for change. These strategies can be labelled as follows.

- *Cooperation* – there is substantial agreement about outcomes and what is the best way forward. Strategies include rational planning, research, consensus decision-making, using group dynamics, and undertaking community work and community and organisational research.
- *Campaign* – there is no consensus, but it is believed that agreement could be achieved by some form of persuasion. Strategies include advocacy, research, education, consciousness-raising, rational persuasion and lobbying.
- *Contest* – there is basic disagreement over outcomes. Strategies include research, organising groups committed to change, building a base in terms of resources and influence, appealing to third parties, disruption to established patterns of doing business.

Given the political nature of policy practice, it is important that students have good communication skills to help them relate to others. Placement supervisors and other agency staff need to be effective role models for students in this regard.

Political realities

Policy formulation is always a matter of compromise and hence is a fundamentally political process. Supervisors, and therefore students, are constrained by the need to avoid unnecessary conflict and to ensure that a range of needs are met so that the policy has a reasonable chance of being accepted and implemented. In the non-government sector, there may be more freedom to negotiate policy that represents a range of views. Whatever the outward appearance, policy is always a compromise at best and an exercise in power at worst. For students on placements with a policy focus, it can be difficult to come to terms with the necessary compromises. The impact of differences in power is a feature of all forms of human service practice and, in the context of policy work, students are forced to confront this reality directly. Supervisors and students have to confront the power that others may yield.

This can impact on how learning is constructed on placement or on the opportunities that are available to learn in this context. It may be the case that writing policy encourages a close exploration of the nature of conflict. It may encourage a study of the nature of compromise, or it may encourage a deep understanding of the benefits of cooperation.

Teaching and learning policy skills

Policy work is largely different from other forms of human service practice; however, the basic principles that underpin assessment and intervention also apply to policy work. What is different is the technical nature of the task, the need to deal with issues at a macro rather than micro level and, perhaps, the nature of relationships that workers form to get the job done. All practice offers opportunities to reflect on the relationship between processes and outcomes, the way workers make use of themselves, and the way they see the connection between individuals and their social environment.

The following example is of a student processing an interaction related to negotiating a policy task within a large organisation. It shows how personalities and structures interconnect.

> The interaction took place at a meeting following a workshop that I had organised to consult with staff who had practical experience in (the issue under consideration). These staff members, who came from city, rural and remote offices for the day, had shown an interest in being involved in the development of relevant resources. All the staff were very interested. However, before I could even finish, Paul interrupted, stating that there was no need for a manual and that it would never be read anyway, as the staff did not have time to read more information. He knew how to run a program to respond to the issue for his region. And he hated manuals!
>
> I felt very uncomfortable; I felt that his comments were directed to me, although in reality I knew better. However, I did feel annoyed that I was put in this position early in my placement and was therefore perhaps unaware of some underlying historical issues. I felt that it was possibly due to my student status and that I was seen to be coming from an academic position without experience in an area in which he was confident. Also, it seemed as though he thought that I was trying to impose my ideas and more work on already overworked staff when I was only doing what I had been asked to do.

Thinking things through in this way helped the student to see that there were many factors at work in Paul's response, and the next interaction was easier. Paul, at a meeting in his office, showed the student the resource he had already developed.

> This was enormously helpful to me as I could now clearly envisage the flow of systems that were required. Paul, I think, now saw the value of his knowledge and how it would be beneficial to staff in other regions. I was also able to explain how we envisaged the format of the guidelines, and Paul

realised that it was going to be divided into smaller units for ease of use and not the large manual that he had envisaged.

From listening to Paul it became apparent to me that his own work role was incredibly busy and I was able to gain some understanding about other issues impacting on his daily work. He said that he had been frustrated at having to spend time at the workshop the previous week, as he essentially saw it as going over issues that he had sorted out within his region. The meeting ended with the relationship intact and we now understood each other's position.

In addition to requiring the analytical skills mentioned earlier, policy practice requires good interpersonal skills, which are used to achieve shared tasks. It is important to identify processes and skills used in the interpersonal aspect of policy practice, just as you would if you were thinking about interpersonal work.

The political nature of policy work – in terms of who has power, and how power is exercised – is important to understanding what is possible and will influence what supervisors will be prepared to let students do. The political affiliations of the level of government responsible for the policy may also indicate what is more or less valuable in policy development. The process of teaching in policy practice is likely to have a strong didactic element, in which the student is given specific directions about sensitive issues, rather than being left to explore for himself or herself. Supervisors are likely to have a clear idea about what is 'right' and 'wrong' in terms of practice, and agencies will have a valued way of doing things, which will influence the learning process. That is, students learn to do what is required, as well as learn about developing policy.

In policy practice, students need to learn to interact with others, identify options from which choices can be made, and analyse why certain outcomes were achieved. Supervisors should use reflective techniques to encourage them.

Practitioners' networks are often central to the effectiveness of policy practice, and supervisors may encourage students to be active in developing their own networks, as well as introducing students to their own contacts. Developing networks requires specific skills, and students are more likely to learn these skills if they are explicitly discussed. Students can watch their supervisor in action in meetings or on the phone. Learning from these observations can be maximised if there is a clear agenda about what skills students should observe.

In some agencies, students may be asked to operate more independently, perhaps working directly with the management committee. In this case, it is essential that students are given very clear guidelines, and have access to regular and timely supervision from the person who takes ultimate responsibility for the work.

EXERCISE 4

FOR THE STUDENT

1 Which of the approaches to learning how to do policy work will best fit with your learning style?
2 What areas of policy work are likely to be challenging?
3 How will you deal with this?

As with community work, it is important for students to have a defined policy task, which might be part of a larger project. As far as possible, they should be involved in the initial conceptualisation of the project; however, if the project has already started when students begin placement, they will need to be filled in about what has happened to this point.

The type of placement agency will determine the range of approaches students can take to policy practice. In government departments, students are most unlikely to be involved in social action, and the change strategies used will be mainly cooperation, or perhaps coercion. In an advocacy organisation, the whole range of strategies may be available.

Writing policy

Students may need to become skilled at writing policy. Policy writing typically has a number of phases: first, proposing that the work should be done; second, preparing working documents for consultation; finally, presenting the finished policy.

Agencies usually have pro formas for presenting policies. Such documents are brief statements of who has responsibility to ensure particular outcomes are achieved or of the circumstances that must be satisfied before particular actions can be taken. They may have longer appendices that spell out the ways in which the policy can be put into practice.

Once approval has been given to proceed, the next task is to work with stakeholders to develop the policy. In your agency, how possible is it to involve the people who will be affected by the policy in the task of setting the policy? If it is difficult, what steps can you take to try to ensure that the policy will be acceptable to them?

The information about recording methods in Chapters 8 and 10 is relevant here, as it is important to record the processes of consultation and the decisions that are reached. The form of reporting will be decided in part by the committee or authority responsible for the worker – in a typical human service agency, workers mostly will be required to write reports on current programs and proposals for new programs.

The proposal format might be similar to one used to propose a project to a management group in an organisation. The areas that need to be covered may be presented in a variety of ways.

The following format, similar to that used in government departments, includes a section in which the results of consultation with others are outlined and identifies further consultation that needs to occur after the proposal is put.

Executive management – XX department
Authority to commence with
[title of major project or policy initiative]

Agenda item no.:	Meeting date:

Background
  1
  2

Assumptions
  3
  4

Results of consultation and advice including implications
  (Results of consultation with internal and external stakeholders)
  5
  6
  7

Further consultation to occur
  8
  9

Risk management
  10 Risks that have been identified as requiring specific management and how they will be managed are as follows:

  11 This risk will be managed by:

Approvals
  12

Action officer	*Name*	*(Telephone number)*

Proposal

1. Objectives of the proposal
2. Summary of events that have led to this proposal
3. Advancement of the organisation's mission and values
4. Time frame
5. Human-resource requirements
6. Extra costs and source of funds
7. Interest groups affected and their views
8. Accordance with government policy, legislation and funding conditions
9. Compliance with current strategic plan
10. Impact of the proposal on the service and its clients
11. Date of commencement
12. Proposed publicity
13. Recommendations (in the form of a motion for the meeting)

Not all proposals would use all of these headings. Here is a more detailed format.

Proposal

1. Project name
2. Project scope (define project parameters)
3. Project outcomes
4. Project outputs
5. Links to strategic plan
6. Project methodology
   - milestones
   - time frame including end date
   - communications strategy
   - ethical considerations
   - evaluation and review
7. Project-management structure

A project sponsor must be identified and any structures for project-management, steering or reference groups must be described, including the following information:

   - role
   - responsibilities
   - membership
   - meeting schedule
   - authorisation and reporting.

8. Project time frame

Phase	Name	Time frame

9. Resourcing

Phase	Name	Time frame

Whatever format is used, the hallmarks of successful project or policy writing are that it should be as brief, as clearly expressed and as coherent as possible, and it should be written in the third person. The aim is to ensure that readers are clear enough about the issues to make an informed decision.

Summary

It is often the case that a placement has some component of policy and research work. The skills in communication, writing, reflection, research and social action that students develop from being involved in policy writing or research projects are invaluable in all human service work.

It is important not to lose sight of the broader policy, organisational and community issues that set the parameters for work with individuals or constrict or enhance the capacity of individuals to live as fully participating members of society. Placement is a good place to start tackling the social face of individual issues.

12

WORKING WITH TEAMS AND GROUPS

Introduction

In general, practitioners in human services spend around a third of their time in direct contact with those for whom the service exists and the remainder in activities related to that work, such as meetings, writing reports and following up contacts on behalf of others. Much of this organisational work is done in teams.

The team-based nature of such practice, and the potential for technology to connect people, suggest that the demand for graduates with team and groupwork skills will increase.

What are teams and groups?

Teams are groups, and a group may be a team working together to accomplish a task. However, while teams are almost always concerned with accomplishing organisational tasks, groupwork may be used as a method of intervention in its own right. Groups and teams may have dynamics in common, but the purpose of these two forms of group and the worker's role in the group may vary.

The term 'team' implies that it is organisationally sanctioned, although it must be acknowledged that not all people who work together form teams. The ideal type of team described in literature is a group of equals who have developed common goals and strategies to achieve more together than they could alone.

Teams can be characterised by:
- the process by which they develop and make decisions, such as conferring, cooperating or consulting (O'Connor, Wilson & Setterlund 2003, p. 172)
- a single, multi-agency or multidisciplinary base that involves specialised skills
- the formal and informal structures the team sets up that determine information flow, decision-making and follow-up action
- the type of leadership, ranging from hierarchical to shared, and from formal to informal
- the work environment, influenced by factors such as any legislative requirements, constitutions and organisational structures (Payne 1982, p. 10).

A group is a collection of individuals who come together for a common purpose. Groups are an integral part of our lives. We are inherently social beings and we have a range of experiences of groups – for example, in families, workplaces, classrooms, sporting associations – that will inform our practice with groups. Some of us may seek out group contact and some may prefer to work independently as often as possible. However, it is hard to imagine having a placement and not having some form of group experience.

EXERCISE 1

FOR THE STUDENT

Try answering the following questions.
1 What do you like most about working with others in a group?
2 What do you like least?

3 How are these answers related to each other?

4 What impact do you think your opinions about working in groups, as identified in questions 1 and 2, have on your behaviour in groups?

5 What do you need to do to enhance your skills in working in groups, both as a leader and as a group member?

All human service organisations use some form of group activity to meet administrative requirements, and many will use groups to make decisions about clients, to discuss strategic directions or to work directly with clients. Group members in workplaces may share some knowledge, skills and values, yet have conflicting or contradictory approaches in other areas. These areas of shared identity and contested identity help to characterise any group. It is important to try to understand these dynamics if you are to work effectively with a group. As in other forms of practice, it is important to be purposive, to be able to analyse what is happening, to identify the skills that are used, and to suggest why things are or are not going well. Benjamin, Bessant and Watts (1997) suggest that the analytical skills required in groupwork centre on:

- checking communication patterns
- checking that the group is moving towards its purpose
- reflecting on the appropriateness of leadership style for the purpose and the group members
- assessing the climate of the group
- checking for understanding of group goals.

EXERCISE 2

FOR THE STUDENTS

Look back at your answers to the questions in Exercise 1 and the list of analytical skills described previously.

1 How do you assess your groupwork skills at this point?

2 Which of these skills will you find easier or harder to teach or learn?

Teamwork

Bearing in mind that a team is one form of group, it is important to use the knowledge you have about groups to understand the opportunities and constraints that working in teams in your placement setting offers. The work environment is a significant factor in whether a team develops and how it develops from a work group. This development can be charted as a process of moving through stages. For example, Brill and Levine (2002, p. 213) describe the stages through which groups move as orientation, accommodation, negotiation, operation and dissolution. Of course, not all teams move along this continuum. The following scenario tracks a team in a hospital through these stages as they develop a new team.

A children's hospital hoped to expand its rehabilitation services for children across a wide geographical area by developing a 'team at a distance'.

Orientation: The original impetus to develop the new team came from the speech pathologist, who was frustrated by the lack of follow-up when children returned home. She received support from other therapists, all of whom were concerned about the slow rate of progress of the children once they left the hospital. The social worker supported the plan, but wanted the group to consider the resources and opportunities that were available at a local level. The idea was supported by the hospital hierarchy, and staff were asked to submit a plan to put it into operation. Staff from each discipline were allocated to the new team, depending on interest and time availability. It was decided that children from areas outside the city would be referred to the team after they had been discharged from in-patient care.

Accommodation: The team met to consider how they would work with children at a distance. This involved considerable discussion about their goals, how they would coordinate their work, how they would communicate with any therapists 'on the ground' and how they could keep other interested parties informed. For many it was difficult because they had relied on face-to-face contact to do their work. The new service inevitably meant that the team would have to train others in therapy procedures and the question arose as to how much parents could be expected to take this role. A social work student on placement was asked to record what was happening, and to identify possible options and a way of evaluating the progress of the team towards meeting their goals. The first children were referred and team members found that the work was more time-consuming than they had thought, and they were continually being pulled away to deal with the immediate demands of children on the wards.

Negotiation: It became clear that team members could only find the time for the new service if one therapist had the responsibility for each child, so a procedure was adopted to identify who the key therapist would be and he or she then negotiated for more specialised input, if necessary. There was tension because not all team members could keep up with the most enthusiastic members. The student highlighted the normality of these tensions from her reading of theory, and this encouraged staff to move from personalities to the structural issues that made the work difficult. Setting goals against which the team's work could be assessed was a long process, but it helped people to become more realistic about what could be achieved.

Operation: The first three months, coinciding with the end of the student's placement, were taken up with getting the team running reasonably efficiently and effectively. Team members were surprised at how much they could cross the boundaries of each discipline and still feel competent. They all acknowledged they had learned a lot from each other. Children seemed to be making more progress with their rehabilitation than had been the case before the team was set up, and parents reported that the extra work for them seemed to be worthwhile. Respecting what each person had to offer was crucial to the program. It was decided to run the program for 12 months and continue to evaluate it.

The conditions under which people work, the leadership effort put into fostering cohesiveness and the personalities involved in a team will all affect the outcomes of teamwork. The development of teams can be interpreted as a product of the forces affecting the team and this developmental approach considers the threats and opportunities the team encounters. Fatout and Rose (1995, pp. 62–7) identify four areas of threats and opportunities, which explain how teams work together: communication, cohesion, control and culture.

The team in the previous scenario worked well because the areas of threat were outweighed by the opportunities offered to improve the service. People in this team were prepared to put the children's needs ahead of their own professional boundaries and come up with an innovative way of delivering a rehabilitation program to children and their families who were at a distance.

Exercise 3 is a useful exercise for students and supervisors to think about how the team in their workplace functions and what their role and tasks are in the team.

EXERCISE 3

FOR THE STUDENT AND SUPERVISOR

Think about teamwork in your workplace or placement agency and answer the following questions.

1 How do you balance client confidentiality with the need to share information in a team?
2 How can you time your work with clients so you fit in with the work and the other team members?
3 How do you handle conflict in teams?
4 How can you involve agency clients in decision-making teams?

Types of teams

The organisational structure of your team is important. It is often the case that you will be a member of more than one team and each may be of a different type, each with its own advantages and limitations. Think about the following types of teams in the context of your agency.

Single discipline team

All members are assumed to share a common practice and skill orientation. The advantages of single discipline teams are that lines of responsibility and accountability are clear, and with a common discipline agendas are more likely to be shared. The disadvantages are that each person in the team is likely to represent a different organisational level (for example, client, worker, team leader, manager) and those in boundary positions between the organisational levels experience the stress of choosing between competing demands.

Multidisciplinary team

Members come from different disciplines and this impacts on the allocation of work. Most multidisciplinary teams have a matrix structure, and team members have dual accountability: on a professional level to a discipline senior and on an administrative level to the team leader.

The main advantages of a multidisciplinary team are that it can facilitate and coordinate the most appropriate response to client needs and provide a single access point for clients. The disadvantages are that workers are left to negotiate the boundaries between their discipline team and work team, and that leadership power is often vested in specific professions and not necessarily in the individuals who are most competent.

Inter-agency teams

Team members come from different agencies and often from different practice areas (for example, child protection and juvenile justice) or represent specific clients. Such teams work well when the task is clearly defined, there is energy for the task and the members trust each other. The advantage of inter-agency teams, if the above conditions are present, is that they develop collaborative work styles, which will benefit the practice areas or clients that are represented by the team. However, there is little recourse if these conditions are not present. This model is threatened by the purchaser/provider funding model for human services, which challenges the traditional cooperative approach between agencies on which these teams rely.

In all teams, regardless of the setting, practitioners have to balance the interests of individual clients and the groups they work with against the interests of individual team members and of employers. As a student, this is an important skill to understand and develop.

Teamwork skills

Other skills that are essential for good communication and cooperative decision-making in groups are active listening, encouraging and balancing participation, clarifying discussion and checking for agreement.

- *Active listening:* Paraphrasing and checking out information is an opportunity to reinforce that important information is heard and shared, and to gain agreement among team members: for example, 'So you are also saying that … ' 'Is that what we are agreeing to try?'
- *Encouraging and balancing participation:* Solicit information from all members, or ask each member in turn to state his or her opinion. Elicit new opinions with questions such as 'Does anyone else have anything to contribute?'
- *Seeking different opinions and encouraging alternative views:* Using open questions – such as 'What are some of the other ways we could assist Mrs B. to stay safe?' instead of closed questions such as 'Is there any other way of helping Mrs B., other than move her into a more secure facility?' – can help the group seek alternatives.
- *Clarifying discussions:* Disagreements often arise from misunderstandings or a failure to appreciate another member's underlying concerns or fears. Use probes such as 'How did you come to this conclusion?' or 'What behaviours of Mrs B. influenced this judgement?'
- *Checking for agreement and understanding:* Check to see if everyone understands a decision and can explain why it is the best. Also ask if everyone is clear about the course of action and the assignment of tasks and roles.

Exercise 4 requires students to evaluate their use of these skills in team meetings.

EXERCISE 4

FOR THE STUDENT

1 Review your behaviour, or the behaviour of others, in a team meeting to understand what made the meeting more or less successful. Focus on the skills outlined above.

2 Prepare for a meeting in which you will lead the team by answering the questions below before the meeting (adapted from Hyer & Howe 2002).

   a What decisions need to be made today?

   b Are you clear about everyone's perspective on these decisions?

   c Is there disagreement among group members about any issues? If so, what accounts for this disagreement?

   d What key questions must be addressed or points resolved to reach decisions?

   e Do you or the group need more information?

   f What are your preferred decisions and what values, knowledge and attitudes are reflected in your preferences?

Groupwork

Berg-Weger and Birkenmaier (2000, pp. 142–3) suggest that there are six models for understanding groupwork as an intervention method, as outlined below. The models are distinguished by their goals and the roles of workers.

Goals	Examples	Role of workers
Social	Resident associations	To facilitate and resource the group
Problem-focused	A range of committees	To advocate on behalf of the group To organise and convene the group
Reciprocal	Caregiver support groups	To mediate the group
Mutual aid and self-help	Alcoholics Anonymous	To educate and support group members
Remedial	Groups for survivors of trauma	To carry out therapy
People working together to achieve change	Groups for perpetrators of abuse	To educate group members and mediate the group

Each places different requirements on the worker, and offers particular challenges and opportunities for teaching and learning. In chairing a committee meeting, the group may use established rules for electing office bearers, setting agendas, reaching decisions and taking responsibility for outcomes. If this is the case, students will need to understand both the rules and the reasoning behind the rules, and develop the skills associated with their role. In some community contexts, students may work with groups to assist them to make decisions about these rules.

Regardless of the model of groupwork, as students and supervisors, you have the chance to apply group theory to practice, to understand and apply group-facilitation skills and to record group processes and outcomes. Issues faced by either students or supervisors may relate to setting up groups, becoming a member of established groups, confidentiality, self-determination and documentation.

Methods of practice

Working with groups

An increasing number of agencies use groupwork to encourage people to achieve their goals. In some placement agencies, students may be encouraged to develop and run groups and, indeed, this may have been part of an agency's motivation for offering a placement. This can be challenging for the student as he or she may be required to develop a proposal for the group, recruit group members, and establish and facilitate the group. Students will need to review coursework information on groupwork, as well as seek ideas and support from both group members and agency staff.

It is more likely that students will join an established group. In this case, the issues relate to establishing themselves as group members – making the transition from observer to participant and, perhaps, to taking responsibility for facilitating the group.

Confidentiality

Group confidentiality always needs to be considered. You may be familiar with confidentiality as it relates to one-on-one practice, but groupwork requires maintaining the confidences of a whole group. How is this different? Will it be different if the group's focus is primarily therapeutic or self-help?

What are the confidentiality issues if you wish to discuss your groupwork practice in your training institution during seminars? What issues do you need to be aware of before you introduce material from placement into this learning group? It is best to know the group rules in advance, and the following exercise will help you to think about the issues surrounding group confidentiality.

EXERCISE 5

FOR THE STUDENT

1 Can group members continue discussions between themselves about material originally raised in the group?
2 Are the rules different if the group is primarily focused on mutual aid or therapy?
3 In what circumstances can you or should you share information raised in the group with a person's individual caseworker?
4 What do you do if one group member tells you something about another group member?
5 What do you do if a group member tells others outside the group what has been discussed?
6 What legal requirements are there for you to share information?

Your answers will probably be influenced by a number of different factors, including existing agency policy, legal mandates and the rules established by the group. As students, your supervisors are responsible for your work, so it follows that they need to know what you are doing. You may need to disclose more of what is discussed than if you were a staff member. However, it may be necessary to discuss this with group members. Issues surrounding confidentiality are often tied to other ethical dilemmas.

EXERCISE 6

FOR THE STUDENT

Consider your response to the following scene.

You work with a group of older people in a residential setting that is designed to help residents regain social skills. The group was originally formed by the worker after an initial assessment was made as to which residents were likely to benefit. The chosen group members were isolated, had felt isolated within the facility and did not have dementia, in an environment in which most people had significant levels of dementia. One resident, who is not popular with others, asks to join in the group. The other group members are very resistant to her joining and want you to exclude this person.

1 What issues does this raise?
2 What would you do?
3 With whom would you discuss this?

Joining the work team

Students starting on placement enter established work groups. A student's entry to a work group is negotiated based on the tasks the student will do, the people who will be responsible for the student's work, the resources that the student will use, the degree to which other workers will be involved in supporting the student and the extent to which other workers can make requests of the student. On the one hand, the whole team may support the placement and be clear about work, resources, and sharing support and education of the student; on the other hand, the supervisor may have forgotten to mention the placement until the student arrives on day one.

Students may immediately feel at home with the team, or they may, even in a well-organised placement, feel like uncomfortable outsiders and wonder how they will last the distance with a team whose values and practice approaches are so different from their own or are so far ahead of where students see themselves in terms of experience. It is important that both students and supervisors pay explicit attention to this process of negotiating entry into established teams to give the placement the best chance of a successful outcome for all, including the clients of the service.

EXERCISE 7

FOR THE SUPERVISOR

Consider the following questions.

1 What organisational issues are likely to make it easy for a student to start in your work team?

2 What issues are likely to make it difficult?

3 Are there any work teams that may not be appropriate for the student to join? (For example, management teams may share sensitive material; peer-supervision teams may make staff feel uncomfortable in front of a student.)

4 Who in your work team or perhaps in the student's training institution might be able to assist with any difficulties you foresee? (For example, perhaps your organisation is facing particular challenges and this will impact on the work you give the student, or a new team member may have had a big impact on team dynamics or staff shortages put pressure on you to give the student extra work.)

FOR THE STUDENT

Consider the following questions.

1 What do you want to learn from the work teams?

2 What did you anticipate would be hard and what would be easy in starting this placement with this work team?

(Think back to what you wanted to achieve on placement.)

3 If you keep a diary, review your entries and look for themes in how you have developed relationships with team members. Discuss these themes (and the associated evidence) with your supervisor and evaluate your progress in joining the team. What can you learn for the future?

Teaching and learning in teams

It is very common for students to report that a number of agency staff, and not just their supervisors, contribute to the students' learning on placement. Although one person usually has ultimate responsibility for the student, other staff can assist with teaching valuable skills and practice methods. It is relatively easy for the supervisor to share the administration and teaching in relation to tasks that need to be covered as part of the requirements of placement with other staff. However, reporting and assessment responsibilities must be made very clear for team teaching to be effective.

Doel et al. (1996, p. 36) suggest that team teaching can be based on cooperation, coordination or collaboration. Cooperation (sharing information about the student) means that one staff member takes responsibility for the student; coordination (sharing planning for the placement) means that staff plan their work to involve the student or support the supervisor; and collaboration (sharing resources) means that the team works closely together sharing responsibility for the student's learning. Exercise 7 helps students and supervisors to identify the current arrangements in the agency.

EXERCISE 8

FOR THE SUPERVISOR

1 Will other staff members provide access for the student to a range of tasks and learning opportunities?

To help you determine the best model for your agency, consider the following issues:

- Who will allocate work to the student?
- Who will provide back-up if you are unavailable?
- What other support networks are available in the agency for the student?
- What consultations will take place between staff about the student's progress?
- Will the student participate in these consultations?

Recording methods

A record of your work is the raw material for learning from your practice. The types of records discussed in Chapters 8 and 10 will be useful for groupwork and teamwork. For example, process reports that chart how the group moved between tasks over time are useful to you both as a participant–observer and as a leader. Video records can be very useful tools for recalling what happened and perhaps seeing and hearing things you missed at the time. Of course, you will need the consent of the group to use this form of recording.

What are some of the topics you might focus on in a report that processes group interactions? These topics will vary depending on whether you are responsible for leading the group or you are a participant–observer. The following topics could be explored:

- preparation for the group sessions – practical and strategic
- the setting of group goals for sessions (To what extent did your goals match those of other members?)
- patterns of communication in the group (Who speaks first, second, and so on? Who is left out? How are the patterns maintained? Do they need to change?)
- patterns of achievement in the group (Do decisions get made? Are issues resolved? Does the group move on or is it 'stuck'?)
- the processing of critical incidents in the group (Were there any instances where members could have made choices that would have resulted in different outcomes?)
- the fit between the leadership style and the group aims
- review of the group processes (What should be maintained and changed in this group? How might this be done?)

Agency records of team or group meetings are likely to be somewhat different. Agency records of groupwork tend to focus on group processes and planning. It is useful to identify a framework that will be suitable for your context. The following areas may be useful to include in your records.

- attendance – who was there and who was missing
- the date of group meetings
- the main topics discussed
- the processes that enabled these topics to be discussed and to be resolved or left unresolved
- the main players and their contributions to these processes
- a sociogram to depict group interactions
- an assessment of the group leader in relation to:
  - their leadership in the session
  - the group's progress towards agreed goals
  - future resources and planning that will be required.

It may be the case that your agency does not have an established recording framework. As a general principle, the more therapeutic the purpose of groupwork, the more likely it is that records will be kept. For other types of groups, the record will often comprise the minutes of the meeting, which summarise the decisions made and the actions group members agreed to take. While this may be a reasonably accurate record of what was discussed, minutes won't generally convey the processes that resulted in these outcomes.

The purpose of the record will have a big impact on the structure you choose. For example, if your records are part of evaluating the usefulness of the group, they will need to make reference to the group's goals. Any records will, of course, need to abide by agency policy in relation to confidentiality. In general, you should not refer to clients by name or include identifying information; however, if you are recording a committee meeting, some comments or action points may be attributed to named individuals.

Summary

Students need to develop confidence in working in teams in the role of student and as future practitioners and managers, as well as working with groups as leaders, facilitators, participants or observers. Placements offer rich experience in this regard, even if the main project of placement is not a group one, and students should be encouraged to reflect on and discuss their experiences in supervision with other team members, using recording methods that are appropriate and useful.

Supervisors need to set the boundaries of teamwork in their agency and ensure that students are adequately prepared either to join established groups or to plan and implement new groups.

13

RURAL AND OVERSEAS PLACEMENTS

Introduction

Rural practice in human services usually takes place in the context of geographic communities at a distance from major urban areas. In 1996 in Australia, one of the most urbanised countries in the world, 14.1 per cent of people were living in settlements with fewer than 1000 people, and 27.3 per cent were living in communities of fewer than 100 000 people (Cheers & Taylor 2001, pp. 206–7). Rural areas traditionally have been defined by a mix of spatial and cultural criteria. It is generally agreed that rurality is associated with distance and low population density, which means that there is a relatively small number of people with whom you repeatedly come in contact. What may start as weak relationships or ties by individual choice, can become stronger because of the circumstances in which people live in rural settings. The strength of the relationships can benefit rural communities, as people are generally willing to work together to achieve specific goals. Sturmey and Edwards (1991) also suggest that, in rural communities, established inequalities and intolerance may be harder to change because stronger ties predominate. Both circumstances offer potential opportunities and limits for all human service practice in rural communities. How is the population distributed in your rural area? What cultural criteria define your rural community?

Rural areas, of course, are not all the same; however, overall they tend to have lower standards of health and education, lower income levels and higher rates of suicide than urban areas. Some rural areas are further disadvantaged by rural restructuring, recession and cutbacks to service provision (Green 2003, p. 209). Other areas are doing well, growing in population and economic activity, and expanding their social infrastructure.

Rural practice

It has been argued that human services practice in rural areas has developed as a distinctive form of practice because of the demands it makes on workers and the opportunities provided by work in small rural communities (Briskman 1999; Cheers 1998; Francis & Henderson 1992; Martinez-Brawley 1990).

Martinez-Brawley (1990) suggests of rural practice that it 'involves the provision of care by members of the community to each other, in mutually supportive relationships and by social workers and other human services personnel working in the community, in partnership with friends, neighbours and volunteers' (p. 216).

It is a form of practice that is community oriented – the practitioner is a part of a community and the work done is shared with the community. This is obvious when the work is community development, supporting informal care networks, lobbying and service development. The worker needs to learn from the community and to share his or her skills with community members. It is often also true when the work is individually focused.

The political realities

The political dimensions of rural communities are very apparent. Rural communities may be the location of 'power struggles, factional disputes, status hierarchies and oppression' (Cheers 1998, p. 233). In rural practice it is harder to remove yourself from these issues. Our behaviour as practitioners and as community members always occurs in a political context that has repercussions for our future work. In this context, the practitioner is trying to be proactive and preventative, to keep abreast of emerging issues, to work with others to identify strategies, and to help build the social infrastructure that enables communities to respond effectively to threats and opportunities. It follows that rural practice requires multiskilled generalist practitioners who are politically astute and able to work with a wide range of life situations and to use methods that range from counselling to social planning.

In rural practice, boundaries between practitioners and clients can be blurred: for example, a worker may discuss with a family their struggles with their child with a disability while at work, then later call on one of the family to fix their plumbing.

The community-oriented nature of practice can be challenging when working with statutory clients or perpetrators of violence. In this context, the worker is clearly an agent of social control as well as someone who is facilitative and empowering. It is challenging for workers to take an empowering approach while in a position of social control (Barber 1991, p. 48) and, for many, rural practice combines these two forms of practice – facilitation and control.

Starting out

Starting placement is a stressful time as you learn how to translate skills and knowledge learned in one context to another. When you are living in a new community as well as working in a new setting, the process of adaptation, both personally and professionally, is often more difficult. Try not to feel overwhelmed when everyone except you seems to know everyone else and know what to do. Normal social skills – demonstrating interest in others, being a good listener, sharing something of yourself, being prepared to ask for advice – will stand you in good stead as you begin a rural placement. Take time to settle into your life in the town, as well as into placement. It is often helpful to join groups in town that match your interests, and to seek out others in a similar position to yourself.

For students from rural areas, the process of adaptation may not be so great; however, it may be difficult to change your identity to that of human services student, if you come from the town or area. You bring your history and knowledge of the area and its people. Your level of comfort is probably what enabled you to ask for a placement in the town in the first place; nevertheless, you may find it more difficult than you thought to relate to people in your home town as a student on placement. For example, people you went to school with may be clients of your agency. Other people, such as those you have played sport with, might greet you with hostility. You may have to exercise authority over those you have seen as authority figures in the past.

All students benefit from some support at this time. It is a good idea to identify people in your network with whom you can discuss issues, let off steam, or talk about something else entirely!

Getting to know your community

This process is likely to be different if you are entering the community for the first time than if you already have established links. If you are new in town, you will need to get advice from your supervisor about who to talk to and where information about the town is kept. Exercise 1 focuses on the features of the community that will be important to understand. It will be helpful also to read about 'insiders' and 'outsiders' in the section of Chapter 10 called 'The political realities' (pp. 103–4).

EXERCISE 1

FOR THE STUDENT

To start to understand your community, think about the following questions.

1 Is your community growing, staying the same or shrinking?
2 How heterogeneous or homogeneous is your community?
3 Are some groups worse off than others in your community?
4 What is the basis for the networks of relationships in your community (for example, religion, length of time in the area, business links, school, and so on)?
5 How do you know the answer to question 4?
6 Are others likely to have a different view to you on issues?

To answer these questions you need to make an assessment of your community, paying attention to geographical, economic, social and political characteristics. It would be a good idea to refer to the section on community profiles in Chapter 10 (pp. 107–8). In your assessment you are trying to identify who lives in the community, who has power and what are the networks. As with any assessment, you need to decide the reason for doing it – you may want to determine the needs or issues of a particular group. You then assess the community from the perspective of this group, paying attention to the impact it has on others.

In this process, remember to take account of where you fit in the community to explore whether you have particular agendas or biases. For instance, you might be hoping to solve a particular community problem, such as getting a refuge for women escaping from domestic violence, and this agenda will filter the information you see as relevant.

EXERCISE 2

FOR THE STUDENT

1 How do others in the community see you?
2 What are they likely to tell you? What sort of information may they withhold, intentionally or not?
3 What biases do you have that will filter out some information but perhaps magnify other information?
4 What knowledge and skills do you have, and how will these impact on your assessment of the community?
5 What evidence do you have to support your assessment?
6 What makes you confident that your assessment will be a suitable basis for ongoing work?

If supervisors have a good understanding of how the community fits together, it will be important to help students discover their own perspective and find the information necessary for their assessment. Students should ensure that they have evidence to support their assessment – their initial ideas should be checked with others who have alternative views.

The issues for placement

Two broad aspects of rural practice impact on rural placements and both relate to ethics. It is sometimes suggested that professional codes of ethics are not always useful in rural practice because of the blurring of workers' roles. The National Association of Social Workers in the United States has recently amended its code of ethics (Martinez-Brawley 2000, p. 254) to cover the complex situations arising from rural practice. It is important for supervisors on rural placements to articulate the ethical standards that are expected of students since it cannot be assumed that those covered in the course will be entirely appropriate.

First, as stated previously, rural workers belong to a community in which they both live and work. They have to manage their work in complex networks of relationships, which provide opportunities to develop relationships that are reciprocal and mutual. They have less privacy than may be the case in urban environments, and this also may be true for clients of the service. Students have to be prepared to use, and work with, the community's wisdom, experience and values

Second, there are often too few services in general and specialised services in particular. This means workers have to be more generalist and have a broader range of skills and knowledge that their city counterparts would refer to more specialised colleagues or other occupational groups. They might struggle to meet the needs and demands of individuals, yet find it hard to refuse service even when they are very busy, because there may be nowhere else for people to go.

There are also practical matters to consider. It is less likely that qualified staff will be available to supervise and more likely to have limited time to devote to supervision. Student placements will often be in a setting with limited resources, and therefore the supervisor and student will need to be innovative in creating student projects and establishing creative ways to problem-solve and learn. Both aspects of rural practice have positive as well as challenging sides for supervisors and students, as highlighted in Exercise 3.

EXERCISE 3

FOR THE STUDENT AND SUPERVISOR

It would be a good idea to do a SWOT analysis of your situation in relation to a particular issue. At each end of one axis write strengths and weaknesses (in the person, situation or relationship), and on the intersecting axis, write opportunities and threats (in terms of progress, learning and change).

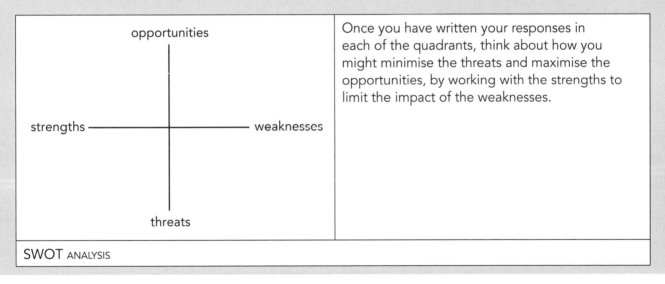

opportunities

strengths ——————————|—————————— weaknesses

threats

Once you have written your responses in each of the quadrants, think about how you might minimise the threats and maximise the opportunities, by working with the strengths to limit the impact of the weaknesses.

SWOT ANALYSIS

The following example shows how an agency uses a SWOT analysis in developing its response to issues of flexible child care in the local area.

- *Strengths*: People know each other; women need child care to take advantages of the work opportunities; the local church is interested in auspicing a child-care service.
- *Weaknesses*: People might learn too much about private family business; parents may not be willing or able to pay for child care; it is not easy to get trained staff.
- *Opportunities*: There is funding available; the service will support stressed families as well as working parents; child care can provide children with a wider range of role models and some protection if abuse is suspected; it will be an opportunity for local people to develop the service they want.

- *Threats:* It challenges the role of women and their extended families in the town; the funding guidelines may not suit local needs; the demands of running the program might exceed the capacity of the auspicing church body.

Students and supervisors could think about ways they could use the strengths in this situation to counteract the weaknesses and use the opportunities provided to respond to the threats.

Other issues

Some of the other issues – professional and personal boundaries, confidentiality, anonymity and joining the community, the political dimensions of placement, generalist or multiskilled practice, and personal safety – that commonly arise in rural placements are outlined below. Consider whether these issues relate to your placement and think about other issues if you need to.

Professional and personal boundaries

Rural practice raises issues about what are appropriate boundaries between workers and clients. People who are clients of a service may also be committee members or fellow parents at school. Workers and clients may have multiple roles as citizens in the community, and the boundaries between these roles may be blurred. Workers and clients will get to know much more about each other than may be the case in larger communities with looser networks. Learning to deal with this blurring of roles is an important task for rural placements.

In taking students on placement, supervisors are overseeing the introduction of a new, temporary worker into the agency and they need to consider how able the agency is to incorporate the student into the agency and the community. Supervisors may need to specify particular tasks and identify particular people with whom students can work to assist them to integrate. Exercise 4 helps students and supervisors to think about the key issues and some strategies.

It is important for students and supervisors to be very clear about the ways in which roles and boundaries are blurred and to be able to raise the matter when either feels that the boundaries need to be strengthened. A supervisor is likely to get feedback from others in the town about how the student is going, particularly if the student is a stranger in town and is not cushioned by their own networks. How are you, as student and supervisor, going to cope with this feedback? Is it different from the feedback supervisors in another setting would receive from other workers in the agency?

EXERCISE 4

FOR THE STUDENT

1 Would it make a difference if clients were primarily known to you or primarily known to your extended family? Why?

2 What general strategies will help you to deal with this blurring of roles?

FOR THE SUPERVISOR

1 What are the boundaries for the student in terms of your relationship with them, the student's relationship with clients, and the student's role in the broader community?

2 What strategies can you offer to the student that will help him or her to deal with the blurring of roles?

Confidentiality

In rural practice, confidentiality is crucial. If you undertake to maintain a client's confidentiality, you must do so, and don't make promises in this regard if they are not within your power to keep. In promising to maintain confidentiality, you also need to take account of your responsibility to community members: for example, a teacher who refers a child to your agency might want to know if the child turned up. What are the implications of telling them or not?

Agencies must ensure that private information is not accessible to staff who have no need to know that information. In your work you are likely to make use of formal and informal resources in the community, and you will need to be accountable for their use to relevant individuals and groups in the community. This will need to be taken into account when entering into agreements about the confidentiality of all client information. For example, what information should an agency give to the local council that provides the agency with a house for use as a refuge for women?

EXERCISE 5

FOR THE STUDENT AND SUPERVISOR

Think about how your agency deals with confidentiality.

1 What are the guidelines about confidentiality in your agency?
2 How does the rural context influence the guidelines?
3 How do these guidelines relate to student placements?
4 Do the guidelines cover situations that might arise in rural settings when public information about a client is incorrect and is potentially damaging to them?
5 If your placement agency is a government service, do the guidelines vary for rural practice?

Anonymity and joining the community

In rural settings, it can be difficult to be anonymous when you are not at work but are out alone or with others doing the shopping or perhaps having one too many drinks at the club. This means that as a human service worker or student you probably will have less freedom to do as you like. Students and supervisors should consider the extent to which students' behaviour outside placement is raised for discussion in supervision.

On the positive side, joining with the community, rather than being isolated, offers the potential to work more effectively with community members, including clients. You are trying to cross the boundary between 'us' and 'them'.

If you are new to town, here are some of the ways to settle in on placement:

- Demonstrate interest in issues that unite people in the town and try to avoid those that are divisive – certainly at the start.
- Comply with group norms as far as is possible within the context of your own standards.
- Highlight the aspects of your personality, skills and lifestyle that are similar to the community you are seeking to join.

EXERCISE 6

FOR THE STUDENT

1 Can you think of particular situations in which you have been, or could be, proactive about joining with the community?
2 What constrains you from and what encourages you to join with the community?

The political dimensions of practice

Human service workers are concerned with issues of social justice, which may bring you into conflict with vested interests in the community. For example, if you support a wife to leave her abusive husband and he is a prominent leader in the community, you may find your organisation comes under fire from a powerful group in the community. Similarly, if you don't support a disempowered group to tackle an important but potentially divisive issue, your ability to attract support for future projects may be jeopardised. Cheers (1998, pp. 235–6) suggests that workers adopt a community perspective and a strategic approach to all their work. This suggests that you need to understand the power structures in the community, how and where decisions are made, who has influence in relation to particular issues, and what issues divide or unite the community.

As a student you are usually relatively powerless in the placement agency and you may not believe you are able to influence decisions. Exercise 7 helps students and supervisors to explore the issue of power further.

These issues can be tricky for supervisors, because they want to ensure that students have the authority to manage tasks, but ultimately don't have the final responsibility.

EXERCISE 7

FOR THE STUDENT

1 How much power do you think you have to influence decisions in your agency and in the community?
2 In your SWOT analysis in Exercise 3, did you identify any ways in which you might be a threat to your organisation or the community?
3 How do you plan to minimise any such threats?

FOR THE SUPERVISOR

Your agency may have a protocol about dealing with people with positional power in the community.
1 How will you convey this protocol to the student?
2 What should a student do if he or she is approached by a community member with positional power?
3 How will you take responsibility for the student's work in this context?

Generalist and multiskilled practice

Martinez-Brawley (1990, p. 239) concludes about community-oriented practice:

> [It] presupposes a great deal of knowledge of the local community. It requires knowledge of local people and strong diplomatic techniques. It requires the ability to interpret events not only in the language of the agency but also in the language of the policymaker, the politician, and the local citizen.

Green (2003, p. 210) suggests that for rural practice workers need a wide knowledge base that includes economics and politics, rural sociology and geography, as well as knowing about a range of intervention strategies. Do you feel you have sufficient knowledge in these areas? Where do you need to develop your knowledge? How will you gather this material in your placement?

Consider the following example of practice to develop a remote-area dementia service in one Australian state. The area covers 414 162 square kilometres, has 30 local government authorities and a population of around 234 000 people, with half living in a large regional town. The author worked for a large statewide non-government provider of residential and community-based aged care.

The need for some form of respite service emerged from work with individuals. Once this need was identified, the agency decided on an appropriate model. It evaluated this model in terms of its ability to support existing care networks and to fit a range of lifestyles of clients. The agency also evaluated whether the model would be acceptable to carers, older people and service providers. They chose the primary health-care approach, which emphasises client choice and self-management, and works with a wide variety of existing 'service providers' (including the school bus, the mental health team and local hotels).

The way forward was to build on local resources; hence, close working relationships were established with existing services to avoid duplication and to access local knowledge. The agency used an advocacy approach with funding bodies to persuade them to fund a program that was somewhat outside the standard guidelines. The funding application was based on research about what had and had not worked previously in local communities and consultation with a range of local people. An advisory committee was set up to give people from different communities a forum for participating in the planning for the program.

A satellite model for outreach services as outlined by Humphreys, Mathews-Cowey and Rolley (1996) was selected, funding for four years was obtained and the service was established. Its worker is located in a small town with back-up from the regional centre, resourced with appropriate transport, communication technology and flexible funding, so, for example, local part-time carers can be paid for when needed. There is ongoing critical evaluation of the service, which involves keeping good data and regularly analysing it. It means that when the service cannot meet needs, it can advocate for change at the political level and modify the service model (Rose-Miller 1999).

Consider the questions in Exercise 8, which are based on this example.

EXERCISE 8

FOR THE STUDENT

1 What knowledge did the agency need to develop the model for practice?
2 What skills did the agency require?
3 If you were in the agency's position, what would you have found the most difficult thing to do? Why?
4 What would have been the easiest? Why?
5 What do your answers suggest about your current knowledge of and skills for rural practice?

Individual members of the community may bring issues to rural workers that stretch their professional skills. In the city, workers can refer clients to a range of specialised services to support their own work. Rural workers develop skills and expertise over time that may exceed those of their urban counterparts.

Rural people may face similar issues to those facing urban people – for example, the need for respite services as outlined in the example above; however, the implications of these issues for people and the options available to them may be quite different, and this will impact on the way you work with them.

You may have to rely heavily on your supervisor's experience of adapting inherently city-based models of intervention to a rural setting. Thinking about the previous example, how might your work to establish a respite service be different if you were located in a large city? How would it be the same?

Having the opportunity to reflect on practice and discuss issues may be harder for students in rural placements, and the training institution may be too distant for regular visits by the liaison person. Students may need to use telephone conferences as a way of maintaining contact if face-to-face meetings are hard to arrange.

Personal safety

A potential issue for rural practitioners is that of personal safety for themselves and their families. In an environment where 'everyone knows everyone else's business', disputes which clients or community members may have with individual workers can escalate quickly. In their study of rural welfare and social workers in Western Victoria in fields of practice labelled 'controversial' or 'conflictual' (including corrections, child protection, mental health, or those that threaten community views on women or children), Green, Gregory and Mason (2003) found that reports of violence and harassment were significantly high. Further, the violence was not generally talked about or acknowledged as an issue that needed to be dealt with (p. 95).

For staff and for students on placement this needs to be challenged for the future wellbeing of all concerned. It is important that students be made aware of situations in which threats of violence could arise, and policies designed and implemented to protect staff and students. If students are exposed to a violent episode, they should be encouraged to discuss it with their supervisor and seek further assistance as needed.

Overseas placements

Most students undertake their fieldwork in local agencies where academic staff are able to liaise with social work supervisors. However, in recent years, an increasing number of students are requesting overseas placements. Students are more aware of the international environment and the burgeoning need for social development workers, or wish to respond to urgent humanitarian crises following wars and natural disasters. In addition, large numbers of international students and others with travel and life experience have requested opportunities to explore the application of skills and knowledge gained from an international placement. The advantages of a global environment, and the technological capacity to communicate easily, have also made the overseas placement a more viable option for social work students.

Undertaking a placement overseas offers students the opportunity to:
* experience another culture and perspective
* enhance appreciation of and ability to apply cross-cultural concepts in practice
* learn more diverse theory and practice, and to integrate them in their work
* bring this learning back and apply it to Australia's multicultural society.

Overseas placements, particularly those located in the developing countries, require different types of arrangements in order to ensure that students are able to gain maximum benefit from the experience and that the receiving agencies are given adequate support. Many of the issues raised above about rural placements are also very relevant to an overseas placement.

Some of the educational issues to consider if you are contemplating an overseas placement include:
* You will need to have a genuine interest in social development and working in developing countries and to have successfully completed the appropriate coursework.
* You must be able to handle cross-cultural work and be prepared to live in often sub-optimal and isolating conditions.
* You must be able to cope with language and cultural differences that may impede the achievement of your learning goals.

- You will appreciate that this placement will enhance your personal learning goals and should be relevant to your future employment.
- You must be able to learn and work without the normal academic supports of liaison, peers and seminars.

Some of the practical things to consider if you are contemplating an overseas placement include:

- **Insurance:** All students undertaking placements are covered by their university for personal and professional liability. This insurance is usually extended for overseas placements, but the university reserves the right to refuse coverage if they believe that there are liability risks because of safety concerns in the country where the student is located. Since the increase in terrorism and civil unrest in many developing countries, universities have been more cautious in agreeing to allow students to take up placements overseas without requiring extra risk management protocols and the students to undertake training.
- **Visas:** Students usually take responsibility for applying for travel documentation, but some countries require written documentation to support their applications. Sufficient time should be allowed for visas to be processed.
- **Accommodation:** The onus may be placed on students to find accommodation that suits their personal needs and budget, but they should investigate possibilities before they leave and seek advice from the local agency or academic contacts.
- **Immunisations:** Working in some countries will require students to be immunised to protect them from local diseases. The Department of Foreign Affairs and Trade offers up-to-date information about safety and health risks at its website: www.smartraveller.gov.au/zw-cgi/view/Advice/

Choosing an overseas placement

Finding a suitable agency to place a social work student is usually a reasonably easy process; the difficulty arises for social work in appointing a supervisor who has the appropriate qualifications to meet Australian Association of Social Work requirements. Many non-government organisations in developing countries don't employ trained social workers, which necessitates a wider search or the recruitment of an academic supervisor from the nearest university that has a Social Work department. Verifying the appropriateness of the qualifications of a potential supervisor is often a lengthy process. Many countries expect payment for supervising a student, and their interpretation of what constitutes a social work task or supervision may be very different from ours.

Ideally, students should seek as much information as possible about the destination country and local conditions, and be adequately briefed by academic staff before travelling to the agency. It can be very helpful to be nominated by two liaison persons, one from a local school of social work (if available) for general support and the other from the training institution, who will fulfil the assessment and monitoring aspects of the placement.

Summary

Rural placements and overseas placements offer students an opportunity to contribute to a community and make a difference. It is important to set up the placement carefully in order to maximise the opportunities of working in a different practice context and minimise its pitfalls. These types of placements may confront students with new or typical human service issues, such as confidentiality and boundaries, but in a more complex way. Rural and overseas placements will also give students the opportunity to work closely with a community and get to understand it. The skills students will learn from this experience will be beneficial whether they end up working in an urban, rural or international setting. Some city-dwellers who 'go bush' or who travel overseas for placement stay there – a testament to the value of the experience for both the student and the town or country.

KEEPING ON COURSE

Most placements have moments in which the participants are aware of specific issues to be addressed – that 'more of the same' won't do. In Part 5, some of the common difficulties students and supervisors face on placement are explored. For most the difficulties are minor and will be quickly resolved, often with significant learning for all. However, in other situations the issues may be more complex and require the assistance of staff from the training institution.

These difficulties may be a result of the impact of difference on placement. Differences of age, culture, gender (dis)ability and more can exacerbate the inequalities in supervisory relationships and amplify other issues that exist. The impact of difference is explored and strategies for overcoming the differences they can make are outlined.

Ethical and legal issues can emerge at all stages of placement. Learning about these can challenge students' and supervisors' sense of what really matters to them. The part played by the training institutions in setting up, supporting, monitoring and evaluating placements is also considered in Part 5.

5

14

CHALLENGING ISSUES IN SUPERVISION

Introduction

As discussed in previous chapters, learning and demonstrating a range of complex tasks within a new and often alien setting will always present challenges for students. They must engage with the learning tasks very quickly and will then be judged as to their level of competency within a relatively short space of time. Not many work settings would make such demands on their staff (Shardlow & Doel 1996, p. 164)!

Any learning also requires change, and change invariably creates anxiety, even in students with experience and proven ability (Ford & Jones 1987). The supervisor may also share this anxiety when teaching and learning tasks threaten his or her sense of competence, control or 'comfort'.

General issues

The difficulties faced by students and supervisors on placement are diverse and, as every situation is unique, there is no standard way to respond when problems arise. Most supervisory relationships experience some normal 'blips', but, in others, the difficulties are a serious barrier to effective teaching and learning.

Problems on placement may manifest, for example, as students experiencing difficulty in producing written work or demonstrating reluctance to engage in reflective practice. Supervisors may be unavailable or ill-prepared for supervision.

Students and supervisors may have to confront the following learning blocks, as described by Megginson and Boydell (1989).

- *Perceptual:* Learners cannot see or recognise the nature of learning required.
- *Cultural:* Learners rigidly adhere to a set of norms that define what is good or bad.
- *Emotional:* The emotional state of learners affects their ability to learn.
- *Intellectual:* Learners may not have the intellectual skills necessary to complete a task.

The underlying reasons why students experience such learning blocks are varied but could include high levels of anxiety, personal or domestic problems, a lack of information and briefing about the work to be undertaken, inappropriate placement tasks, or an inflexible teaching or learning style.

Problems experienced by all parties on placement can emanate from different sources. The student's personality may not be suited to human service work, or he or she may experience emotional problems that interfere with his or her judgement. The problems may originate in the rigid teaching style of the supervisor or his or her inability to provide support and direction. The supervisory relationship may be impaired by communication and value conflicts that impact on the level of trust between the student and supervisor.

Other typical problems are a result of the lack of resources or space in the placement agency, or the agency not accepting the student or not offering a suitable project for the student to focus on. Perhaps the training course has not prepared the student adequately with the skills and knowledge needed for placement.

Case studies of common difficulties

Consider the following three scenarios – each explores some common difficulties that arise in placements. Possible ways to understand these difficulties and some action plans are suggested for each scenario.

'No problem' supervision

Supervisor:	Female, aged 38, experienced welfare worker.
Student:	Male, aged 27, no welfare experience but has done some voluntary work and paid work in hospitality.
Scenario:	The student is likeable and hard-working and engages well with the elderly clients in a day-care centre. Although he seems to be relaxed in his role of student, his supervisor senses that he is not engaged in some aspects of his work. During team meetings, for example, he looks bored and rarely contributes to the discussion. When he does talk, he usually suggests very practical and superficial solutions to often complex problems. He accepts the cases offered without asking many questions and rarely seeks out his supervisor or another team member to check out any concerns.

When the supervisor raises these concerns in supervision, the student acknowledges them but is then silent. The sessions can be frustrating for the supervisor as the student does not come with any agenda items and looks to the supervisor to raise topics. When the supervisor asks how things have been going, the student will generally reply that things have been going well. If the supervisor persists in questioning the student, she feels that they are just going through the motions and filling in time. |

While it is possible that the student is resistant to supervision, there are other explanations that need to be considered first. The student may feel that he has to prove he is a competent worker and that any expression of need or inadequacy would reflect badly on him. The supervisor may have unwittingly conveyed an impression that supervision is about exposing problems and addressing things that are not going well. If this is the case, the student could equate supervision with failure.

Yet other explanations are possible: the student may feel that his practical and concrete suggestions are being undervalued by the supervisor, or perhaps he feels threatened by her process skills. Being fairly inexperienced, he may be relying on what he has learned as a volunteer and has not yet developed the particular knowledge and skills needed in this placement. Given this, he may not yet be able to articulate his needs in the way the supervisor expects. In addition, if he is unfamiliar or uncomfortable with using process skills, he is unlikely to be able to use them in supervision. It could also be a dynamic created by gender or age differences or another psychodynamic reaction.

The supervisor needs to resist prematurely interpreting the student's behaviour as resistance and explore whether it is more an expression of her own frustration. Confronting the student with her initial interpretation may lead the student to defend himself and really become resistant. Recognising that the problem exists between them and does not belong to either one of them is an important first step and shows that the supervisor is not using her status and power to demand that the student changes.

The onus is on the supervisor to provide a safe and structured environment to explore the underlying reasons for the student's behaviour. She could renegotiate the supervision contract to ensure that process issues are made part of supervision with the aim of enhancing the student's learning rather than 'correcting his mistakes'. The learning agreement could be reviewed to include more reflective and process methods. If the student shares that he feels ill-equipped to apply process skills, the supervisor could offer some educational input to assist the student to use both practical and process skills (Brown & Bourne 1996, p. 99). The supervisor also needs to consider what stage the placement is at and whether this is the student's first placement, as both these factors will impact on his depth of understanding of practice issues.

'One of us' supervision

Supervisor:	Female, aged 46, very experienced, handles a small caseload and has management responsibility for a large child-protection agency.
Student:	Female, aged 42, was a teacher before doing a welfare course. This is her first placement.
Scenario:	Although the supervisor is extremely busy, she agreed to take the student because she wants her agency to develop closer ties to the university and to encourage more graduates to work there. The student is strong academically and was pleased to be assigned to child protection for her first placement, as she is keen to specialise in this field and is confident that she can handle the work.
	In the first few weeks, the student is fully occupied in on-the-job training about complex legislative and reporting mechanisms. Most of her time is spent with other team members. Her supervisor checks how she is going but does not offer any formal supervision time. The supervisor promises to block out some time when the three-week orientation period is over. At this first supervision session, the student presents a draft learning agreement and the supervisor suggests a fairly full caseload that will be overseen by the supervisor and other team members. In the following three weeks, the student works long hours but she loves the work she is doing and it seems that most of the staff work this schedule. Supervision continues but the times are frequently changed or cut short because of the supervisor's hectic workload. The supervisor often tells the student that she is doing well and the student greatly admires the supervisor's professional skills. They often talk about aspects of their private lives because of their similar age and shared interest in child protection.
	During the sixth week of placement, the student presents a report in court that is strongly criticised by the magistrate and the student is very upset. She becomes even more upset when the supervisor also criticises her work and suggests that she may have to extend her placement.

In this scenario, it appears that the student believed she could transfer her previous teaching skills to the new learning environment and work without supervision. It is possible that in her teaching career she was rewarded for hard work and 'not rocking the boat'. This assumption was not challenged by the supervisor, who may have chosen the student in the hope that her maturity would mean that she would need less supervision.

It is likely that the student felt that she should have the necessary skills to undertake the work; hence she had difficulty asking for direction from the supervisor, who was extremely busy. She may have played down her needs in order to protect the supervisor and not be seen as creating extra work.

The supervisor, in attempting to create an equal and open relationship, failed to establish a supervision environment in which the student's learning goals were clear. The supervisor and student may have unconsciously colluded in minimising any problems – the supervisor is relieved that the student is not too demanding of her time and rewards her by personal chats and positive feedback. However, when the student experiences a learning difficulty, the supervisor takes a fairly punitive response as a defence for her guilt over not spending more time with the student.

The identified problem in the student's work provides the catalyst for a reflective discussion. Both the student and supervisor need to acknowledge that supervision is not what it should be and that neither of them is to blame, but it is something they need to sort out together. Perhaps they could brainstorm the possible reasons for why the supervisory relationship did not develop sufficiently. They need to renegotiate the supervision contract to set some strong boundaries and outline how they will work together in the future. They also need to review the learning agreement to ensure that the student feels safe to embrace the role of learner and not feel that she should have the skills of a paid worker. The student may have entrenched views that make it difficult for her to assume the role of student, in which case the 'unlearning' can be challenging and perhaps the liaison person from the training institution could help to facilitate dialogue about this.

Mature-aged learners face a number of issues in placement that can have a detrimental impact on their learning. They may fear failure or believe that others will expect them to be more knowledgeable because they have had more life experience. They are often juggling family commitments and coursework requirements, or they may experience resistance from family and peers to their student status.

Also, the age differential between the supervisor and the student may impact on the supervisory relationship, as the student may feel equally or more competent than the supervisor (Razack 2000, p. 197).

'Personal problems' supervision

Supervisor:	Male, aged 35, experienced family counsellor.
Student:	Male, aged 24, trained youth worker and now doing final placement in welfare course.
Scenario:	The student was very pleased to be offered a placement in an intensive family-support agency and has been working hard with families in which there are varying levels of abuse and neglect. Supervision sessions have been regular and supportive, with opportunities for both parties to reflect and share knowledge and ideas. The supervisor is happy about the student's obvious dedication to his work and his willingness to work late some nights in order to see families who can't come to the centre during the day. About six weeks into a 14-week placement, the student rings in to say he is sick and does not come in for two days. In the following week, he has to take another day off, although he offers to make up the time by doing longer hours for the next few weeks.
	During supervision, the supervisor notices that the student becomes very angry about a client he is seeing, who continues to abuse his children and has refused to take responsibility for his drinking. The student wants to encourage the client's wife to take legal action to prevent the father having access to his children until 'he gets his act together'. When the supervisor challenges the student about his unexplained anger, the student becomes very agitated and then asks to be excused for the rest of the day because he is feeling unwell again. He does not come back to work for another two days and when he does return he wants to continue working with the family that was the cause of his emotional outburst. The supervisor tells the student that he is reluctant to see the student proceed any further with this case until they can discuss the student's atypical behaviour. The student replies that this particular case reminds him of his 'bastard' father, but that he doesn't want to talk about it further.

The student's out-of-character outburst and his absences from the placement suggest that issues from his past have been triggered by working with the family. The client or his behaviour reminds the student of his father, which makes him feel angry.

Students often enter the human service field because they have had significant life experiences and they feel that they can help others who have had similar experiences. This can lead to over-identification with some clients, perhaps triggering emotional trauma or making the student less able to be objective and maintain professional boundaries. The situation may be made more complex by the fact that the issues stirred up in the student have extended beyond the client relationship and are affecting his supervisory relationship. The fact that both the client and the supervisor are male may be significant, and this may undermine the capacity of the supervisor and student to sort their relationship.

If the placement does trigger past emotional issues, the student may not feel comfortable or willing to reveal this to the supervisor. Some research has shown that the majority of students are opposed to sharing such information with their supervisor (Razack 2000, p. 201).

The student's behaviour has the potential to interfere with his judgement, so it may not be an option for the supervisor to agree not to discuss the personal aspects of the student's practice. A balance needs to be found between the student's right to privacy and the supervisor's right to information. The relationship between the supervisor and student is critical in this context so that the student's personal issues can be raised and discussed (Razack 2000, p. 200). The supervisor must be sensitive to the student's emotional needs and assess the level of difficulty or trauma.

The supervisor is not responsible for counselling the student about his past, but he can help the student to understand how his relationship with his father impacts on his practice. This transference – or unconscious replaying of past dynamics within a current relationship – is more likely because of the unequal power in the student's relationship with the supervisor (Brown & Bourne 1996, p. 91). Reflective tools such as process records, journals or the Kolb learning cycle could be used to encourage the student to re-create sessions with the family and analyse his feelings in the interaction. Particular cases or issues that may cause the student to feel vulnerable may need to be temporarily or permanently avoided. As a consequence, the supervision contract could need to be redrafted and the learning agreement modified. The liaison person from the training institution could be contacted for advice or support, and the institution may need to give permission if the placement goals are to alter significantly. The student could be referred to a counselling service or could take time out from the placement until he feels able to function in the placement.

Strategies

The common features of the action plans that have been suggested for the three scenarios are as follows:

- Early identification and acknowledgement by both parties of what is happening is crucial. Since both students and supervisors are likely to have a vested interest in the success of the placement, they may be reluctant to deal with the problems (Shardlow & Doel 1996, p. 168), but they won't disappear and will only become more acute as the placement progresses. For example, in the final scenario, the student became progressively immobilised and emotionally affected by the placement.
- Often problems in placements start out as small issues, concerns or 'niggles' that cannot be clearly defined. It is only when these small things accumulate that the main problem becomes evident. Records – journals, process records and supervision summaries – provide evidence and examples that enhance discussion of the issues. For instance, the student in the second scenario could have identified the difficulties earlier if she had used more reflective tools.
- Students should be made to feel that the 'problematic' behaviour is a shared concern, and supervisors should not overreact and assume that the behaviour will manifest in other areas of practice.
- A strong supervisory relationship, in which open discussion of concerns can take place, is essential in resolving difficulties.
- Supervision and learning contracts are important documents that identify, record and structure strategies for resolving placement issues.

The following exercise can help students and supervisors explore situations in which they are getting 'bogged down' or in which the outcomes are not what they expected.

EXERCISE 1

FOR THE STUDENT AND SUPERVISOR

Think broadly about your placement and more specifically about your supervisory relationship.

1 In this placement, do you feel that you are actually doing what you think or say you do?
2 If not, why not?
3 To what extent are your feelings congruent with your reasoning or understanding about practice?
4 Is your verbal behaviour consistent with your non-verbal behaviour?
5 To what extent are your goals for placement being met?
6 Are you able to focus on your own behaviour in the supervisory relationship? Are you more likely to blame others?

Specific issues

If you felt some level of discomfort in answering these questions, it could be that there are specific issues in your supervisory relationship that will need to be addressed. In the following section, some typical issues in supervisory relationships are discussed: game playing, mirroring, unmet learning needs and conflict. An issue that is likely to cause discomfort and perhaps conflict is unsatisfactory student performance. This is dealt with in more detail in Chapter 18.

Game playing

Game playing is a covert transaction in which one or more people have an ulterior agenda – usually to punish the other person or people – and is a negative expression of unmet emotional needs. In environments that are alienating, game playing is one way to survive (but not thrive!). Because games are based on dishonest or covert transactions, they never satisfy the real or underlying and sometimes legitimate needs. Neither party will win, but all involved and others, such as clients or other staff members, can certainly lose.

Game playing in placement thrives in environments in which some or all of these factors are present: responsibilities are unclear and there is no placement contract, there is no feedback or permission to express feelings or needs, or difference is not acknowledged.

As a student or supervisor, you might suspect you are in a game when:
- you frequently feel bad or uncomfortable with the same person or group
- you go into interactions knowing what you want, but always do what the other person wants
- you try to help someone and you end up feeling punished
- you never get to say what you really want, or what you say gets twisted.

Kadushin (1976) suggests that many of the games that are played in supervision act out the drama triangle. This concept comes from transactional analysis theory and describes the ways in which the three roles of persecutor, victim and rescuer can get passed around. These three psychological positions can be adopted during an interaction as a defence to avoid a range of feelings. Hughes and Pengelly (1997) argue that this dynamic is fostered by a persecutory environment, while Morrison (2001) suggests the drama triangle is an attempt to deal with the struggle for power that is present in much supervisory interaction. An example of the drama triangle follows.

Supervisor to student: *I just wanted to check that you were right for today.*
(The rescuer speaks to the victim.)

Student to supervisor: *Yes, of course, didn't we cover that yesterday?*

(To avoid being perceived as the victim, the student goes on the attack and adopts the persecutor role, putting the supervisor in the role of victim.)

Supervisor to student: *Well, there's no need to adopt that tone!*
                               I was simply checking.

(Responding to the perceived attack and put in the victim role, the supervisor adopts the role of persecutor and puts the student back in the victim role. Alternatively, the supervisor may, having been put in the victim role, choose to put the student in the position of rescuer and say something like, 'Yes, of course we did. I've just got so much on my mind, I wasn't sure this morning what we said.')

If there were significant differences between the supervisor and student in this example in terms of gender, age, ethnicity and so on, these transactions would need to be explored in the wider context of structured expectations and inequalities. The meaning of unhealthy processes, including games, needs to be understood at an interpersonal, institutional and societal level. Many supervisory games mirror discrimination as they are based on distorted assumptions and stereotypes and are exacerbated by role confusion, pressure, and threats to established patterns of thinking and behaving.

Game playing in supervision may be initiated by the supervisor, the student or both; however, even if one party has not initiated the game playing, they may have some responsibility for maintaining it – it takes two to play and the game may have different pay-offs for each party. Any problems in the supervisory relationship cannot be resolved while this is occurring.

Kadushin (1976) categorises the games that are typically played in supervision in the following way. If you experience some or all of the signals outlined above, you might want to consider whether any of these games are being played out in your supervisory relationship.

Recognising that these processes are occurring, and naming the processes, is the first and most significant step in assisting students and supervisors to no longer feel the need to use or be involved in such processes.

Purpose of the game	Game
Redefining the relationship (This game dilutes the power of supervisors to be critical of students' practice or behaviour.)	Treat me, don't beat me. Evaluation is not for friends. Let's sort it out over a drink.
Reducing power (In this game, students challenge the expertise and knowledge of supervisors.)	So, what do you know about it? If you knew Dostoyevsky like I know Dostoyevsky …
Controlling the situation (This game diverts attention away from the issue at hand because it may be threatening.)	I have a little list.
Heading them off at the pass! (In this game, students get supervisors off the track in order to avoid difficult or confronting situations.)	What you don't know won't hurt me. I wonder why you really said this? One good question deserves another.
Manipulating demand levels (In this game, students overstep professional boundaries in order to join with the supervisor and avoid issues such as negative feedback.)	You and me against the organisation. I know it's my session, but you look busy.

Mirroring

Mirroring or paralleling is the unconscious process through which the dynamic of relationships with clients or other people is reproduced in the relationship between the student and the supervisor. Mirroring stems from the way in which individuals, groups or organisations adopt unconscious defence mechanisms when confronted with stressful feelings.

This stress often stems from the distress felt by students who work with people who are poor, powerless and in pain, and from the helplessness on their part or the part of their supervisors to do anything about this distress. In the face of such stress, students and supervisors may deny, minimise, blame, project or rationalise feelings that would otherwise threaten to overwhelm them. If one aim of supervision is to help students maintain their objectivity, then supervisors must be alert to the mirroring process in supervision.

Morrison (1993) asserts that what workers cannot 'swallow' they 'spit out', using processes such as *denial* (He's such a competent worker, it's just not possible); *blaming* (If only you'd done what I asked you); *collusion* (I couldn't raise that issue, it would ruin my relationship with X); *minimisation* (It's nothing really); and *invalidation* (You haven't got enough experience to comment).

Strategies for game playing and mirroring

Exercise 2 comprises questions for students and supervisors to tackle unhealthy processes in supervision, based on the strategies suggested by Morrison (1993, p. 98). It is important not to discount your 'gut' feelings – they are telling you something important – and remember that everyone gets caught up in such processes at times.

EXERCISE 2

FOR THE STUDENT AND SUPERVISOR

ANALYSE THE SEQUENCE
Think about an unhelpful process in your supervisory relationship and consider the following questions.

1 How did this process start? What do you think it relates to (for example, issues of power inequality, other relationships affecting it)?
2 Who starts it?
3 If you don't start it, how do you get hooked into it?
4 What are the different stages you each go through?
5 How do you end up feeling?
6 Is there a hidden pay-off for either of you?
7 What does it allow you both to avoid?
8 How does it affect your practice?

It may be useful for you to check out what you think is happening with a trusted colleague or fellow student who knows you well. The following strategies to interrupt these processes can be used by supervisors and students in supervision sessions.

- Tell the other person that you are feeling angry, frustrated, and so on.
- Ask how the other person is feeling.
- Name the process you think is happening.
- Ask the other person who their behaviour or feelings most remind them of among their clients (or other people).
- Ask whether the other person has experienced this process before in interactions or in previous supervisory relationships.
- Explore what would happen if these processes were not occurring – what would be the costs or potential benefits?
- Clarify what you both want to achieve for the placement.
- Pool ideas for how your discussions could be more productive (for example, staying on the issue, listening to the other person, and so on).
- Agree to ground rules to which you both can keep.

- Make a note of the processes you have found effective in tackling challenges in supervision.

These processes need to be dealt with, otherwise they can become damaging to others in the agency, clients, and students and supervisors.

Unmet learning needs

Students may be uncomfortable about supervision because they believe that their learning needs are not being met. This checklist of frequently mentioned student needs, adapted from Shardlow and Doel (1996, p. 71), is a useful way of exploring whether unmet needs are a potential source of unhelpful processes in the supervisory relationship.

- Students need recognition of their existing strengths, so it is not assumed that they are 'starting from scratch' in everything they do.
- Students need guided practice. They can be given opportunities to practise skills in a controlled environment so they are not prematurely given responsibility.
- Students should not be placed in situations beyond their level of competence.
- Students need to be given the opportunity to learn complex tasks in small steps.
- Students need to observe practice in order to replicate it, otherwise they will have to rely on intuitive methods.
- Students need to feel that they can make a mistake without it having disastrous consequences.
- Students should be able to experiment with different learning approaches if the chosen methods are not working.

Strategies

Many of these issues can be dealt with before they become problems, if the placement is set up with clear agreements and processes for resolving difficulties, as outlined in Part 2 and particularly in Chapter 5.

Conflict

Conflict is an inevitable part of interaction with others whenever people are involved in promoting change. The way students and supervisors respond to conflict can prevent or promote an escalation of difficulties in supervision; however, some degree of conflict is inevitable.

Conflict in supervision is generally a result of a perceived difference of interests and values. It can be seen as a positive force, enabling new options to emerge and challenging negative ways of working. It may result in better communication, more clearly defined structures, more resources and a resolution of competing demands. If an equitable process is used to manage the conflict, there is an opportunity for growth and development. It is a negative experience, however, when it develops to the point that individuals and not issues are the focus for the conflict.

The way people interact in conflict depends upon their culture – that is, the shared meanings, knowledge and processes they use to perceive and interpret social realities. If there is a breakdown in these shared meanings, knowledge and processes, it results in conflict.

Carlopio, Andrewartha and Armstrong (1997) identify the four main sources of conflict as: personal differences (the conflict focuses on perceptions and expectations); poor information processes (the conflict focuses on misinformation and misrepresentation); role incompatibility (the conflict focuses on goals and responsibilities); and environmental stress (the conflict focuses on resources and conditions).

Sources of conflict can also be located in the roles or positions people adopt in their interactions with others. The source may be:

- *Organisational:* Are structures or procedures getting in the way, or is the physical environment an issue?

- *Cultural:* Are assumptions about class, gender or race, for example, causing conflict? Is the worker oblivious to or aware of the cultural norms of the other?
- *Interpersonal:* Are styles, behaviours or non-verbal messages making the conflict worse? Are the values of the people involved clearly at variance?
- *Intrapersonal:* Is the supervisor or student caught in an inner conflict? Has the situation triggered a transfer of feelings that belong somewhere other than the current situation?

Strategies

Conflict passes through a number of stages. Understanding the process of conflict assists supervisors and students to hear what the issue is and be aware of the approach the other is taking in response to the conflict. The stages of conflict are commonly defined as:

1 *Articulation:* Stating that the conflict exists and identifying the cause of conflict.
2 *Mobilisation:* Seeking out others or other information to support your point of view.
3 *Personalisation:* Picking on attributes of the person with whom you have the conflict in order to discredit them. This usually escalates the conflict.
4 *Redefinition:* Rethinking your options.
5 *Institutionalisation:* Institutionalising the conflict or its resolution.

A conflict will not necessarily pass through all these stages or in this order. The successful resolution of conflict usually requires that the issues, rather than the people, be addressed. That is, students or supervisors identify and respond to the messages that are being sent, without trading insults or attacking the other person. Using statements that start with 'I' rather than 'you' helps to keep students and supervisors on track. For example, a supervisor or student might say 'I get the impression that this is really important to you and it needs to be resolved', rather than 'You are being very pigheaded about this and digging in your toes'.

Summary

The supervisory relationship is no different from other forms of human interaction – a degree of discomfort, conflict, game playing and transference is to be expected at times, especially since the relationship between students and supervisors is inherently unequal and must be formed quite quickly, often in pressured and stressful environments.

Issues in this important relationship should not develop to the point where they prevent either or both parties from acting competently and effectively. Understanding the causes and processes of such problems can help students and supervisors to become aware of the problems and take action sooner rather than later – in which case, resolving the issues can be an important learning experience for both.

15

WORKING WITH DIFFERENCE

Introduction

Placements are an important opportunity to engage with different ways of viewing and acting in the world. They create a complicated set of relationships. At a minimum there are five sets of relationships: student–colleague or community members, student–supervisor, supervisor–client, student–training body and supervisor–training body. Any of these may be characterised by cultural and power differences. Where such differences devalue people, it is essential that students and supervisors try to understand the impact of this difference on their practice.

The different levels of power in society and their potential to be linked to discrimination in human services practice and supervision are explored in this chapter. Difference associated with inequality, as Thompson (1993) notes, occurs at three different levels: the personal, the cultural and the structural. Discrimination at the personal level is the result of the potential in people for stereotyping and prejudice. At the cultural level, it is a failure to appreciate the significance which different cultures ascribe to events. At a structural level, discrimination occurs if social forces are not taken into account and social policies maintain the status quo that privileges some at the expense of others.

Factors such as difference between urban and rural lifestyles, in levels of physical ability, in class and education, as well as in race, culture, sexual orientation, age and gender, influence students' implicit and explicit assumptions and values, their behaviour and how they represent themselves to the world. For example, Ryde (2000) suggests that people who come from an individualistic culture may assume that people in a more group-oriented culture suppress individual wishes. The group-oriented culture may assume that individual needs are best met by paying attention to the needs of the group.

Understanding ourselves

We all have a number of identities. Some are ascribed to us by society and may make us more or less powerful in social situations. Students will have explored these issues in their courses before going on placement; however, it is useful to review this in the context of placement, thinking about colleagues or clients. Students and supervisors should consider characteristics such as age, gender, sexual orientation, class, ethnic and cultural background, previous work and family experiences, sporting achievements, lifestyle, role as student or supervisor, and so on. The following exercise encourages students and supervisors to consider issues of power and identity.

EXERCISE 1

FOR THE STUDENT AND SUPERVISOR

1 List five characteristics that give you more power and five that give you less power.
2 Identify which of these characteristics are public aspects of your identity. If you can choose whether or not to reveal the characteristics, which ones do you tend not to disclose and why?

3 In your agency, do any characteristics in particular make you feel powerless? (Consider the extent to which you are marginalised or included, have your confidence and self-esteem raised or lowered, feel you have choices or are constrained.)

People tend to build relations based on similarities, but if workers ignore areas of difference they are in danger of perpetuating the institutionalised oppression they seek to address in their practice. It is important that differences are named and valued and the inherent power differential is recognised. If we are not aware of how these characteristics position us in society, then it is likely that we belong to the group in society with power, and that this power exists at the expense of those who are different (Doel et al. 1996, p. 52).

We also can learn from other cultures in ways that can inform and enrich our practice. For example, Māori approaches to juvenile justice, which involve shaming processes, have had effective outcomes with Anglo-Australian youth (O'Connor, Wilson & Setterlund 2003, p. 63). The main barrier to an equal exchange of ideas and practices is, perhaps, the inability of those whose backgrounds reflect the dominant culture to step outside their comfort zone and take on ideas that challenge their frames of reference.

Understanding difference

Consider the following scenario.

> I had gone shopping with Brian, a young man with a learning disability. We were working, at his request, on his budgeting skills and had spent time beforehand thinking about the various items that he needed now, and the things he would need to save for. It was pension day, a high point in Brian's life. When we arrived in the shopping centre Brian wanted to look at new CDs, although these had not been on our shopping list. In the store I tried to discuss with Brian how purchasing the CDs would affect his other plans, and indeed make it hard for him to get by for the next fortnight. He just was not interested. It was about *now*, having something that would give him pleasure. I gave up, but it was hard to share in his pleasure in the purchases.

The disparity here between what was planned and what actually happened has just as much to do with a culture of poverty as it does with Brian's learning disability. Although the student existed on much the same income as Brian, she knew that it was a temporary state of affairs. She had other ways to feel good about herself and did not share Brian's cultural understanding of money, gratification or sense of self-worth. Think of similar examples from placement in which unacknowledged cultural differences have got in the way of effective practice.

Age, gender and race can impact on the supervisory relationship, particularly if one person has characteristics that are less socially valued. An indigenous young female supervisor with an older male Anglo student may have to negotiate some issues for the placement to be successful. Similarly, students from minority groups face considerable challenges as they learn human service practice in the dominant culture. The following exercise, by Doel et al. (1996), helps students and supervisors to explore the dynamics of supervisory relationships in which either the similarities or differences between the student and supervisor are stronger.

EXERCISE 2

FOR THE STUDENT AND SUPERVISOR

Use the triggers in the box and think about the dynamics of a supervisory relationship in which the student and supervisor are similar in terms of their race, age, gender and ability. Then consider the dynamics if the student and supervisor are very different in these same characteristics.

making assumptions	support networks	fear
ethnocentrism	difference	power differential
ascribing expertise	dumping	collusion
political correctness	over-identification	stereotyping

How students evaluate the usefulness of theoretical approaches to understanding people and society and how change might occur is influenced by culture. In human service work, the commitment to redressing injustice and working together to address issues that unnecessarily constrain people's life choices, as well as demonstrating an abiding respect for people, should be universal. The challenge is to apply these commonalities in a way that is respectful of difference. Smart and Gray (2000) suggest that the following areas of cultural difference need to be considered during placement.

- *Individualism:* Anglo-Saxon cultures view individualism as a marker of maturity and believe that the individual is entitled to be self-determining and in control of his or her life. This view is not universal and in many cultures the focus on self is seen as a marker of immaturity. In such cultures, individuals must take account of their place in the family and their interdependence.

- *Spirituality:* Practice in human services in most Western countries is underpinned by scientific notions of human behaviour and social functioning in which the emphasis is on rational thought and deductive reasoning. As a consequence, little attention is paid to the religious and spiritual beliefs that influence the way people operate in and perceive the world. In other cultures, causes for individual and family problems may be found in the spiritual realm and perhaps attributed to physical features of the environment, and hence healing should pay attention to these dimensions.

- *Family:* Students are likely to meet families or family members who challenge their assumptions about family life. This may be a consequence of the reasons for which the families become involved with human services – for example, families supporting adult children with disabilities – or because of cultural differences.

- *Boundaries:* What constitutes appropriate boundaries between professional and unprofessional behaviour vary from culture to culture. This may relate to physical contact, the meaning of time and the ways time should be used, and the amount of social contact that is appropriate between the worker and the people with whom they work.

Ryde (2000) suggests the following exercise as a way of understanding cultural differences. It highlights the interaction of different elements and challenges you to think about difference in more than a one-dimensional way (pp. 39–40).

EXERCISE 3

FOR THE STUDENT AND SUPERVISOR

Locate yourself in relation to these four quadrants. (For example, you may come from a group-oriented culture that is high on emotional expressiveness, in which case you would place yourself at some point in the bottom left.)

Now think about how you understand human nature and locate yourself. Do the same exercise to think about how you relate to hierarchy and deal with conflict. Can you think of factors that are relevant to your situation?

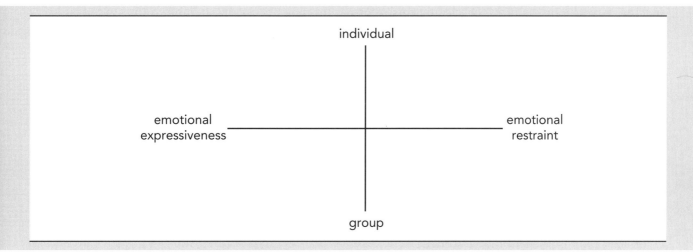

Sometimes placement brings students from minority cultures into contact with mainstream families and communities. Sometimes it provides an opportunity for students from the dominant culture to be more involved in the life of minority communities. There are significant issues for all concerned when people from minority groups are forced into contact with workers from different cultures, particularly in statutory contexts such as child protection, juvenile justice or mental health. Students need support to understand, for instance, which aspects of a situation relate to cultural issues and which relate to a specific family or individual. They also need to understand how intervention in people's lives, particularly that enforced by legislation, has the potential to do damage.

Students from minority groups and cultures may work with clients from the dominant culture and face both prejudice and their own lack of certainty about the prevailing cultural norms. Alternatively, they may choose to do placement in agencies that cater to a target group that shares their language and culture, but they may have to deal with other aspects of difference.

It is important for both supervisors and students to acknowledge the limits of their cultural knowledge and skills in general and the uses and limits of their cultural knowledge in particular contexts. They need to develop an awareness of their biases and prejudices, which may limit the options they make available to others.

Physical and mental (dis)ability and placement

A significant number of students, as well as supervisors, live with disabilities. There is not a great deal of information about placement for students with disabilities, yet it is an issue that needs to be discussed in negotiating placement. It is essential that a student's disability does not become the focus of placement. As for all students, the focus should be on the student's learning. Students with a disability need to achieve at the same standard as other students, although the means to achieve this standard may be different.

Disclosure

In planning placement, some students who have a disability that is not evident may choose not to disclose their disability, believing that this will restrict their choices and chances on placement. This is very understandable, but risky. It is highly likely that the moment of disclosure will come and perhaps damage the trust in the supervisory relationship. Also, the student may not get appropriate education and support, or may be asked to do inappropriate work by the supervisor or other staff. It is possible that the student or clients or community members may be put at unnecessary risk.

It is difficult for the training institution if it knows that a student has a disability to keep that information from the placement agency. Non-disclosure may introduce duty-of-care and ethical issues. At a pragmatic level, not telling agencies the student has a disability may have future implications for the training institution. It is much better if the student is in control of the process of telling a prospective supervisor about the specific issues he or she faces. Disclosing this information may be less threatening to the student if he or she has a sensory deficit or mobility or learning disability. The student may be more reluctant if he or she experiences a mental-health disability or has acquired brain injuries, particularly if the student is doing placement in a relatively small community.

Tension may result because the student understandably wishes to keep the information within as small a circle as possible, and therefore doesn't want to say anything until the offer of placement is almost sure, yet the supervisor may need to know this information before deciding whether to offer placement.

Cooley and Salvaggio (2002) identify possible obstacles for students with a disability on placement (pp. 54–5). To what extent do you think these might apply to your situation? Students could:
- experience stigmatising and labelling, restricting their options
- be limited in their choices for placements – the general shortage of placements impacts more on students with disabilities
- be seen more as a client than a student
- be viewed by the agency as an occupational health and safety risk
- experience negative attitudes from some staff
- not be taken seriously as an emerging practitioner if tasks are modified to take account of disability, or if the supervisor overcompensates
- have difficulties with the physical environment.

Students with disabilities who have met course requirements leading to placement have as much right as other students to an appropriate placement. However, some placements may not be suitable for students with certain disabilities. This is a reality for all students, whether they have a disability or not (Cooley & Salvaggio 2002, p. 57). For instance, some placement settings are in high demand and not all students who want to do placements in these settings will be able to. Cooley and Salvaggio (2002) also point out that there may be distinct advantages for agencies that are prepared to offer placements to students with disabilities, such as raising awareness of disabilities and reducing the barriers between the agency and people with disabilities.

Preparing for placement

Placement will be a success for everyone if potential challenges resulting from a student's disability are, as far as possible, identified and planned for. Training institutions can provide considerable assistance by supporting students with disabilities on placement practically and by identifying helpful teaching strategies. Planning for the placement will involve:
- understanding the impact of the particular disability on the student and being aware that this impact may change over time and in different circumstances
- negotiating appropriate tasks and determining any arrangements if the student's abilities are likely to vary or if they become unwell
- outlining the agency's expectations of the student in terms of the student communicating about his or her health status
- negotiating support that the training institution or disability support agencies can offer
- modifying aspects of the placement to take account of the student's disability, where necessary.

As with cultural differences, a student's mental or physical (dis)ability can magnify the power differences between student and supervisor and make it difficult for them to be clear about what is expected. The student is required to meet the same standard of performance as other students, although the placement tasks undertaken and the approach to teaching and learning may vary. The following exercise for supervisors will help them consider what may need to be modified in their agency if a student has a disability that requires this.

EXERCISE 4

FOR THE SUPERVISOR

1 To what extent could the working arrangements in your agency impact on someone with this specific disability? Can you modify these working arrangements, if necessary? (Don't assume that special arrangements will be required.)

2 What information do others in the agency need to know about the student's disability and who will let them know this information?

3 What modifications, if any, need to be made to the tasks the student is asked to do?

4 In what way might you need to change your approach to help the student to learn? (For example, if a student has head injuries that affect memory, taping supervision sessions so that the student can replay them may help.)

The following exercise gives students an experience of difference and increases their self-awareness. It involves the use of symbols such as photos and common objects or symbols that students make using plasticine. Strength cards, such as some agencies use with clients, could also be used as the stimulus. The exercise works best in a group but can be undertaken between the supervisor and student. A group has the added benefit of learning from others, and learning not to impose your own interpretations on the sense others may make of the topic.

EXERCISE 5

FOR THE STUDENT AND SUPERVISOR

Step 1   The student selects an object or card from the collection. Alternatively, the student can choose to make an object with plasticine.

Step 2   Without speaking, the student writes responses to the following questions.

1 Why did you select this object or card? Why did you make this object?

2 Looking at this object, what life experience comes to mind for you?

3 Name three feelings that arise in you when you look at the object.

4 What are you thinking now?

Step 3   Share your reactions with the supervisor (or group). The supervisor can ask about the meaning of the colours for the student today or always, and whether the pictures or words on the card influenced the student.

Step 4   The student should pay attention to anything that he or she chose to withhold during the exercise and notice if this occurred in this situation only or whether this is typical behaviour. If it is only in the current situation, what is the student learning about himself or herself or the situation?

If the exercise is done in a group, there is the added learning of not interpreting or imposing on another's choice or meanings given.

Difference – teaching and learning methods

Both students and supervisors need to pay attention to how difference affects their supervisory relationship, particularly in regard to power associated with difference. The power people have according to their broader role in society and by virtue of their personality can intensify or diminish the power they may have as students or supervisors in the supervisory relationship. The presence of a disability, or other structurally devalued characteristics, can amplify existing power issues. Teaching and learning methods used on placement must seek to minimise such power differences.

It is also important to acknowledge that students and supervisors are products of their own cultures and that they are not culturally neutral. What they should be aiming to achieve is an open approach to understanding the impact which difference makes to their lives and the lives of clients, their practice as human service workers, and their roles as teachers and learners on placement. This openness is not necessarily easy to achieve – people are often blind to their prejudices, and the issues related to difference are very complex.

The placement setting should also be considered: on what cultural, professional and legal assumptions is the setting based? The assumptions are often painfully obvious in agencies with statutory obligations that reflect dominant cultural views and where people from minority groups are over-represented in the client group. In these contexts, the system may be seen as racist and victim-blaming, but if supervisors and students are open to exploring these issues, it is a great opportunity for learning about discrimination and its effects, as well as learning to work within the system to minimise the effects of cultural prejudices on individuals. Think about other agencies in which there is a good fit between the culture of the organisation and the needs of those who use its services. How did this come about? Even though it is doing a good job, it may still exclude some people.

As newcomers to an agency, students may be more aware of the culture than supervisors who are used to it. Students often comment on how quickly they became 'acclimatised' to the agency, and their initial reactions, sometimes even negative ones, can be very useful to consider, as demonstrated in the following scenario.

> Sally arrived for her first day of placement at a busy adult mental-health centre and found her way through a throng of people waiting outside the front door. She waited her turn to speak to the receptionist in a full waiting room. She felt a sense of relief as a locked door was opened for her, but then had to face her nervousness at meeting the many people who staffed the centre.
>
> Two weeks later, Sally's supervisor asked her what it was like for her to come to the centre for the first time and find her way through all the people who were waiting for attention. The memory flooded back for Sally. She found it scary for many reasons: she felt anticipation and apprehension about her new placement and concern about her capacity to cope. She felt frightened of mental illness and she was aware of how cultural stereotypes had caused this fear. She was anxious about working with people who had very different experiences from her own, and she felt quite vulnerable and lacking in confidence. She was also concerned that she might be damaged by working with the clients and the overall experience of social work. The supervisor then asked her what it was like for her to enter the building now. Sally replied: 'I just love it!'

Sally's experiences can be interpreted as the shock of meeting a new culture and acclimatisation. Her supervisor introduces a reflective dialogue in which she recognises that Sally has experienced rapid change, part of which was Sally finding her feet in the centre. Sally could use her experience to understand how visiting the centre impacts on people with mental illness, as well as analyse what she recognised as her capacity to fit in with the group in power.

Strategies

Hawkins and Shohet (2000) describe different modes of supervision to assist students to work with difference. The following approaches to supervision may be useful.

- Discuss explicitly the cultural contexts of clients and seek to understand in cultural terms the issues raised by clients and the way they raise them.
- Discuss ways of responding appropriately in this context.

- Discuss the ways in which the cultural differences between student and client and/or the student and supervisor can be seen in the relationships.
- Explore the cultural assumptions made by the student and the supervisor.
- Discuss the social, organisational and political issues that are a result of difference.

In addition to being useful in supervision, these approaches can assist students in their work with clients and to make links between individual experiences and political and social structures. It is important for students to feel safe in discussions of their experiences, whether they come from minority or dominant groups. 'Their social identity and the extent to which they have internalised society's dominant ideologies and values will determine how they respond to issues of privilege and oppression' (Smart & Gray 2000, p. 103).

Summary

Human service practice aims to address structural and individual inequality by recognising the diversity of people's needs and empowering people who have less power and status in the dominant culture. Students need to understand how their attitudes and values are created by their own culture in order to develop awareness of prejudices and stereotypes that may inhibit effective practice with people who are different from them. Agencies also need to be aware of the impact that diversity and difference may have in placements and be prepared to modify their practice to ensure that students are given equitable access to learning opportunities.

16

ETHICAL AND LEGAL ISSUES

Introduction

Issues of legal liability and ethical behaviour have become increasingly clear and pressing in human services, as in society in general (Kiser 2000, p. 118). As human services become more diverse and decision-making more complex, practitioners must continue to recognise the legal and ethical foundations of practice and be aware of how legal and ethical issues impinge on their work. Placements bring together a number of systems: the agency that provides the placement, the clients who use the agency, the supervisor, agency staff, the student and the training institution. The relationships between these systems are to some extent mediated by legal requirements – duty of care, occupational health and safety, anti-discriminatory practice – as well as by laws and protocols governing the behaviour of citizens. The ethical and legal considerations of placement relate to implementing these rules in a just and fair way, as well as to the teaching and learning of the law and ethics.

To act illegally is to act unethically, and many forms of unethical practice are considered offences in society. In this chapter, the legal and ethical issues that underpin student placements, as well as how students can learn about ethical practice on placement, are considered.

Legal responsibilities

Each profession has its own set of standards or principles of conduct known as a code of ethics. Other obligations are determined by the legislation and various regulations that govern the activities in human service agencies (Alle-Corliss & Alle-Corliss 1998, p. 139). These responsibilities need to be recognised and understood by students and supervisors embarking on placement.

Responsibilities of the training institution

The training institution has an obligation to provide a duty of care to students and agencies – to act with due diligence, to try to pre-empt potential hazards and minimise risk to students and placement agencies (including staff and clients). At the same time, it must ensure that students are treated fairly, that anti-discrimination legislation is complied with and that students are placed in safe environments. In different jurisdictions, the legislation affecting these relationships varies. For example, in some states security checks are required for students who work with children, or people with disability.

Training institutions provide insurance that typically covers students, or those with whom they work, for personal injury while on placement, including while using motor vehicles on placement. It also covers professional indemnity to protect students for actions clients may take against them or, indeed, that students may take against placement supervisors. The training institution must ensure that agencies and students are clear about what is covered by the insurance.

Some training institutions formalise the relationship with the agency using a contract that specifies the duties and rights of the parties involved. This generally covers the topic of insurance. It is important to clarify matters before things go wrong. Exercise 1 assists students and supervisors to consider the responsibilities of each party involved in placement. Some questions may require research.

EXERCISE 1

FOR THE STUDENT AND SUPERVISOR

1 What are the responsibilities and rights of all parties involved in placement?
2 What is the nature of the agreement between your training institution and your agency?
3 What are the training institution's obligations towards students and supervisors?
4 What are the student's obligations to the placement agency?
5 To what extent are these obligations required by legislation?
6 What does the insurance for students and supervisors in your placement cover?
7 What are you required to do to be covered by this insurance?
8 If you are not clear about the answers to questions 1 to 7, what information do you need to find out?

Other legal issues that impact on the process of organising and conducting placements – fairness in the allocation of placements, the sharing of information by the training institution with students and prospective supervisors, and assessment of students' performance – are not easily dealt with in contracts.

Although training institutions and agencies are bound by anti-discrimination legislation, not all placements are available to all students: for example, some agencies that provide services to women don't take male students; some agencies require students to demonstrate at least a tolerance of specific religious beliefs; and some agencies may not offer placements to students with a criminal record. Agencies may specify characteristics they prefer: for instance, the student must have prior experience or should not be a school leaver or, alternatively, a mature-age student. In this regard, the agency's position in terms of the legislation may be tenuous.

Most training institutions have policies about placement for students with specific issues that are likely to impact on their experience of placement. For example, if a student with a history of mental illness requests a placement in this area, the training institution may suggest that the student discuss their experience with the prospective supervisor before placement is finalised. In this way, the institution is balancing its duty of care to clients and agencies with the student's right to do placement in an area that is important to them.

Other institutions may take the approach that students and agencies are entitled to make their own assessment about doing or offering a placement. Agencies may expect, however, that the training body will share relevant information about the student. Legally, students' confidentiality is protected, but agencies may argue that they are entitled to information about students so that they can make informed choices about whether a particular student will be acceptable to the agency clients.

It is important that training institutions and students are clear about what information is shared with prospective supervisors. It is common practice for the institution to use the information gathered from the students in interviews or in forms as a basis for allocating placements. In general, students should be aware that the information they provide can be given to agencies, unless students specifically request otherwise. However, legislation such as the *Privacy Act 2000* limits the amount of information that can be passed on and it is important for all parties to be aware of such requirements.

Equally, students are entitled to information about any safety, health and insurance issues with placements. Increasingly, students are being asked to be immunised against hepatitis and to be aware of particular health issues in particular agencies. Students may also argue that they are entitled to know something of the quality of the placement previous students have experienced in a particular agency.

Exercise 2 explores these issues for students and supervisors in more detail.

EXERCISE 2

FOR THE SUPERVISOR

1 What information has been shared between the different parties involved in placement? Do you think this is appropriate?

2 What types of information about the prospective student could present you and your agency with challenges?

3 What legal and ethical principles are most important in making your decision about taking a student on placement?

FOR THE STUDENT

1 What issues do you think are important to raise with your training institution and placement agency?

2 What legal and ethical principles underpin your decision about what information you would pass on to the agency?

3 What information did you have about the agency before you came on placement and was it adequate?

4 Do you think the information the agency was given about you was appropriate?

The reality for training institutions is that generally they don't 'own' placements. They are provided as a 'favour' by agencies who expect certain returns for the time and energy put into providing placement. If the training institution determines that the requirements of the agency are discriminatory, and they are unable to get the agency to change, the institution may choose not to use the agency or to fall into line. They are unlikely to take the matter further.

Consider the following scenario. The questions in Exercise 3 are based on this scenario and ask supervisors and students to consider how they would deal with complex issues.

S. is ready to do her final placement. S. comes from a reasonably large regional centre and she wants to do her final placement there. She had considerable difficulty in a previous placement and was moved to another placement setting because the personal problems between her and her supervisor could not be resolved by the liaison person from the training institution. Eventually S. met the course requirements and passed the placement.

S. believed that her first supervisor was prejudiced against her because S. is gay and her supervisor continually asked her how her sexual orientation was impacting on her work. S. thought this was inappropriate. Her supervisor believed that S. developed inappropriate relationships with clients, that she promised more than she could deliver, and that she could not be trusted to tell the supervisor what was happening with her clients.

S. does not want the report from her first supervisor to be sent to her prospective supervisor, as she feels it will prejudice the supervisor and not give her a fair chance of passing.

EXERCISE 3

FOR THE STUDENT AND SUPERVISOR

1 How would you deal with this situation if you were the liaison person at the training institution?

2 To what extent would your approach be influenced by legal requirements, your values or knowledge of the field?

3 What would be the implications if your decision turns out to be inappropriate?

Although training institutions provide guidelines for assessing students on placement and may be actively involved in this process, a number of issues, discussed in more detail in Part 6, make the interpretation of these guidelines difficult.

Responsibilities of the agency

Once a placement is established, a range of ethical and legal issues – related to the duty to protect students and clients and to use assessment criteria in a fair way – should be considered by the agency and supervisor.

Duty of care to clients

Agencies have a duty of care to clients and should consider the following guidelines when offering placements to ensure that their clients will be protected.

- The agency should feel reasonably certain that the student has the skills required for work with the clients.
- The agency should ensure that clients are aware that the person they are seeing is a student. The clients must agree to this.
- The supervisor should agree with the student on a process to ensure that the supervisor knows about the work done with clients.

It is clearly stated in most agreements between training bodies and agencies providing placements that supervisors are responsible for the work done by students and, in turn, students are obliged to keep their supervisors informed of their activities with colleagues and clients. Supervisors are equally obliged to ensure that reports on work are appropriate. This is a straightforward process when the relationship between the student and the supervisor is open and the student is competent to do placement tasks. It becomes more of an issue if there are problems, in which case it may be time to contact the liaison person appointed by the training institution.

In general terms, if a student acts inappropriately with a client, the student must be withdrawn from contact with clients and probably from the agency. However, students and supervisors are also obliged to exercise caution in making negative comments about students, supervisors or institutions, as defamation laws may apply. It is better to focus on the facts rather than make broad generalisations when making an assessment of either a supervisor's or a student's behaviour.

Duty of care to students

As discussed in previous chapters, students usually have less power and control over what happens in the agency; therefore, it is important to protect students by providing fair and consistent treatment. In particular, supervisors must be mindful of the following issues.

- *Be aware of the limitations of a student's ability.* Students should not be asked to perform work for which they don't have the knowledge or skills, or be sent into situations in which their safety is at risk. They should not be given inappropriate responsibility for decision-making or for the running of a project or agency. A good example is that of a first-year student who was told to drive a bus of adolescents to a function. In addition to feeling concern about driving a large vehicle, the student felt uncomfortable about being given responsibility for the safety of a group whose behaviour was very antisocial.

- *Try to give students useful learning opportunities.* Students' time should not be consumed by tasks that don't meet the educational requirements of the course. However, it is reasonable to ask students to do some of the less skilled tasks that staff share, such as answering telephones or getting milk for morning tea.
- *Ensure that the student's quality of work is adequate.* Supervisors are liable to ensure that the student's work is of a competent standard by observing the student's work or asking colleagues to do so, by requesting and reading reports, by regularly discussing practice issues with the student, and so on.
- *Don't neglect the student.* Students require supervision to oversee and guide their practice and to ensure that the clients' needs are being met. Supervisors must provide back-up supervision in their absence.
- *Inform the student about confidentiality requirements.* Supervisors must spell out the circumstances in which information about clients and the agency can be shared and with whom. Students need to understand agency protocols such as getting written permission from clients, if necessary, and disguising the identity of clients and staff when talking about their work with other staff or students and in field seminars.
- *Ensure that the student's work is assessed fairly.* Supervisors are liable if they fail students unjustifiably, as failing will have professional and financial implications for the student. Hence, training body protocols and principles of natural justice should be followed.

Generally, human service placements have relied on goodwill. By ensuring that statements of goals and objectives and evaluation criteria are clear to all parties, problems are usually avoided. However, as cases of malpractice become more common, human service practitioners and agencies must be cognisant of the legislation that underpins their practice. In turn, students on placements must understand the important legislation pertaining to most settings and practice areas – for example, child abuse and neglect, permanent care, domestic violence, family law, social security, sexual harassment and assault, mental health and disability.

Evaluating students

An important aspect of duty of care for students is how supervisors and agencies assess their performance. Exercise 4 assists supervisors to examine their assessment processes to see whether they are being fair to their student and have taken account of the rights and responsibilities of both parties. Students are asked to consider whether they are clear about the assessment process. These processes are examined in more detail in Chapter 18.

EXERCISE 4

FOR THE SUPERVISOR

1 How well was the student prepared for placement? What is a reasonable standard of competence, given the student's level of preparation?

2 Was your agency able to respond to the needs of the student on this placement?

3 Were you able to offer an adequate placement at this time? Did you have sufficient time and skills for the task?

4 What evidence do you have for passing the student on assessment criteria?

5 Do you think that the assessment criteria are clear? Do the criteria adequately measure the student's level of competence?

6 Is there a clear appeals process if there are problems with assessment? What would you need to do to prepare for an appeal?

Ethical practice

Reflection about ethical issues involves systematic exploration of how we ought to act in relation to others – what we see as right or wrong, or good or bad. Our moral framework in our relationships with others and the way we interpret society are underpinned by our values. Ethics and values influence our choices when a range of actions is possible and determine how we exercise power.

Failure to meet the legal obligations of placement also constitutes unethical practice. Ethics are at the heart of the student–supervisor relationship, and attending to ethical issues is a way of coping constructively with the power imbalance in this relationship and the complex nature of each of the roles. The supervisor needs to model ethical practice and to provide a context in which ethical issues can be identified and discussed.

Ethical supervision

As previously discussed, supervisors have a duty of care for their clients and the student. They are guided by the laws of society and the policies and procedures of their employer and the training institution. Codes of ethics provide guidelines, but practitioners still need to exercise professional discretion.

Clear agreements about rights and responsibilities, as well as what will be required for students to be successful on placement, are necessary to clarify the boundaries and expectations of supervision. This is discussed in more detail in Chapter 5.

The ethical principles that underpin worker–client relationships are also relevant to supervisor–student relationships (Corey, Corey & Callanan 1998, pp. 12–13). Some moral principles that should direct the relationship between the supervisor and student, as developed by Briggs and Kane (2000, pp. 132–6), are explored in the following section.

- *Autonomy:* the promotion of self-determination. Supervisors should assist students to develop their capacity to make informed choices about their practice, within organisational and legal limitations. Issues arise when students don't have the capacity to make sound choices – that is, their choices may compromise clients or the agency or, perhaps, their own futures. The challenge for a supervisor is that it can be difficult to gauge a student's competence for a given task and, in some contexts, the individualism inherent in the principle of autonomy is not always appropriate in contexts in which other rights may override those of the student.
- *Non-maleficence:* do no harm. Supervisors and students should not do things that, intentionally or otherwise, put clients or themselves at risk. This is a basic principle in all human service work. In the context of placement, students should not take on work they are not competent to do, and supervisors should ensure that students are not put in risky situations.
- *Beneficence:* promoting good for others. The focus of all parties on placement should be on facilitating the growth of the student and clients. The principle of beneficence depends on cultural definitions of what is 'good' – in professional terms, some broad goals will be agreed to, but there may be debate as to how to put these into practice in particular situations.
- *Justice:* providing equal opportunities to all regardless of age, gender, ethnicity, disability, class, religion, sexual orientation or cultural background. Not all human services are just, and this can be challenging

for students and their supervisors. The principle of justice also requires that students are treated consistently, fairly and impartially, particularly in relation to the supervisor's assessment of their practice.

- *Fidelity:* making honest promises and honouring these commitments. This is a basic principle in most occupations; in placements it requires the student and supervisor to be committed to meeting the obligations they have to each other or renegotiating the obligations if conditions change significantly.
- *Veracity:* being truthful. It is difficult to be entirely truthful on all occasions, but students and supervisors certainly should not mislead others by omitting important information or falsifying information. Both should operate on the basis of informed consent, so that supervisors agree to a student's plan knowing the student's intentions. Students are entitled to know supervisors' opinions of their performance and on what the opinions are based.

Students and supervisors could think of an example from their experience in which they have been conscious of applying these principles or where they have experienced difficulties in meeting the expectations raised by each principle.

Both in practice and in the supervisory relationship, students and supervisors may be faced with ethical problems or disputes that require resolution. These principles may assist them to think through these disputes, but in practice there are few absolutes. Emotions play a part in the way disputes are resolved, however well these principles are applied. Therefore, it is important to draw on the views of a third party – perhaps the training institution's liaison person – early on.

The ethical basis of practice

In discussing practice, it is important to pay attention to the ethical base of human service work, as well as its knowledge and skills. The discussion about integrating theory and practice in Chapter 9 also applies to learning about the ethical dimensions of practice. In the following scenario, the student discusses his lack of acceptance of, and therefore respect for, a committee member in a particular situation recognised by reflecting on his practice.

I had prepared quite well for the committee meeting. H., the chair, had contacted me to let me know what he hoped to cover, and I had done my homework. Finally we seemed to be under way now that all the structures were in place. Maybe J. would not be able to dominate the meetings with her long, rambling discussions about what the area used to be like. I was wrong. J. had the bit between her teeth. She took exception to the way the council people had treated her when she went to get the planning information. H. got short with her and I found myself doing the same. I remember the thought dashed through my head, 'I'm not surprised you got short shrift at the council, you silly old woman.' Later, I was pretty ashamed of myself, and only hope that J. didn't notice my reaction – she does a lot of work and people trust her.

The student noted that he reflected broader attitudes to denigrating older people, particularly older women, and that these attitudes had made it seem all right, at least temporarily, to run the risk of hurting J. and perhaps what the group was trying to achieve. In Briggs and Kane's (2000) terms, the student compromised on the broad values of justice and beneficence by treating J. as troublesome rather than troubled. More specifically, the student failed to demonstrate respect and did not treat her equally to others, largely because he adopted the culturally sanctioned stereotype of older people as being of less worth than younger people.

In reflecting on this scenario, the student learns about the interaction of behaviour and attitudes and raises questions about what constitutes appropriate and reasonable behaviour.

A profession's code of ethics is a guide for professional behaviour and outlines what it means to be a member of the profession, protects people who use services from incompetent practice, and protects workers from malpractice lawsuits. The Australian Association of Social Workers' *Code of Ethics* (1999) states that when a worker seeks to promote justice and fairness, reduce barriers, and expand choice and potential for all persons, the worker must pay special regard to those who are disadvantaged, vulnerable, oppressed or who have exceptional needs. Understanding this aim will influence a practitioner's professional behaviour. For example, a practitioner works with a group of young people, some of whom are being excluded by other members of the group. The practitioner considers that the young people being excluded are in the most vulnerable position; therefore, the rights of those doing the excluding are secondary. The practitioner feels that the only ethical thing to do is to advocate on behalf of the excluded members, even though it could be argued that all young people are disadvantaged in society.

Agencies often have similar codes of conduct, which provide a framework for thinking through situations encountered on placement. Exercise 5 helps students to identify this framework.

EXERCISE 5

For the student

Read any relevant codes of ethics or conduct and think about how these should direct your practice.
1 Are there any differences between your agency's codes and the codes of your profession?
2 Which aspects of these codes are harder and easier to apply in your agency?
3 Why is it hard or easy to apply them?

To think about the ethical basis of your practice you need to link specific events with general ideas and principles. Banks (2001) outlines four principles for human service practice, none of which are straightforward in meaning or in their implications for practice, but are a useful framework. It is important that this framework reflects your cultural situation, so you should consider whether these principles, written by a British author, are appropriate to your situation.

- Practitioners must respect and promote individuals' rights to self-determination by creating an environment that assists people to be more self-determining. However, there are very real limits to self-determination in many welfare systems – it is not always morally right to promote one person's rights at the expense of others.
- Practitioners should promote welfare or wellbeing by improving the interactions between individuals and the society they live in. However, there is always the potential for conflict between welfare for the individual and welfare for the majority.
- Practitioners should strive to be equal in their treatment of others, to provide equal opportunities and to aim for equity in outcomes.
- Practitioners should apply the principle of distributive justice (justice based on need, rather than 'just deserts'). This is a challenge for workers, as they are often gatekeepers between the resources and people who need those resources.

It is likely that there will be ethical issues in all practice situations. For example, if a worker advocates for a client on a waiting list for public housing to be moved up the list, using their knowledge of policies, it raises ethical issues because in doing so the worker has pushed others down the list. Ethical problems can arise when a worker knows what to do but feels uncomfortable doing it: for example, taking a child into care. To students on placement, such ethical problems can be very confronting. Taking the following steps may help students to cope with such situations.
1 Define the ethical issue(s). In ethical dilemmas workers are confronted with a choice between two mutually exclusive courses of action: for example, a worker may be bound to confidentiality but feel a

duty to warn others about a client's behaviour. A worker may want to distribute resources based on a client's merit or need, rather than distribute the resources in equal shares. The way the issue is defined gives the worker a clear direction and encourages them to explore the situation further.

2 Gather useful information from books, from the Internet, or by analysing the situation itself or discussing it with others. Take the time to explore at least some of the many perspectives on the issue(s).

3 Identify broad ethical principles that could guide action. A number of writers define different sets of principles (see, for example, Beauchamp & Childress 1994; Loewenberg & Dolgoff 1992). The principles previously outlined by Briggs and Kane (2000) and Banks (2001) may also be useful.

4 Refer to your profession's code of ethics or the agency's code of conduct for guidance.

5 Think about the client's world view and hopes, society's values and your values. Quite often it is the worker's values that have the most impact on how situations are defined and resolved, yet reflective practice depends on your ability as a worker to take these factors into account and subject your values to the scrutiny of others.

6 Define your options and arrive at a resolution. The options must be real and possible. In reflecting on the ethical basis of your practice, you need to keep an open mind and entertain a range of possible outcomes.

Think about a situation from your practice and apply these stages, or do the same for the following scenario.

Mrs D. is 94 and lives alone in her own home, which has very basic facilities. She is a pensioner with a small amount of savings reserved to pay for her funeral. She is now very frail and at times her memory is not reliable; however, she has not been diagnosed with dementia. Mrs D. is almost blind and can only walk with assistance. She spends most of her day in bed and gets assistance with meals, washing, shopping and dressing from a community agency twice a day. She is determined to stay in her own home and seems prepared to accept the loneliness that goes with her lifestyle. Mrs D. has one daughter who lives reasonably close. The daughter maintains regular contact and does a range of practical tasks. She has a history of mental illness and finds her mother's situation very stressful. She is constantly worried that her mother has fallen or that someone has broken in. She is often on the phone to the community agency pushing them to withdraw services so that her mother will be forced to go to a nursing home and she won't have to worry. At the same time, the agency is finding it increasingly difficult to maintain the level of service to Mrs D., who gets more than any other client, due to the increased demand for community care.

Summary

The onus is on students and supervisors to be cognisant of the legal requirements for human service practice and to work in an ethical and reflective manner that reflects the broad social values of justice, fairness, autonomy, equality and equity, as well as personal and agency values. The formal legal requirements and codes of ethics and conduct should be clearly outlined by the training institution and the placement agency and be agreed to by supervisors, students and the training institution in some form of contract or agreement.

17

ROLES AND RESPONSIBILITIES OF THE TRAINING INSTITUTION

Introduction

Agencies provide a valuable educational role for human service courses. Students and supervisors can look to the training institution to provide resources and support for placement and to undertake certain tasks. This is particularly important in the current climate in which there is an ever-increasing focus on productivity and agencies receive minimal support for supervising students.

In Chapter 2, some of the factors that prospective supervisors need to consider before agreeing to take a placement are outlined. In addition, agencies should consider whether the staff capacity and resources of the training institution are adequate. Courses vary enormously, so supervisors should decide how much support they will need and whether the institution is able to match these requirements. For instance, an experienced supervisor may feel confident to take responsibility for the development of the learning agreement but may require input from the liaison person about how the student can be included in an ongoing community project.

The training institution has three main responsibilities: to outline the structure for the teaching and learning framework for placement; to provide back-up where necessary to ensure that a placement remains viable; and to offer support to students and supervisors if any difficulties arise.

The teaching and learning framework

Although human service training institutions vary considerably, students and supervisors can expect the training course to provide the following support structures:

- *Orientation and preparatory seminars:* these should ensure that supervisors and students are clear about their responsibilities; some programs also offer debriefing and reflection sessions after placement finishes.
- *Training:* general training about the placement experience for new supervisors, and more advanced or specific training for experienced supervisors.
- *Course syllabus:* should be provided to supervisors so that they understand placement in the context of the total learning environment.
- *Clear written documentation for agencies, supervisors and students:* details performance expectations and guidelines.
- *Liaison person:* the formal link between the training course and the agency, and promotes and monitors the placement.
- *Agreement between the training institution, student and agency:* Outlines the legal requirements and responsibilities, including grievance procedures.
- *Criteria for evaluation:* see Chapter 18 for more information.
- *Student seminars during the placement:* to help students integrate learning from placement with classroom teaching.

- *Clear procedures for students who are unable to reach a pass standard:* see Chapter 18 for more information (AASWWE 1991, p. 126).

Resources

A major dilemma for human services training courses is their dependence on the practitioners and agencies to offer placements, when both training institutions and agencies are struggling with their own workplace issues about doing more with less (Cleak, Hawkins & Hess 2000, p. 160). It is not unreasonable for an agency to negotiate for resources from the training institution in order to create or sustain a viable placement or to supplement the agency's resources. Collaborative partnerships between training courses and agencies can provide considerable resources in terms of research and educational exchanges.

Some of the useful ways that the training course can contribute to innovative learning opportunities in a placement are:
- providing off-site supervision if supervision is not available within the agency, or if problems arise, such as sudden illness or a crisis in the agency
- providing access to oral, written, audiovisual or technological materials to enrich and enhance students' and supervisors' teaching and learning
- giving input of the staff's specialist knowledge and skills so that the agency and student can complete placement tasks
- offering access to libraries, computers, workshops and research staff
- providing agency staff with workshops or access to course subjects either free or at a reduced rate
- carrying out extra liaison visits to support placements with difficulties, such as repeat placements.

Liaison

The liaison person is appointed by the training course to assist students to achieve a worthwhile learning experience and to support the supervisor in his or her teaching role (AASWWE 1991, p. 128). This person is an employee of the training program and provides personal contact during the placement and has responsibility for verifying and recommending the final grade. As each training institution has its own requirements for the liaison role, it is only possible here to talk about expectations in general terms.

The liaison experience may vary from meetings for a 'cup of tea and a chat', to formal sessions in which there is a tight agenda and the student and supervisor are 'interrogated' by the liaison person. The expectations of the liaison person will vary according to the requirements of the different training courses and the circumstances of the placement – whether it is a full-time or part-time placement, first or final placement, and so on. Unfortunately, it is often not until the placement develops problems that the supervisor and student explore the broader role of the liaison person.

The responsibilities of the liaison person

The general functions of liaison, adapted from the School of Social Work and Social Policy (2003a) at La Trobe University, are as follows:
- *Monitoring and evaluation:* The liaison person has an important role in assessing, in conjunction with the students and supervisors, the quality of the student's placement experience and the extent to which the aims and objectives of the placement have been achieved.
- *Education:* The liaison person is a link between classroom teaching and agency practice. Liaison visits should broaden and enrich the educational experience in order to optimise student learning.
- *Support and problem-solving:* At times, the placement experience creates difficulties that require outside intervention. The liaison person should be accessible to both students and supervisors for support

and advice. The liaison person can be directive with either students or supervisors to ensure that they undertake the required tasks for the successful completion of the placement.

Structure of liaison

The tripartite relationship between the student, the supervisor and the training institution ideally will be one in which there is open and shared communication. The liaison person is at a disadvantage, as he or she will not see much, if any, of the student's work in the agency yet is still responsible for assigning a grade for the placement (Royse, Dhooper & Rompf 1993, p. 50). Therefore, students and supervisors should provide as much evidence of the student's work as possible.

Supervisors and students should have access to their liaison person between formal meetings for consultation and to discuss issues of concern. As the level of support offered may vary between training institutions, this should be discussed at the outset of placement to avoid disappointment or confusion.

Liaison meetings

Liaison meetings are an opportunity for students and supervisors to reflect on the progress of the placement, to discuss any concerns and points of difference, and to review learning goals and achievements. Both students and supervisors may be somewhat anxious about these meetings because they usually involve assessment.

It is likely that students will have had contact with their liaison person in the classroom, and this may have set up positive or negative expectations. The following scenario illustrates how this can impact on a student's experience of placement.

> Mai noted in her diary that she had been quite concerned that her liaison person, Juan, would find plenty to criticise. She had always been wary of him at her training institution and thought he was quite intolerant of people who did not express themselves clearly. She wrote: 'I am determined to be organised, to be clear about what I am doing and to leave him as little room as possible to be critical.' Later she noted: 'Well, I'm pleased I was prepared but he almost seemed like a different person to the one I know in the classroom! It was really helpful having him go through what was expected, and he had some good ideas about how I could make the most from this placement – I might even ring him up if I'm stuck!'

Sometimes students and supervisors collude to keep the true state of the placement from the liaison person because they fear having to examine the difficulties more than they fear continuing with the current arrangement. A typical scenario follows.

> The liaison person at the training institution was interviewing a student for her second placement, having liaised with this student on her first placement. The liaison person had been concerned about what was happening on the first placement and had gone back to do an extra visit, but had not been able to get to the bottom of the problems. At the interview for the second placement, she started by asking the student what had happened on her first placement. The student burst into tears and described how difficult it had been. The liaison person asked the student why she hadn't said anything, and the student replied that she couldn't talk to her supervisor about it – the supervisor just changed the subject if the student objected to anything, and she seemed to be under pressure from her senior and didn't want any more challenges. The experience had been terrible for the student, and the liaison person had been unable to help.

Establishing clear expectations about liaison helps to overcome some of these issues. It may be the case that in some placement settings the student and the supervisor always have time on their own with the liaison person, as well as meeting together. If this is not the case, if the liaison person asks to see them separately it may signal that there are problems. Clarifying these expectations at the outset should prevent such misinterpretations.

The first meeting

The first liaison visit should occur when the learning agreement has been formed, at least as a draft, and the student and supervisor can offer some examples of the student's work. The agenda for the first visit could include the following areas for discussion and negotiation.

1 *Overview:* The student and supervisor share general information about the agency, orientation program, and any highlights and concerns arising from orientation. The student should be encouraged to take the lead in this discussion so that both the supervisor and liaison person can gauge how well the student has engaged with the agency and understood the setting and agency tasks.

2 *Learning agreement:* The student and supervisor introduce the learning agreement. The liaison person reviews and endorses the agreement and suggests any necessary changes to meet the training institution's expectations, and considers whether the main evaluation criteria are covered and whether the tasks are realistic and balanced.

3 *Placement experience:* The student describes the tasks undertaken and indicates any achievements and constraints on learning so far. The liaison person asks if there are any potential areas of concern that could interfere with the achievement of the student's learning goals. The liaison person asks questions like 'What has been developing well?', 'What is presently proving to be a challenge?' and 'Are there any concerns about the learning at this stage?'

4 *Future planning:* The liaison person asks, 'What do you need from me at this stage?' The supervisor and/or student may request additional resources or support, and the liaison person clarifies his or her availability and outlines any constraints on offering resources or support. All parties discuss the agenda and timing of the next meeting, then close the meeting.

The example on page 171 of a liaison report can be used to discuss and record the progress of the first meeting.

Subsequent meeting(s)

In the subsequent meeting(s), the focus will be on doing a midway evaluation of the placement and reviewing the work achieved to date.

1 *Placement experience:* The liaison person asks questions like 'What have you mainly been involved in doing?' and 'What are the main strengths of this placement so far?' All parties need to discuss whether modifications to the learning agreement – due to agency constraints, student performance, and so on – are needed. The liaison person considers if the proposed changes present any issues for the completion of the placement.

2 *Review of achievements:* During this meeting, the liaison person reviews the student's achievements in relation to the learning goals. The student presents his or her work in the form of project or case summaries, reports or examples of practice. The liaison person asks questions like, 'How do you think you have developed so far on the professional level?', 'How have you applied theory in a placement task?', 'Have you experienced a critical incident on your placement and can you share what this was about?'

3 *Future planning:* The liaison person and supervisor affirm the learning that has been achieved and identify, in conjunction with the student, what still remains to be done. The liaison person asks questions like 'What do you need to address for the remainder of the placement?'

Student ....

Agency ....

Date placement commenced ....

Date of visit ....

Number of days absent from placement

The learning agreement has been discussed and finalised   Yes/No

If the learning agreement has not been finalised it will be done by .... and forwarded to the liaison person.

The progress of the placement has been discussed and there are no issues or potential problems with either the learning opportunities offered by the placement or the student's performance
Yes (*Go to signatures*) / No (*Complete 1.1–1.3*)

1.1   The following issues have been identified:

....

....

....

....

....

1.2   The following strategies to address these issues have been agreed on:

....

....

....

....

....

1.3   Review of progress on implementation of strategies will occur on .... by means of:

....

....

....

....

....

Liaison person .... Signature ....

Date ....

Supervisor .... Signature ....

Task supervisor .... Signature ....

Student .... Signature ....

Adapted from the School of Social Work & Social Policy, 2003, La Trobe University, Bundoora.

The final meeting

The focus of the final meeting is on reviewing, assessing and terminating the placement. Chapters 18 and 19 cover these processes in more depth. The liaison person and supervisor give the student explicit feedback as to whether he or she has achieved the level of competency required for the placement. The liaison person asks questions like 'How has this placement differed from what you initially expected?', 'What do you think went well?', 'Why did it go well?', 'What do you think went less well?', 'How might you do it differently if you were to do it again?'

It is appropriate for the liaison person to give feedback on the contribution and quality of the supervision. If it is the policy of the course for the liaison person to provide written progress reports, the student and supervisor should be able to request a copy. This report should clearly document any concerns or issues that have been raised and any decisions about how they will be addressed (Bedford 2003).

Summary

The training institution is responsible for resourcing agencies and students, and for providing educational support to enhance students' learning opportunities. The liaison person offers agencies and students an outside perspective on placement, assisting the student and supervisor to review and evaluate the placement and resolve issues. The liaison person is a valuable resource for agencies, providing back-up supervision, if necessary, and ensuring that the placement remains on track in terms of the student's learning and the supervisor's teaching.

EVALUATING, ASSESSING AND FINISHING PLACEMENT

How will you know as a supervisor or student when the standard of work is competent and the goals of placement have been achieved? Evaluation should ideally identify the growth and learning that have been achieved and where further improvement is needed.

In Chapter 18, a framework for evaluation to assess both students' and supervisors' performances on placement is outlined. The difficulties of the assessment process and how to deal with issues such as managing failure are explored. In Chapter 19, the processes for finishing placement well are reviewed.

6

18

ASSESSMENT AND EVALUATION – STUDENTS AND SUPERVISORS

Introduction

The term 'evaluation' is used to refer to the ongoing process of feedback about a student's work, while 'assessment' refers to the process used to decide on the standard of work or to defined events such as the mid-placement assessment. Evaluation and assessment must be closely linked so that there are few surprises in the assessment phase because the ongoing evaluation has been clear and focused and has identified opportunities for students to develop their practice.

Evaluation occurs from the first week and is ongoing. It is not confined to the periodic formal sessions scheduled for this purpose (Brennan 1982, p. 76). An approving nod or a shake of the head are all subtle forms of evaluation.

It is not only the student who is assessed. Supervisors are also evaluated during the placement process, at least informally, by the student, the training institution and, to some extent, by their colleagues and superiors in the workplace (Brennan 1982, p. 46).

Resource and time constraints make supervisors more reluctant to take on the burden of assessment (Hughes & Heycox 2000, p. 95), yet it is crucial that graduates who intend to work in human services have been assessed as competent. The supervisor stands in the middle of a tangle of organisational relationships, facing the demanding task of being both assessor of and advocate for the student (Beddoe 2000, p. 44). While it may be easy for the supervisor to facilitate the student's learning, the process of examining, judging and identifying faults in the student's practice, which is part of the educator's role, may be more difficult (Hughes & Heycox 2000, p. 92). Although avoiding this process may help the supervisory relationship in the short term, it will not help the student learn and may put the supervisor at risk in terms of duty of care to clients, the community and the profession.

Evaluating students' practice

The processes of evaluation and assessment in placement assume that there are normative standards for achieving competence as a practitioner, yet how do students, supervisors and training institutions know when students have achieved competence? Is it when students demonstrate progress towards competent practice and show the ability to learn? Is it when students achieve all of the learning goals outlined in the learning agreement? Is it when students can develop good working relationships with a range of people? Does it make a difference if it is a first or final placement?

From these questions, it may be clear that judging the value of practice or behaviour is not an easy process. So, before a student can be evaluated, what is good practice and how it will be measured must be decided on and agreed to from the outset. This is an important part of negotiating the learning agreement, as outlined in Chapter 5. Training institutions provide guidelines on how to evaluate students' practice. How supervisors carry out this evaluation in the context of their agencies is an important aspect to consider.

The liaison person from the training institution can help students and supervisors to determine clear and achievable goals for evaluation.

For evaluation to be effective, it must take account of the following four requirements:

- The criteria for what will be evaluated are well developed.
- The evaluation tools and procedures for evaluation and assessment are clear.
- The evaluation documentation has been clearly articulated.
- The measures of practice have been agreed to by all relevant parties.

The evaluation criteria

As reported by Doel et al. (1996, p. 167), a number of studies have identified a lack of clear criteria as one of the difficulties in assessing practice competence. Criteria to evaluate skills, knowledge and values should be specific and consistent.

An example of criteria developed to assess one aspect of the placement curriculum used by the School of Social Work and Applied Human Sciences at the University of Queensland, Australia is shown on page 176.

Note that most of the criteria described above are based on process evaluation – whether the student can apply relevant knowledge and skills and follow accepted procedures to develop effective relationships – rather than evaluation of outcomes for the client group. Such criteria are more commonly used in human services, as measures of outcomes are usually too hard to define and test (Brennan 1982, p. 80).

In this module, students' practice is evaluated on a continuum from 'unsatisfactory' to 'high standard' practice. There is a large gap between the two extremes and there will always be disagreement about which point in the middle of the scale should be judged as 'good enough'. To evaluate students fairly, supervisors and training institutions need to develop standards that define what constitutes good, competent or unsatisfactory practice.

This example comprises a learning goal from the 'Doing' framework of experiential learning, as outlined in Chapter 2, Exercise 5. The goal is for students to develop skills in being assertive in group situations. Examples of specific criteria are identified that supervisors and students could use to determine the degree to which students are assertive in group situations.

Unsatisfactory practice	Competent practice	Good practice
The student remains silent during most group forums and avoids opportunities to contribute.	The student is able to present ideas in staff meetings but remains intimidated by the senior staff.	The student is able to chair a meeting and behave assertively when handling conflicting views of members.
The student lacks confidence in expressing their point of view in supervision.	After rehearsing in supervision, the student feels more comfortable about presenting cases in team meetings.	The student actively participates in staff meetings.
The student is unable to contribute at a professional level at team meetings in which the student's clients are discussed.		The student is able to express and defend his or her ideas in group supervision, even when these ideas differ from those of other students.
		The student contributes ideas and opinions in team meetings in which staff from other disciplines are present.

Module 3   Relationships

Work completed

Tick the required tasks completed at this stage (as specified in the curriculum for Module 3).
Written work:

_____ process report

_____ process report/reflection sheet/analysis of critical incident

_____ an inventory of skills/knowledge

Observation by liaison person on two occasions:

Date _____ (1st occasion)

Date _____ (2nd occasion)

Notes on any other tasks undertaken in this module

....

....

....

....

Evaluation of performance at this stage

Circle the appropriate point on this continuum for this student.

Students are able to develop constructive, purposive relationships with people in a range of roles (for example, colleagues, service users, community members) and with people who are different from themselves.

1	2	3	4	5	6
Unsatisfactory			Pass		High standard

Students can describe how their behaviour might have contributed to developing such relationships.

1	2	3	4	5	6
Unsatisfactory			Pass		High standard

Students are able to make links between this understanding as to how they have developed purposive relationships and relevant theory about knowledge, skills and values.

1	2	3	4	5	6
Unsatisfactory			Pass		High standard

Students are able to describe and evaluate the effectiveness of the patterns and principles evident in their interactions.

1	2	3	4	5	6
Unsatisfactory			Pass		High standard

Students are able to modify their behaviour in the light of this understanding where necessary.

1	2	3	4	5	6
Unsatisfactory			Pass		High standard

Comments on achievements and issues relating to this module

....

....

....

....

These considerations are helpful in evaluating students. Is it acceptable for a student to pass placement even though he or she has not demonstrated competent practice for all criteria? How is the overall assessment determined when the student has demonstrated examples of both unsatisfactory and competent practice? Often supervisors only consider these issues when a student's performance is of concern, but it is helpful to prepare for this particular challenge. Grades in placements are usually 'pass/fail' or 'satisfactory/unsatisfactory'. This reflects the difficulty in making a precise assessment, and the grades do not reflect the considerable variation in students' abilities, placement sites and supervisory styles.

It is important to seek guidance from the training institution and colleagues about assessment issues. Often the overall view the supervisor has of a student impacts on whether faults are highlighted or overlooked. If the supervisor predominantly focuses on a student's faults, it may be necessary to review the future of the placement as the student is less likely to progress in such an environment and the supervisor could feel uncomfortable about assigning work. If the supervisory relationship does not encourage the student to learn, the student may have to be placed in another agency or the student and supervisor may be able to identify, with assistance, what has gone wrong so as to create a more productive teaching and learning environment.

Learning on placement is a developmental process and some minor 'mistakes' should be overlooked in this context. Willingness and ability to learn, openness to examining practice, and a capacity to form good working relationships are the key indicators that a novice practitioner is likely to be successful. However, the training institution and the supervisor may judge some mistakes to be too important, particularly if they involve unethical practice such as inappropriate disclosure of information, or inappropriate relationships with clients or staff, and the placement may be terminated.

Principles of evaluation

Evidence suggests that supervisors tend to rely on retrospective self-reports by students as the main vehicle of assessment of a student's work (Shardlow & Doel 1996, p. 141). This can be a limiting and sometimes unreliable approach to assessment, especially as students tend to be unduly self-critical or sometimes too optimistic about their real abilities.

Shardlow and Doel (1996, p. 157) suggest four principles to guide whatever method of assessment is put in place for the placement.

- *Accuracy:* What methods of learning are used to assess the student's competence, and do they accurately reflect the student's ability? For example, does the student's process record show the ability to reflect on practice or the ability to accurately remember information?

    Using the learning goal used in the previous example (develop skills in being assertive in group situations), the student's ability to chair a meeting or present to a team meeting may be a reflection of his or her confidence rather than a demonstration of assertiveness skills, particularly in situations of conflict.

- *Fairness:* Students usually feel pressure to perform competently from the start of placement. Although it is impossible to eliminate this pressure, discussion about and understanding of the assessment criteria will promote fairness. For instance, supervisors and students might agree that for the first interviews the focus will be on encouraging the student to do the best job they can, rather than on drawing conclusions about the overall capacity of the student. Shardlow and Doel (1996, p. 159) suggest that sampling students' work in a planned way can free them to take risks in other unassessed areas of their work.

- *Efficiency:* Teaching and learning methods on placement, including evaluation methods, should make the best possible use of the time available.

- *Congruence:* There should be a good 'fit' between the methods used, the student's actual practice and the evaluation of that practice. For example, a student undertaking groupwork as one of their placement tasks may rely on client feedback as the main method of assessing their learning and competence, but this may not be adequate to evaluate the student's broader interpersonal skills or satisfy curriculum requirements.

Evaluation and assessment measures

The standard the student is expected to achieve on placement will be interpreted differently according to whether it is the standard of the training institution, the agency, the industry or profession, or the student. It is unlikely that all parties will agree.

Training institutions are likely to take professional standards or statements of competency in industry standards into account in setting the assessment criteria for placements, but there may be debate about how accurately or how thoroughly they have done so. The training institution and the agency may have different opinions about what students need to learn. At a personal level, students may find some of the tasks set by the training institution or agency difficult and therefore cannot achieve their own standard. To deal with this, the learning agreement should spell out the criteria for learning and assessment (see Chapter 5).

In some training courses, placement may be graded on the basis of assignments, journals or exams in which students reflect on their learning on placement. The advantages of these assessment methods are that teachers can compare and contrast work, and students can identify themes in their practice, consolidate learning, and make links between practice and the theory that underpins it. The disadvantages are that these methods rely on the student's capacity to conceptualise practice and don't really evaluate what was actually done on placement.

It is very important to use written assessment methods to support decisions about the student's level of performance. It is both a skill that students must develop and a requirement of the training institution. The institution will nominate core tasks that all students must complete for assessment.

Brennan (1982, p. 92) notes that the procedures for collection and analysis of assessment data must be spelled out. These procedures help the student to build a 'portfolio' of completed learning tasks, which will give the student confidence and will ensure that evidence of achievement is readily available at assessment times.

In addition to any written methods, evaluation ideally should combine direct observation of practice with assessment of the following skills:

- how students access and use feedback
- how students make sense of what they have done and explain their practice to others
- whether students work constructively with organisational staff as well as clients and communities.

The observations other people have made about the student will be taken into account in the evaluation process. It is a good idea for the supervisor to ask whether colleagues who wish to comment on a student's activities are prepared for the information to be passed on to the student.

Evaluating supervisors' practice

This process can be more difficult for training institutions and students than student evaluation is for training institutions and supervisors, for two main reasons: (1) if the evaluation of the supervisor is more negative than positive, the agency may be unwilling to take future placements; and (2) it is difficult for anyone external to the supervisory relationship to observe supervisory practices.

Nevertheless, students and training institutions do evaluate the quality of placements, and these evaluations affect decisions about whether agencies will be requested to take future placements and about the type of students referred for placement. In Chapter 19, a framework for students to evaluate supervisors is outlined.

Some training institutions require students to give formal feedback to supervisors. This is another opportunity to reflect on and review the placement in general and the supervisory relationship in particular. Students need to consider how to offer this feedback so that they are comfortable, as they may fear reprisal if the evaluation is negative. Some ideas about how to give constructive feedback are covered in Chapter 7 (pp. 66–8).

The evaluation criteria

Most training institutions don't have specific criteria for evaluating supervisors, so students, liaison staff and supervisors may need to develop their own. Clearly, the feedback of students is the main focus of assessment and evaluation.

At this stage, it will be helpful for supervisors to review the material in Part 2 about expectations of placement and supervision. Part of evaluation for supervisors will be to decide whether they have met these expectations. Taking students on placement is often part of supervisors' professional development – they progress from being competent practitioners to testing their ability to teach practice. They also may be trying their wings in a management role. Taking a student may reflect their commitment to the profession, their interest in expanding their skills or improving their curriculum vitae, or their need for assistance to complete a particular task. How they evaluate themselves will be influenced by their reasons for supervising placements and this will impact on the experience students will be evaluating.

The same continuum of 'good' to 'unsatisfactory' used to evaluate students can be applied to evaluating supervisors. It is important for supervisors to pay attention to supervisory practices that they consider 'good' as well as 'competent' in rating themselves. Self-reviews of supervisor's behaviour (pp. 61–4) are also useful.

Supervisors should try to focus on their behaviour and the opportunities and constraints of the agency, rather than on the characteristics of the student. For example, in considering the typical criterion 'Ability to be student focused', supervisors might conclude that, due to a particularly stressful time in the agency in the middle of placement, they were not able to respond to the students' learning needs when there was the opportunity to do so.

The criteria outlined below are broad, and supervisors might wish to expand them to suit their context. For example, the criterion 'Ability to be student focused' could comprise indicators such as their flexibility in allocating work, their ability to negotiate with other staff for work for students, their ability to assess students' learning needs, their capacity to vary the teaching methods used, the quality of their preparation for supervision, and so on.

Supervisors and students can use these broad categories and criteria to assess the quality of placement supervision.
- The match between the student's learning needs and teaching resources and skills of the agency:
    - The work extends student's learning.
    - The agency and supervisor are able to be student-focused not just agency-focused.
    - The levels of vulnerability and risk experienced by the student facilitate rather than threaten learning.
    - The agency politics and resources support a student placement.
- The qualities of the supervisory relationship:
    - openness
    - 'adult to adult' communication patterns
    - respect for each other
    - trust in each other.
- The teaching skills of the supervisor:
    - uses flexible teaching methods to facilitate the student's learning

- makes links between specific situations and broad practice or ethical principles
- links research findings to practice
- identifies goals and measures progress against these goals.
- The level of enjoyment and the gains from the experience:
  - Supervision is a source of energy and excitement.
  - The student has an increased understanding of practice.

Forms for evaluating supervisory experiences vary from simple checklists to rating scales and detailed narratives. The following evaluation to be completed by students is adapted from Collins, Thomlison and Grinnell (1992, p. 199). This format may be equally useful for the supervisor to give feedback to the student.

- *Availability:* Did the supervisor keep to the scheduled supervision times? Were the supervision times frequent enough and of sufficient length? Did the supervisor assign someone else to supervision if he or she was going to be absent?
- *Approachability:* Was contact with the supervisor encouraged? Did the supervisor make use of informal opportunities for teaching and learning?
- *Knowledge base:* Was the supervisor open to learning from you? Did the supervisor direct you to useful sources of learning?
- *Able to direct learning:* Was the supervisor able to guide and direct your learning, particularly at the start of placement? Were any tasks too simple or too complex? Did the supervisor suggest relevant assignments? Did the supervisor help to integrate your learning with your classroom knowledge?
- *Use of self:* Was your supervisor able to analyse your abilities and help you understand your strengths and weaknesses? Were the teaching techniques used by the supervisor effective?
- *Expectations:* Were the supervisor's expectations too high or too low? Did the supervisor clearly explain his or her expectations for placement?
- *Feedback:* How would you assess the feedback you received in terms of quality, regularity, fairness?
- *Conflict:* If you experienced conflict in the relationship, was the supervisor able to resolve this effectively? Was the supervisor able to listen to your point of view?
- *Level of autonomy:* Did the supervisor allow you to take risks you were comfortable with and support you to do this? Was this in balance?
- *Evaluation process:* Was the evaluation ongoing and open? Was it fair?
- *Finishing with the agency and staff:* Were the staff, including your supervisor, supportive? Did you feel comfortable? Did the agency offer a comfortable learning environment?

In the instance that students feel that the supervisory relationship was unsatisfactory, it might be helpful to use Rosenblatt and Mayer's (1975) characteristics of poor supervision to assist students to identify the underlying problem. The four styles can be located along two continua as shown.

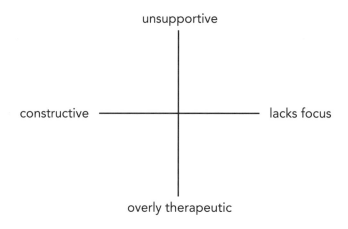

Just as supervisors are required to provide examples to back up their assessment of students, the students' review and evaluation of the supervisor in the agency context needs to be based on specific evidence. It is important for students to recall any instances that challenge the conclusions they reach and include them in the final assessment.

Evaluation and assessment measures

Supervisors often ask training institutions to provide feedback on their work with students. This can be difficult since the liaison person is unlikely to have seen supervisors in action and is relying on the impressions of the student and the supervisor's self-reports. When students raise issues with staff at the training institution they may not want the discussion to go any further, and, unless the matter is serious, this feedback is often not given to the supervisor.

The more open supervisors can be in discussion about what they have been trying to achieve and their successes and failures, the more confident the training body will be about sending students in the future.

The supervisor's team leader and peers can be a useful source of feedback on supervisory practice. Taping supervision and reviewing the tapes using the formats in Chapter 7 can give supervisors some hard data on what they did and did not say and can also be a basis for feedback from students on the usefulness of the session.

All interactions can usefully be scrutinised. A quick passing comment may have had more impact – positive or negative – than an hour of carefully prepared supervision. Unless students are encouraged to give supervisors feedback, they may never know the impact they have on students.

The same range of standards used by students may also set the benchmarks against which supervisors evaluate their practice: the training institution's standards, professional or industry standards, agency standards and personal standards.

However, unlike the standards applied to a student's performance on placement, the standards for supervisors may be less developed or only apply to ideal settings. In many settings, supervisors have to compromise between the standards. For example, supervisors might have to ask students to spend time on a specific project even though the students have requested more variety in their placement, or supervisors may find that their time to prepare for supervision is compromised by the activities of the agency.

Supervisors should identify their standards about whether they are doing a 'good enough' job as a supervisor. It can be easy to get stuck between meeting the needs of the agency, clients and community members, and their own standards and those of students. Having a clear set of achievable objectives is one way of avoiding the trap of trying to be all things to all people. Exercise 1 gives supervisors some ideas about how to identify these objectives.

EXERCISE 1

FOR THE SUPERVISOR

Rank the following tasks from most to least important. Then answer the questions for each task, followed by the general questions at the end of the exercise.

To spend sufficient time with the student on tasks designated by the training institution

How much time does this represent in terms of the overall supervision time available?

To prioritise the student's learning needs ahead of what is more convenient for the agency and clients

What principles do you use in resolving any conflicts between these competing interests?

To meet my needs in relation to offering a student placement

How would you describe these needs?

To extend the student's learning beyond the competencies required by your agency

How good is the fit between the agency's day-to-day work and your idea of professional practice?

1 Has your ranking changed? Why/why not?

2 How do you resolve conflict between the needs of the student and the training institution, the needs of the agency and your own needs as a supervisor?

In Chapter 7, some methods to record supervision sessions were outlined. These records can be reviewed to look for patterns. Supervisors could ask for feedback from students on a particular aspect of each session. Supervisors might, for example, enquire about their effectiveness in each of the supervisory functions – educational, administrative, management and support. They might review this feedback in light of the learning agreement and assess whether they are consistently assisting students to meet their goals.

Training institutions often run sessions to train supervisors and, in well-developed courses, the institution will give supervisors various activities that can be used to evaluate their practice. Supervisors should try to make explicit links in their records on supervision between their behaviour, their assessment of what happened and their goals for supervision. Completing assessments of students is a good opportunity for supervisors to review their practice and set goals based on their evaluation.

Assessment events

Ongoing evaluation processes should be linked to the assessment events, in which issues raised by evaluation using the criteria discussed earlier can be summarised. Sometimes supervisors may not be aware of the issues that haven't been discussed with students until all the criteria are reviewed together.

The training institution usually outlines a timetable of assessment events showing how and when assessment and accompanying documentation should be completed. Assessment typically occurs mid-placement and at the end of placement, although liaison meetings are another means of evaluating students' progress. Supervisors and students may also decide on other assessment events, such as a presentation, completion of a project or evaluation of a program.

These events give all parties the opportunity to review the direction, pace and progress of learning. Without them it is too easy to keep busy without reflecting on the learning that has occurred (Hughes & Heycox 2000, p. 88).

Mid-placement assessment

The purpose of the mid-placement assessment is to review the learning to date against the goals set at the beginning of placement, to highlight the student's achievements and identify ongoing learning needs, and to revise the goals to direct the remaining time of the placement.

The mid-placement assessment may indicate that some goals are unattainable or unnecessary. This could be disappointing for the student because they have to accept that their enthusiasm for running a group, for instance, must be redirected to acquiring more experience in another learning area. Other goals may have become crucial in the light of the mid-placement review.

Feedback from the supervisor to the student in the mid-placement assessment, as far as possible, should be clear, objective, specific and timely. It is easier for a student to accept and use feedback if it balances the positive and the less-than-positive aspects of practice and focuses on the issues rather than the personality of the student. If any party believes that the negatives of a particular placement outweigh the positives, then the mid-placement review is a good time to check if the placement continues to be viable.

Final assessment

The purpose of the final assessment is to make a decision about whether students have met the placement criteria of the training institution. In general, students need to demonstrate that they have achieved a satisfactory level of competence.

The assessment report may have a long shelf life. If this is the student's first placement, the report may be sent to their next supervisor and it will probably be used in planning the next placement, or students may use the report to gain credit in further studies.

It is important that what is written is discussed as openly as possible, that critical and positive comments are made on the basis of specific examples, and that the limitations of the agency with respect to the student's learning are noted.

Deciding to fail a student

One of the more difficult situations for supervisors and students occurs when students are assessed as not meeting the training institution's assessment criteria. This situation can be dealt with more 'cleanly' if the standards required for passing placement were clearly articulated at the outset, students were given appropriate tasks and adequate support, supervisors regularly evaluated their own performance and modified their behaviour to meet students' needs, and supervisors documented what had been tried and what was achieved.

Some reasons as to why it is difficult for supervisors to judge that a student is not ready to practise, adapted from Doel et al. (1996, p. 181), follow. The supervisor may:

- be aware of the academic, financial and personal consequences for the student
- develop a closeness to the student and an understanding of his or her difficulties
- lack confidence to assess the student in the absence of reliable and useful criteria for evaluation
- lack confidence to assess the student for fear that their judgement may be biased
- have trouble describing the basis of the student's learning difficulties
- have difficulties pinpointing evidence to back up concerns
- lack support from agency colleagues or program staff
- fear that the student's failure reflects on his or her teaching abilities
- fear a negative reaction from the student
- be aware of the 'all-or-nothing' effect of the pass/fail choice
- experience a lack of sufficient rigour in the assessment process.

Supervisors form relationships with students and have been trained to be non-judgemental and to accept people and avoid imposing their values on them (Collins, Thomlison and Grinnell 1992, p. 170). Then supervisors have to judge students and impose professional standards and values on their performance.

As students become aware that their performance is seen as problematic, it can be difficult to continue to share their work honestly with their supervisor. Supervisors may feel obliged to focus on the problematic areas of students' performance, and it is difficult for students to hear that there is anything positive in their work. If students continue to fail to demonstrate that they are able to learn from their experience, it is difficult for the supervisor to continue to allocate work so that the student can learn. A cycle of failure is established that reinforces the negatives and makes it hard to find a way forward. It is important that the process of evaluation is assessed at this point, as well as the performance of students and supervisors.

Strategies

It is never easy to decide that a student is not at a pass standard, but the following checklist will help supervisors feel more confident that they have been fair. The methods and strategies discussed have been outlined in more detail in the chapters referred to in the following points.

- *Agreements:* The learning agreement and supervision contract are specific ways to discuss, record and examine the competencies expected for placement. The value of the agreements lies less in the paperwork than in the processes by which they have been established (see Chapter 5).
- *Open communication:* If there has been good communication in supervision and the teaching and learning environment is open and supportive, there should be no surprises for either the student or the supervisor (see Chapter 8).
- *Feedback:* Students and supervisors need to be given specific feedback about their performance so that they are clear about what work or behaviour is problematic and needs to be addressed (see Chapter 7).
- *Records:* It is unfair to comment on behaviour if it had not already been raised as an issue in supervision. Students and supervisors are advised to record such issues because students may have grounds to appeal a fail grade if they are not told about a problem at an earlier assessment (Hughes & Heycox 2000, p. 88). (See Chapter 7.)
- *Consultation:* Supervisors should not have to make the decision about failing a student on their own. Seeking the opinions of task supervisors, colleagues who have had supervision experience, senior staff and program staff broadens the range of ways that a student's performance can be evaluated.

The training institution will be involved in the assessment process and should have established processes for handling such situations. These will be outlined in the documentation provided by the institution. A supervisor's final assessment is usually a recommendation to the training institution, which is ultimately responsible for the final grade. Depending on the policy of the training institution, the student may be given an extended placement or failed.

To test out the extent to which the process of assessment and evaluation respects the rights of students, supports supervisors and follows due process, students and supervisors could complete the following exercise, adapted from Doel et al. (1996, p. 161).

EXERCISE 2

FOR THE STUDENT AND SUPERVISOR

1 What do you think was fair and unfair about the way your work was assessed?
2 What other methods would you have liked to use as the basis of assessment?
3 Were there any aspects of the assessment that were too positive or too negative?

Summary

It is important to remember that there are numerous steps to achieving competency. Placement should begin or continue the journey rather than be the final stop, so supervisors, students and training institutions should have realistic expectations. The assessment and evaluation process is three-way, and each party – student, supervisor, liaison person – should feel equipped to both give and receive feedback about performance. This should be done in an open, constructive manner in which the constraints on agencies, supervisors and students should be acknowledged and the strengths of the placement highlighted. If an effective and ongoing evaluation process is carried out, the focus of assessment will be familiar to all and will build on the learning.

19

FINISHING WELL

Introduction

The end of placement should feel like a plane landing – it should be relatively smooth with a sense of arrival and an understanding of where you are (Shardlow & Doel 1996, p. 101). There is plenty written about beginning placement, but discussions about ending placement tend to focus on the final evaluation rather than the actual process of finishing. The ending should be as important as the beginning and is an opportunity to model good practice in the management of change-oriented relationships (Beddoe 2000, p. 53).

The term 'termination' is generally used to describe endings in human service contexts (Kiser 2000, p. 227). In this chapter, some of the emotional and practical aspects of terminating the placement effectively are discussed.

How to begin the ending!

The ending of placement should be anticipated from the outset. It does not need to be over-emphasised, but there should be an explicit acknowledgement of expectations about finishing with clients, projects and staff. Agencies may have specific requests of students, such as asking them for feedback to the agency about its placement processes or doing a presentation at a staff meeting. Such requests should be documented in the learning agreement.

Ford and Jones (1987, p. 144) suggest that the following tasks should be carried out as part of termination: students should complete their work properly; deal with feelings about finishing, work through any unfinished business and ritualise the end through a ceremony. In addition to these tasks, students and supervisors must carry out the final assessment and give feedback to each other. Chapter 18 outlines how to do this in more detail.

Completing the work

Most placements necessitate student contact with service users and service providers, as well as agency staff. Ideally, agencies will have already informed clients and staff about the length of time students will work at the agency so they will have anticipated the end of the relationship.

Before leaving, students must inform their supervisors and relevant staff about the status of their cases, projects and research activities, and any tasks that needed to be handed to other workers.

Sometimes supervisors and students may lose interest towards the end of placement and prematurely disengage from teaching and learning tasks. This can have negative consequences for the final assessment if the supervisor views this as the student neglecting his or her responsibilities, or if the student believes that the supervisor is abandoning his or her role prematurely.

Towards the end of placement, the final assessment will probably dominate the content of the supervision sessions. Even if evaluation has been ongoing, students and supervisors will still need to complete the assessment documentation. Beddoe (2000) suggests that it is useful for supervisors to try and balance the requirement to complete this documentation with helping students to view the assessment as a milestone in their development – part of their continuous learning for the future (p. 52).

Dealing with feelings

Kiser (2000) emphasises the importance of intensive review and reflection as the student leaves the placement and offers some general guidelines for positive termination. These guidelines follow the general principles for terminating within helping relationships (p. 227).

Awareness of previous experiences with termination

Students have experience in endings and saying goodbye to friends, family members, places and people, and have established patterns of emotional reaction and behaviour in these situations. Students will feel more in control by approaching termination with some self-awareness about how they handled these previous situations: did they avoid, confront or minimise the event?

Some relationships will be more significant than others, and students may feel regret and loss about leaving them. Reflective tools such as think sheets and journals, and other learning and teaching methods such as role-playing, can help prepare students to handle difficult partings.

Awareness of needs and wants

Ending relationships often creates conflicting and mixed emotions, the result of which is that the students may experience a wide range of reactions to the simultaneous task of staying engaged and letting go (Kiser 2000, p. 11). Supervisors and students can share similar feelings of wanting to move on and feeling tired of the responsibilities of the role, yet wanting to continue to enjoy the work. When students have trouble letting go, they may postpone termination tasks by:

- minimising the significance of the ending and hence avoiding making plans for farewells, transferring tasks, and so on
- denying the end of the placement and so missing the opportunity to participate in the termination events
- prematurely disengaging from the placement by withdrawing their interest from agency activities.

To assist students to overcome their resistance to terminating placement or to just dealing with the ending, supervisors should encourage them to reflect on and express their feelings. Supervisors should ensure there is time and space to acknowledge and share these feelings as the end of the placement gets closer. Some strategies to do this include adding the topic of termination to the supervision agenda and suggesting that students devote time to reflecting about termination in their journal or diary. Students can discuss this process with the liaison person from the training institution or can raise it in field seminars to hear how other students deal with ending.

It is imperative that both students and supervisors have the opportunity to review the experience. In thinking back over the placement, they will identify certain learning experiences that were momentous in shaping their learning – even if the experience was unpleasant or seemingly insignificant at the time (Kiser 2000, p. 232). It can be difficult to recognise the value of a particular event when it is happening, so this time at the end is crucial.

Working through unfinished business

The extent of any unfinished business with the placement will largely depend on the nature of the supervisory relationship and the experiences that supervisors and students have shared together. It can be a time of emotional intensity; even when the placement journey has been relatively smooth, disappointment, residual anger or resentment may not have been explicitly expressed. In deciding whether to raise unresolved issues in the end stage, supervisors and students should consider the following questions: Is now the appropriate time to bring up these issues? Will it enhance the learning for both parties? Will it result in any unintended or negative consequences?

For example, a student may have been unhappy about the fact that placement did not offer enough exposure to different kinds of practice. The supervisor may have hoped that the student could have worked more autonomously on tasks. This feedback would be valuable information for both and would not pose particular difficulties if it had been raised and worked on throughout placement. Would it matter if the student or the supervisor decided not to give feedback about this? Would both gain if the feedback is given?

Doel et al. (1996) suggest that it is sometimes preferable to wait until after the placement is completed to give feedback. A written report may be a constructive way to offer sensitive feedback.

Giving and receiving critical feedback can be awkward, but at this stage in the relationship it is hoped that the student and the supervisor have both practised the positive techniques of giving and receiving feedback and are able to be open to any ideas to keep improving their practice.

Ritualising the end

A formalised ceremony or ritual that marks the finish of the placement is a useful strategy to assist the student, the supervisor and the agency deal with some of the issues raised above. Some supervisors mark the occasion with a lunch, dinner or afternoon tea; sometimes the student will organise something as well. These are public occasions where contributions are acknowledged and people are thanked.

Effective termination of placement offers students the opportunity to reflect on the dreams, fantasies and fears that catapulted them into the placement and gives them insights that will enhance their future career decisions.

Evaluating performance

The final activity for terminating placement is the formal evaluation of the performance of the supervisor and the student. As with clients, acknowledging the learning and growth that has occurred reinforces a sense of pride and completion. Tools such as the journal, process records and the final assessment will endorse this process by recording the completion of tasks against the initial learning goals. The processes and tools of evaluation are discussed in Chapter 18.

Planning for the future

The review process should also involve discussion about the next placement or future employment if students are finishing their training course. In the former situation, there will still be learning goals to be achieved; and in the next placement, students' work will need to demonstrate greater depth and supervisors will need to give students more autonomy and develop more complex learning goals with them. In the final assessment, there is usually a section in which the knowledge and skills the student needs to develop further are outlined.

By now, students will have an idea about the work of other agencies. This exposure can help students to form tentative goals for the future. At the end of placement, they are in a position to think about where they want to do their next placement or which work settings will complement and extend their learning. Exercise 1 helps students to consider the next step after placement.

EXERCISE 1

FOR THE STUDENT

Think about the following questions in light of the placement you are about to complete.

1 Would you prefer to work in a smaller or larger agency?

2 Would you like to work with a different client group or use different practice methods or focus on other issues? If so, what are your preferred options?

3 Have you identified through self-reflection areas of practice that you particularly enjoy or in which you have particular shortcomings?

4 What skills and knowledge can you transfer to a new setting?

5 What specific learning issues have been identified in this placement that require more attention in your next placement?

Students and supervisors may find it useful to reread Chapters 1 and 2 and consider some of the initial questions raised about choosing placement settings and preparing for placement. Exercise 2 requires students and supervisors to answer similar questions, but with the benefit of hindsight.

EXERCISE 2

FOR THE SUPERVISOR

1 Were you ready to have a student?

2 What did you learn about your teaching style?

3 What did you learn about your approach to practice?

4 Which learning tasks were particularly helpful and which ones did not work as well as expected?

5 What did you like most about teaching the student?

6 What did you find difficult about teaching the student?

7 Which questions will you definitely ask at the pre-placement meeting next time?

8 Was your agency able to offer a stable working environment for the student?

9 Was your agency able to offer appropriate tasks for the student, or were there too many constraints (for example, legal requirements or accountability issues)?

10 Were the agency staff able to support the student and offer appropriate task supervision or co-supervision?

FOR THE STUDENT

1 What did you find out about yourself as a learner?

2 What do you now know about your knowledge, skills and value frameworks?

3 Did the placement offer the structure and work that you wanted and needed to experience?

4 Did you have a 'good enough' match with your supervisor? If not, why?

5 Are there any attributes that would be essential for your next supervisor to have?

Your career

An important task at the end of this placement is to consider the meaning of the experience for your future, both professionally and personally (Doel et al. 1996, p. 228).

Some students may feel elated and more passionate and committed to the human service profession, but others may feel disillusioned and confused about the meaning of their placement experience for their future in this area. If a student is experiencing the latter, talking to the supervisor, a trusted person or a staff member from the training institution may help. Sometimes, these emotions are symptomatic of work exhaustion and tiredness, especially if the student has been juggling work, domestic tasks and placement.

Exercise 3, adapted from Doel et al. (1996, p. 229), may be helpful in reflecting on the placement experience and whether a career in the human services is the best choice for you at this stage in your life.

EXERCISE 3

FOR THE STUDENT

Answer the following questions.
1 Why did you choose to work in human services?
2 What did you enjoy about the work in this placement?
3 What did you not enjoy about the work in this placement?
4 Do you feel symptoms of burn-out?
5 Has your perception of human services changed since you commenced this placement?

Placement and its evaluation are significant events in students' careers. Similar evaluations will take place throughout their careers because evaluation is an essential component of accountability within the profession and assists professional growth and development (Kiser 2000, p. 223). Students' ability to embrace the learning situation in placement and their appreciation of the value of supervision will give them a better understanding of why and whether they want to be a worker in the human services and what kind of worker they want to be.

For supervisors, agreeing to take a student on placement engages them in a complicated web of roles and responsibilities, yet it offers them the chance to reflect on their practice, to assist another to learn in a demanding profession and perhaps to reveal further options as they continue to develop as practitioners.

Working in human services is an important and rewarding career but can also be complex and demanding. Practitioners must continue to examine and reflect on their practice to remain effective. It is hoped that students emerge from placement recognising that learning is a lifelong endeavour.

REFERENCES

AASWWE (Australian Association of Social Work and Welfare Education) 1991, *A Handbook for Field Educators in Social Work and Social Welfare*, Charles Sturt University, Bathurst.

Abbott, A. & Lyster, S. 1998, 'The use of constructive criticism in field education', *The Clinical Supervisor*, vol. 17, no. 2, pp. 43–57.

Alle-Corliss, L. & Alle-Corliss, R. 1998, *Human Service Agencies: An Orientation to Fieldwork*, Brooks/Cole, Pacific Grove.

Australian Association of Social Workers 1999, *Code of Ethics*, Australian Association of Social Workers, <www.aasw. asn.au/acrobat/national/code_of_ethics_99.pdf>, 2003.

Banks, S. 2001, *Ethics and Values in Social Work*, 2nd edn, Palgrave, Basingstoke.

Barber, J. 1991, *Beyond Casework*, Macmillan, London.

Bateman, N. 1995, *Advocacy Skills: A Handbook for Human Service Professionals*, Arena, Aldershot.

Beauchamp, T. & Childress, J. 1994, *Principles of Biomedical Ethics*, Oxford University Press, New York.

Beddoe, E. 2000, 'The supervisory relationship', in L. Cooper & L. Briggs (eds), *Fieldwork in the Human Services: Theory and Practice for Field Educators, Practice Teachers and Supervisors*, Allen & Unwin, Sydney.

Bedford, I. 2003, Placement liaison visits, unpublished paper, School of Social Work and Social Policy, La Trobe University, Albury–Wodonga.

Benjamin, J., Bessant, J. & Watts, R. 1997, *Making Groups Work: Rethinking Practice*, Allen & Unwin, Sydney.

Berg-Weger, M. & Birkenmaier, J. 2000, *The Practicum Companion for Social Work: Integrating Class and Field Work*, Allyn & Bacon, Boston.

Bogo, M. 2006, *Social Work Practice: Concepts, Processes, and Interviewing*, Columbia University Press, New York.

Bogo, M. & Vayda, E. 1998, *The Practice of Field Instruction in Social Work: Theory and Process*, 2nd edn, Columbia University Press, New York.

Bolio, D., Keogh, R. & Walker, D. 1985, *Reflection: Turning Experience into Learning*, Kogan Page, London.

Brennan, E. 1982, 'Evaluation of field teaching and learning', in B. Sheafor & L. Jenkins (eds), *Quality Field Instruction in Social Work*, Longman, New York.

Briggs, L. & Kane, R. 2000, 'Ethics in fieldwork', in L. Cooper & L. Briggs (eds), *Fieldwork in the Human Services: Theory and Practice for Field Educators, Practice Teachers and Supervisors*, Allen & Unwin, Sydney.

Brill, N. & Levine, J. 2002, *Working with People: The Helping Process*, 7th edn, Allyn & Bacon, Boston.

Briskman, L. 1999, 'Setting the scene: Unravelling rural practice', in L. Briskman & M. Lynn (eds), *Challenging Rural Practice*, Deakin University Press, Geelong.

Brown, A. & Bourne, I. 1996, *The Social Work Supervisor*, Open University Press, Buckingham.

Bucknell, D. 2000, 'Practice teaching: Problem to solution', *Social Work Education*, vol. 19, no. 2, pp. 125–44.

Carlopio, J., Andrewartha, G. & Armstrong, H. 1997, *Developing Management Skills in Australia*, Longman, Melbourne.

Cheers, B. 1998, *Welfare Bushed: Social Care in Rural Australia*, Ashgate, Brookfield.

Cheers, B. & Taylor, J. 2001, 'Social work in rural and remote Australia', in M. Alston & J. McKinnon (eds), *Social Work: Fields of Practice*, Oxford University Press, Melbourne.

Cleak, H., Hawkins, L. & Hess, L. 2000, 'Innovative field options', in L. Cooper & L. Briggs (eds), *Fieldwork in the Human Services: Theory and Practice for Field Educators, Practice Teachers and Supervisors*, Allen & Unwin, Sydney.

Coley, S. & Scheinberg, C. 1990, *Proposal Writing*, Sage, Newbury Park.

Collins, D., Thomlison, B. & Grinnell, R. 1992, *The Social Work Practicum: A Student Guide*, Peacock, Illinois.

Cooley, B. & Salvaggio, R. 2002, 'Ditching the "dis" in disability: Supervising students who have a disability', *Australian Social Work*, vol. 55, no. 1, pp. 50–9.

Corey, M. & Corey, G. 1998, *Becoming a Helper*, 3rd edn, Brooks/Cole, Pacific Grove.

Corey, G., Corey, M. & Callanan, P. 1998, *Issues and Ethics in the Helping Professions*, 5th edn, Brooks/Cole, Pacific Grove.

Cournoyer, B. 2000, *The Social Work Skills Workbook*, Brooks/Cole, Pacific Grove.

Cox, D. & Pawar, M. 2006, *International Social Work: Issues, Strategies and Programs*, Footprint Books, NSW.

Davys, A. 2000, 'Reflective learning in supervision', in L. Beddoe & J. Worrall (eds), *From Rhetoric to Reality: Proceedings of the Supervision Conference*, Auckland College of Education.

Doel, M., Shardlow, S., Sawdon, C. & Sawdon, D. 1996, *Teaching Social Work Practice*, Arena, Aldershot.

Drury Hudson, J. 1997, 'A model of professional knowledge for social work practice', *Australian Social Work*, vol. 50, no. 3, pp. 35–44.

Egan, G. 2000, *The Skilled Helper: A Systematic Approach to Effective Helping*, Brookes/Cole, Pacific Grove.

Ellis, G. 2000, 'Reflective learning and supervision', in L. Cooper & L. Briggs (eds), *Fieldwork in the Human Services*, Allen & Unwin, Sydney.

Fatout, M. & Rose, S. 1995, *Task Groups in the Social Services*, Sage, Thousand Oaks.

Fook, J. 2002, *Social Work: Critical Theory and Practice*, London, Sage.

Fook, J. & Gardner, F. 2004, 'Critical reflection training – general briefing notes', presented at the CSSW Field Education Introductory Workshop, La Trobe University, February 2004.

Fook, J., Ryan, M. & Hawkins, L. 2000, *Professional Expertise: Practice, Theory and Education for Working with Uncertainty*, Whiting & Birch, London.

Ford, K. & Jones, A. 1987, *Student Supervision*, Macmillan, London.

Fox, R. & Gutheil, I. 2000, 'Process recording: A means for conceptualising and evaluating practice', *Journal of Teaching in Social Work*, vol. 20, no. 1/2, pp. 39–55.

Francis, D. & Henderson, P. 1992, *Working with Rural Communities*, Macmillan, London.

Gardiner, D. 1989, *The Anatomy of Supervision*, Society for Research into Higher Education and Open University Press, Milton Keynes.

Gardner, F. 2006, *Working with Human Service Organisations*, Oxford University Press, South Melbourne.

Globerman, J. & Bogo, M. 2003, 'Changing times: Understanding social workers' motivation to be field instructors', *Social Work*, vol. 48, no. 1, pp. 65–73.

Green, R. 2003, 'Social work in rural areas: A personal and professional challenge', *Australian Social Work*, vol. 56, no. 3, pp. 209–19.

Green, R., Gregory, R. & Mason, R. 2003, 'It's no picnic: Personal and family safety for rural social workers', *Australian Social Work*, vol. 56, no. 2, pp. 94–106.

Hawkins, P. & Shohet, R. 2000, *Supervision in the Helping Profession*, Open University, Buckingham.

Healy, K. 2005, *Social Work Theories in Context: Creating Frameworks for Practice*, Palgrave Macmillan, Houndmill.

Henderson, P. & Thomas, D. N., 2002, *Skills in Neighbourhood Work*, 3rd edn, Routledge, London.

Heron, J. 1990, *Helping the Client: A Creative Practical Guide*, Sage, London.

Honey, P. & Mumford, A. 1986, *The Manual of Learning Styles*, Ardingly House, Maidenhead.

Howe, D. 1987, *An Introduction to Social Work Theory*, Wildwood House, Aldershot.

Hughes, L. & Heycox, K. 2000, 'Assessment of performance', in L. Cooper & L. Briggs (eds), *Fieldwork in the Human Services: Theory and Practice for Field Educators, Practice Teachers and Supervisors*, Allen & Unwin, Sydney.

Hughes, L. & Pengelly, P. 1997, *Staff Supervision in a Turbulent Environment: Managing Process and Task in Front Line Services*, Jessica Kingsley, London.

Humphreys, J., Mathews-Cowey, S. & Rolley, F. 1996, *Health Service Frameworks for Small Rural and Remote Communities: Issues and Options*, University of New England, Armidale.

Hyer, K. & Howe, J. 2002, 'Using this book as a teaching tool', in M. Mezey, C. Cassel, M. Bottrell, K. Hyer, J. Howe & T. Fulmer, *Ethical Patient Care*, The Johns Hopkins University Press, Baltimore.

Irwin, J. 2000, 'Making the most of supervision', in A. O'Hara & Z. Weber, *Skills for Human Service Practice*, Oxford University Press, South Melbourne.

Ixer, G. 1999, 'There's no such thing as reflection', *British Journal of Social Work*, vol. 29, pp. 513–27.

Jones, A. & May, J. 1992, *Working in Human Service Organisations*, Longman, South Melbourne.

Kadushin, A. 1976, *Supervision in Social Work*, Columbia University Press, New York.

Kelly, A. & Sewell, S. 1988, *With Head, Heart and Hand: Dimensions of Community Building*, Boolarong Press, Brisbane.

Kiser, P. 2000, *Getting the Most from Your Human Service Internship: Learning from Experience*, Brooks/Cole, Pacific Grove.

Kolb, D. 1984, *Experiential Learning: Experience as the Source of Learning and Development*, Prentice-Hall, New Jersey.

Loewenberg, F. & Dolgoff, R. 1992, *Ethical Decisions for Social Work Practice*, F. E. Peacock, Itasca.

Maidment, J. 2000, 'Student learning and integration of theory with practice', in L. Cooper & L. Briggs (eds), *Fieldwork in the Human Services: Theory and Practice for Field Educators, Practice Teachers and Supervisors*, Allen & Unwin, Sydney.

Maidment, J. & Egan, R. 2004, *Practice Skills in Social Work and Welfare*, Allen & Unwin, Sydney.

Martinez-Brawley, E. 1990, *Perspectives on the Small Community: Humanistic Views for Practitioners*, NASW Press, Washington DC.

Martinez-Brawley, E. 2000, *Close to Home: Human Services and the Small Community*, NASW Press, Washington DC.

Megginson, D. & Boydell, T. 1989, *A Manager's Guide to Coaching*, British Association for Commercial and Industrial Education, London.

Moore, D. 2000, 'Managing fieldwork', in L. Cooper & L. Briggs (eds), *Fieldwork in the Human Services: Theory and Practice for Field Educators, Practice Teachers and Supervisors*, Allen & Unwin, Sydney.

Morrison, T. 1993, *Supervision in Social Care*, Pavilion, Brighton.

Morrison, T. 2001, *Staff Supervision in Social Care: Making a Real Difference for Staff and Service Users*, Pavilion, Brighton.

Napier, L. 2006, 'Practising critical reflection', in A. O'Hara & Z. Weber, *Skills for Human Service Practice*, Oxford University Press, South Melbourne.

Noble, C. 2001, 'Researching field practice in social work education', *Journal of Social Work*, vol. 1, no. 3, pp. 347–59.

O'Connor, I., Wilson, J. & Setterlund, D. 2003, *Social Work and Welfare Practice*, Pearson Education Australia, Melbourne.

Payne, M. 1982, *Working in Teams*, Macmillan, London.

Pettes, D. E. 1979, *Staff and Student Supervision: A Task-centred Approach*, Allen & Unwin, Sydney.

Razack, N. 2000, 'Students at risk in the field', in L. Cooper & L. Briggs (eds), *Fieldwork in the Human Services: Theory and Practice for Field Educators, Practice Teachers and Supervisors*, Allen & Unwin, Sydney.

Rees, S. 1991, *Achieving Power: Practice and Policy in Social Welfare*, Allen & Unwin, Sydney.

Regan, S. 1977, *The Think Sheet: A Framework for Analysing Student Learning Interactions*, PIT Press, Melbourne.

Reynolds, L. 1965, *Teaching and Learning in the Practice of Social Work*, Russell & Russell, New York.

Rogers, G. & Langevin, P. 2000, 'Negotiated learning contracts', in L. Cooper & L. Briggs (eds), *Fieldwork in the Human Services: Theory and Practice for Field Educators, Practice Teachers and Supervisors*, Allen & Unwin, Sydney.

Rose-Miller, M. 1999, 'Beyond the black stump – who cares?', *Proceedings of the Joint AASW, IFSW, APASW and AASWWE Conference*, Brisbane, vol. 2, pp. 210–15.

Rosenblatt, A. & Mayer, J. 1975, 'Objectionable supervisory styles: Students' views', *Social Work*, vol. 20, no. 3, pp. 184–9.

Royse, D., Dhooper, S. & Rompf, E. 1993, *Field Instruction: A Guide for Social Work Students*, Longman, New York.

Ryde, J. 2000, 'Supervising across difference', *International Journal of Psychotherapy*, vol. 5, no. 1, pp. 37–48.

Schön, D. 1983, *The Reflective Practitioner*, Temple Smith, London.

Schön, D. 1987, *Educating the Reflective Practitioner*, Jossey-Bass, San Francisco.

Schön, D. 1995, *The Reflective Practitioner: How Professionals Think in Action*, Basic Books, New York.

School of Social Work and Social Policy, 2003a, *Field Education Handbook 2003*, La Trobe University, Victoria.

School of Social Work and Social Policy, 2003b, *Information and Evaluation Handbook*, La Trobe University, Victoria.

Shardlow, S. & Doel, M. 1996, *Practice Learning and Teaching*, British Association of Social Workers, Macmillan, Basingstoke.

Smart, R. & Gray, M. 2000, 'Working with cultural difference', in L. Cooper & L. Briggs (eds), *Fieldwork in the Human Services: Theory and Practice for Field Educators, Practice Teachers and Supervisors*, Allen & Unwin, Sydney.

Sturmey, R. & Edwards, H. 1991, *The Survival Skills Training Package. Community Services and Health Workforces in Rural and Remote Areas: Needs and Recommendations Study*, Department of Health, Housing and Community Services, Canberra.

Thompson, N. 1993, *Anti-discriminatory Practice*, Macmillan, Basingstoke.

Thompson, N. 2005, *Understanding Social Work: Preparing for Practice*, Macmillan, Basingstoke.

Trevithick, P. 2000, *Social Work Skills: A Practice Handbook*, Open University Press, Buckingham.

Victorian Combined Schools of Social Work 2003, questionnaire, Victorian Combined Schools of Social Work, Victoria.

Watson, J. 1999, *The Minute Taker's Handbook,* 2nd edn, Self-Counsel Press, Bellingham, BC.

Western, D. 2003, 'Reflection, connection and narrative: Journaling as a social work intervention', *Victorian Social Work*: *AASW Newsletter*, Winter, pp. 6–7.

Wilson, J. 2000, 'Approaches to supervision in fieldwork', in L. Cooper & L. Briggs (eds), *Fieldwork in the Human Services: Theory and Practice for Field Educators, Practice Teachers and Supervisors*, Allen & Unwin, Sydney.

INDEX

A

abstract conceptualisation (AC) learning strategy 19–22
accommodation (teamwork stage) 120
accountability 56, 121
accuracy principle 177
acquire-it-as-you-go-along approach (to student
    induction) 33
action planning 95–7
active experimentation (AE) learning strategy 19–22
active listening 122
activist learning category 22
administrative supervisory function 55–6
agencies
    agency records 81–2, 126
    choosing a student 15
    and groupwork 123–6
    fields 7
    inter-agency teams 121
    knowledge regarding 9
    legal responsibilities of 161–3
    mapping 27–8
    motivations for student placement 14–15
    and placement allocation 15
    and policy practice 115
    preparing for student placement 13–22
    and skills 8
    and student work 13–14
    surviving in a human service agency 27–30
    types of 6
    understanding services and structures of (student) 35, 37
    visiting agencies 88–9
    and workplace issues 14
agreements
    and duty of care 161–2
    example 43–4
    and failing students 184
    learning agreements 39–44
    placement contracts 46–7
    presenting and reviewing 43
    supervision contracts 45–6, 57
aims definition 42
analysis 94–5, 96, 97, 131–2
analytical skills 119
anonymity 133–4
anti-discriminatory legislation 159
assertive communication 27
assessment 4–6, 32, 56, 73, 107, 174–84
atheoretical 'agony aunt' syndrome 17
attributes (supervisors) 10
audio recording 85–6
authoritative supervisory relationship 60–1
authority 17
autonomy 29, 163

B

being learning element 40, 43
beneficence principle 163

Bogo and Vayda's integration of theory and practice loop 94–7
Bogo's reflective evaluation 53
bottom-up practice 101
boundaries (professional and personal) 132, 152

C

campaign strategy (for change) 112
change 100–2, 103, 111–12, 148–9
circular questions 61, 63
clients 6–7
    and duty of care 161–2
code of ethics 165
co-working 86
    stages of 105
collective supervision 69
communication 112, 27, 35, 36
    open communication 184
    teamwork skills 122
    techniques 61–4
community development *see* community work
community profiles 107–8
community resources (use of) 17
community work 100–8
concept maps 82–3
conceptualising (theory and practice loop stage) 94–5
concrete experience (CE) learning strategy 19–22
confidentiality 14, 123–4, 133, 162
conflict 17, 27, 29–30, 35, 122, 148–9
congruence principle 177–8
'constructivist' tradition 52
consultation 115, 184
contest strategy (for change) 112
contracts 45–7, 57, 70–1
cooperation strategy (for change) 112
critical incidents 80–1, 107
critical reflection 50–4

D

decision-making processes 101–2
developmental stages [model] 17
diaries 27, 37, 77–9, 107
    work diaries 106
difference/diversity 59–60, 92, 146
    difference—teaching and learning methods 155–7
    understanding difference 151–5
    working with 150–6
directives 62, 63
disability 153–5
disclosure 153–4
discussion tools 75–83
documentation 106–8
doing learning element 21, 40, 44
domestic issues (and placement choice) 8
duty of care 161–2

E

ecological environments 33–4
educational approaches 50–4
educational methods 21
educational supervisory function 55–6
efficiency principle 177
emancipatory reflection 53
empirical knowledge 92
empowerment 102–3, 104–5
enabling supervisory function 55–6
encouragement 62, 63
environments 21, 29, 33–4
ethical issues 158–66
ethics, values and professional practice (core learning area) 41
evaluation 41, 105
    Bogo's reflective evaluation 53
    and conceptualising (theory and practice loop stage) 94–5
    criteria 175–7, 179–81
    and the critical reflective approach 52–3
    evaluating learning 43
    evaluating students' practice 174–8
    evaluation and assessment measures 178, 181–2
    of orientation programs 37–8
    principles of 177–8
    of students 162
    students and supervisors 174–84
    supervisors' practice 178–82
    see also assessment
experiencing (theory and practice loop stage) 94, 95, 97
experimental learning model (Kolb) 22

F

fairness principle 177
family life 152
facilitative supervisory relationship 60–1
feedback 182, 184
    feedback stage of co-working 105
    giving and receiving feedback 66–8
    guidelines for 67–8
    purposes of 66
    student feedback 37–8
fidelity principle 164
field placement *see* placement
final assessment 183–4
framework (personal) identification 5–6

G

game playing 145–6
Gardiner's learning interaction levels 18–19
generalist practice 134–6
goals 29, 40–1, 43–4, 123–6
government agencies 6
group contracts 70–1
group decisions 101
group supervision 69–71
groups and teams 118–27

H

Honey and Mumford's *Learning Styles Questionnaire* 22
human services 7, 27–30, 119, 167–8

I

identities, understanding ourselves 150–1
immunisation 8
individualised learning approach 17
individualism 152
inductive (inferential) learning 93
information 62, 63
    and discussion tools 75–83
    and learning stages 78
    presentation of 33
    and *Privacy Act 2000* 159
insurance 14, 158–9
integration (theory and practice) 91–7
interaction processes 27
inter-agency teams 121
inter-agency work *see* top-down practice
interpretation 62, 63
intervention 77
interviews 9, 10, 26
intuition 52

J

journals 27, 37, 77–9, 106, 107
justice principle 163–4

K

key target groups 6–7
knowing learning element 40, 44
knowing-in-action concept 52
knowledge 77
    and ideas 104
    and practice skills 103–5
    and rural practice 135
    and teamwork 119
    types of 91–3
    using knowledge in supervision 104–5
knowledge in practice (core learning area) 41
Kolb's experimental learning model 22, 51, 71

L

Langevin and Rogers' learning elements 21, 40, 43–4
learning
    core areas 41
    devising methods and strategies 42
    difference—teaching and learning methods 155–7
    elements of 21, 40, 43–4
    evaluating 43
    Gardiner's learning interaction levels 18–19
    Honey and Mumford's *Learning Styles Questionnaire* 22
    Kolb's experimental learning model 22, 51, 71
    learning modes, environments and educational methods 21
    linking learning and practice in placement 90–7
    on placement 50–4, 55–71, 73–89, 90–7
    Schön's adult learning model 50, 52
    solution-focussed learning approach 51
    stages of 17
    strategies for and styles of 19–22
    teaching and learning activities 86–9
    teaching and learning approach 74–5

the teaching and learning framework 167–8
teaching and learning in teams 125–6
teaching and learning policy skills 113–14
teaching and learning tools 73–89
unmet learning needs 148
learning agreements 39–44
learning blocks 140
learning principles 32–3
learning strategies/styles 19–22, 33
    assessing 19–20
    basic learning strategies 20–1
Learning Styles Questionnaire (Honey and Mumford) 22
legal issues 158–66
legislation 37, 159
liaison 168–72, 175
linear questions 61, 63
location (placement) 8
log sheets 106–7

M

mapping 27–8
    concept maps 82–3
meetings 9, 169–72
mid-placement assessment 182
mirroring 146–8
modelling 83–4
multidisciplinary team 121
multiskilled practice 134–6
Mumford and Honey's *Learning Styles Questionnaire* 22

N

narratives 81
negotiation (teamwork stage) 120
non-government organisations (NGOs) 6
non-maleficence principle 163
'no problem' supervision 141
norms and rules 36
not-for-profit organisations 6

O

observation 26–7, 77
    and community profiles 107–8
    observation stage of co-working 105
    observing students' work 85
observation tools 83–6
'one of us' supervision 142–3
open communication 27, 184
operation (teamwork stage) 120
organisational analyses 35–6, 82
organisational context (core learning area) 41
orientation stage of teamwork 119–20
orientation programs 32, 33–8
overseas placements 128–37

P

participation 122
pathologising 17
personal interests 8
personal knowledge 92
'personal problems' supervision 143–4

personal safety 136
perspective (profession) 17
placement
    allocation of 15
    and anonymity 133–4
    basic models for student induction 33
    beginning—student perspective 26–30
    beginning—supervisor perspective 31–8
    and boundaries 132
    choosing 4
    contracts and agreements for 39–47
    cultural difference considerations 152
    definition 2–3
    and disability 153–5
    finishing 108, 185–9
    the first weeks (student) 26–7
    game playing in 145–6
    goals of 3–4
    issues for rural placement 130–6
    linking learning and practice in placement 90–7
    placement settings 6–8
    planning for 4–11
    and practical considerations 8, 9
    pre-placement interviews 9, 10
    preparing for 13–22
    rural and overseas placements 128–37
    and self-assessment 4, 5–6
    stages of 3
    starting out in rural placement 129–30
placement contracts 46–7
planned program approach (to student induction) 33
planning stage of co-working 105
police clearance/checks 8, 14
policy/policy practice 111–17
    examples 109
    and research 109–17
    writing policy 115–17
policy skills 113–14
political realities 102–3, 113, 129
portfolio *see* journals
power 59, 60, 150–1
practical considerations (of placement choice) 8, 9
practical reflection 53
practice 27
    bottom-up and top-down practice 101
    and the critical reflective approach 52–3
    describing approaches to 16–17
    developing good supervisory practice 55–71
    ethical practice 163–6
    evaluating students' practice 174–8
    evaluating supervisors' practice 178–82
    generalist and multiskilled practice 134–6
    knowledge and practice skills 103–5
    knowledge in practice (core learning area) 41
    linking learning and practice in placement 90–7
    methods and contexts of 100–8, 109–17, 118–27, 128–37
    personal safety in rural practice 136
    policy practice 111–17
    political dimensions of 134
    praxis (integration of theory and practice) 93–7
    and process recording 75–7

professional practice, ethics and values (core learning
    area) 41
    recording methods 126–7
    research practice 110–11
    rural practice 128–9
    understanding the context of 33–4
    working with groups 123–6
practice wisdom 92
practicuum *see* placement
pragmatist learning category 22
praxis (integration of theory and practice) 93–7
pre-placement interviews/meetings 9, 10
presentations (student) 88, 115
principle/practice gap 5–6
Privacy Act 2000 159
private organisations 6
problematising 17
procedural wisdom 93
process recording 75–7
process reports 106–7
processes, skills and relationships (core learning area) 41
professional development and self-learning (core learning
    area) 41
professional identity 17
profiles, community 107–8
proposals, policy writing and 115

Q

questioning 61–4, 77

R

reading 27, 88
reassurance 62, 63
recording 27
    in community work 108
    methods for 126–7
    process recording 75–7
    requirements for 37
records
    agency records 81–2, 126
    and failing students 184
reflecting (theory and practice loop stage) 94–7
reflection 37, 62, 63, 93, 114
    on critical incidents 80–1
    critical reflection 50–4
reflection-in-action concept 52
reflective observation (RO) learning strategy 19–22
reflective tools
    agency records 81–2, 126
    audio and video recording 85–6
    co-working 86
    concept maps 82–3
    diaries and journals 27, 37, 77–9, 106, 107
    modelling 83–4
    narratives 81
    observing students' work 85
    organisational analyses 35–6, 82
    process recording 75–7
    reflection on critical incidents 80–1
    think sheets 80
reflector learning category 22

reflexive questions 61
relationships
    and knowledge and practice skills 103
    and liaison structure 169
    in rural communities 131
    supervisory relationship 59–64, 140
relationships, skills and processes (core learning area) 41
research (core learning area) 41
    and empirical knowledge 92
    and policy 109–17
research practice 109, 110–11
resources (use of) 17, 26
    access to 29
    human services resources 168
responsibilities
    linking theory and practice 90
    legal responsibilities of agencies 161–3
    legal responsibilities of training institutions 158–61
    of the liaison person 168–9
    roles and responsibilities of training institutions 167–72
    supervisors and students 46–7, 53
Rogers and Langevin's learning elements 21, 40, 43–4
role play 86–7
rules and norms 36
rural placements 128–37
rural practice 128–9

S

Schön's adult learning model 50, 52
self-assessment 4–6, 32
self-awareness 76–7, 155
self-learning and professional development (core learning
    area) 41
service delivery 29, 35
sessions 61–8, 87–8
settings (placement) 6–8
single discipline team 121
skills
    to gain from placement 8
    and group activity 119
    knowledge and practice skills 103–5
    policy skills 113–14
    and research practice 112
    skills, knowledge and experience audits 5
    teamwork skills 122
skills training 87–8
skills, processes and relationships (core learning area) 41
social change approaches 112
social distancing 17
social planning *see* top-down practice
social policies 37
    social policy as core learning area 41
solution-focussed learning approach 51
spirituality 152
strategic questions 61, 63
students
    assessment and evaluation 174–84
    beginning placement—student perspective 26–30
    completing placement work 185–6
    dealing with feelings 186
    evaluating students' practice 174–8

evaluation of 162
failing students 183–4
finishing placement well 185–9
general issues facing and case studies 140–5
meeting (placement) 22–4
meeting staff 34–5
motivations for placement 14–15
observing students' work 85
and orientation programs 32, 33–8
and placement allocation 15
and placement contracts 46–7
and placement—the first weeks 26–7
planning for the future 187–9
ritualising placement end 187
student presentations 88
student unit supervision 71
student work/tasks 13–14
and supervision contracts
surviving in a human service agency 27–30
working through unfinished business 186–7
supervision contracts 45–6, 57
supervision sessions 61–8
    recording 65–6
    structuring 64–5
    techniques and content 61–4
supervisors/supervision
    assessment and evaluation 174–84
    beginning placement—supervisor perspective 31–8
    challenging issues in supervision 140–9
    clarifying expectations 23
    collective supervision 69
    describing approaches to practice 16–17
    developing good supervisory practice 55–71
    developing the supervisory relationship 59–64
    early models 50
    evaluating supervisors' practice 178–82
    expectations of supervision 56–9
    functions of supervision 55–6
    general issues discussions 32
    group supervision 69–71
    learning principles 32–3
    meeting students 22–4
    meeting with supervisors 10–11
    motivations for student placement 14–15
    the orientation program 32, 33–8
    and placement contracts 46–7
    and placement—the first weeks 31–2
    poor supervision characteristics 180
    preparing for placement 13–22
    readiness of (taking students) 16–22
    Schön's adult learning model 50, 52
    student unit supervision 71
    and supervision contracts 45–6
    supervision sessions 61–8
    task supervision 68–9

teaching others 17–22
    using knowledge in supervision 104–5
supervisory relationship 59–64, 140
supportive supervisory function 55–6
SWOT analysis 131–2

T

task supervision 68–9
tasks/work (student) 13–14, 40–4, 53–4, 56, 85–6, 114
Taylor's critical incident technique 53–4
teaching
    difference—teaching and learning methods 155–7
    on placement 50–4, 55–71, 73–89, 90–7
    teaching and learning activities 86–9
    teaching and learning approach 74–5
    the teaching and learning framework 167–8
    teaching and learning in teams 125–6
    teaching and learning policy skills 113–14
    teaching and learning tools 73–89
    teaching methods and learning strategies 19–22
    teaching others 17–22
teams and groups 118–27
technical reflection 53
tension 29, 101–2, 122, 154
theoretical knowledge 92
theories 90–7
theorist learning category 22
think sheets 80
thinking learning element 21, 40, 44
time constraints 8
tools (for teaching and learning) 73–89
top-down practice 101
training institutions
    legal responsibilities of 158–61
    and liaison 168–72
    and placement allocation 15
    and placement organisation 4
    roles and responsibilities of 167–72
    skills training 87–8
transport (and placement choice) 8

V

values, ethics and professional practice (core learning area) 41
Vayda and Bogo's integration of theory and practice loop 94–7
veracity principle 164
video recording 85–6
views/opinions (alternate) 122
visiting agencies 88–9

W

work diaries 106
work/tasks (student) 13–14, 40–4, 53–4, 56, 85–6, 114
workload constraints 8
workplace issues 14